POLITICAL LEARNING AND REDEMOCRATIZATION IN LATIN AMERICA: DO POLITICIANS LEARN FROM POLITICAL CRISES?

Political Learning and Redemocratization in Latin America:

Do Politicians Learn from Political Crises?

Edited by

Jennifer L. McCoy

North·South Center Press
UNIVERSITY OF MIAMI

The publisher of this book is the North-South Center Press at the University of Miami.

The mission of the North-South Center is to promote better relations and serve as a catalyst for change among the United States, Canada, and the nations of Latin America and the Caribbean by advancing knowledge and understanding of the major political, social, economic, and cultural issues affecting the nations and peoples of the Western Hemisphere.

© 2000 North-South Center Press at the University of Miami.

 Published by the North-South Center Press at the University of Miami and distributed by Lynne Rienner Publishers, Inc., 1800 30th Street, Suite 314, Boulder, CO 80301-1026. All rights reserved under International and Pan-American Conventions. No portion of the contents may be reproduced or transmitted in any form, or by any means, including photocopying, recording, or any information storage retrieval system, without prior permission in writing from the North-South Center Press.

All copyright inquiries should be addressed to the publisher: North-South Center Press, 1500 Monza Avenue, Coral Gables, Florida 33146-3027, U.S.A., phone 305-284-8912, fax 305-284-5089, or e-mail mmapes@miami.edu.

To order or to return books, contact Lynne Rienner Publishers, Inc., 1800 30th Street, Suite 314, Boulder, CO 80301-1026, 303-444-6684, fax 303-444-0824.

Library of Congress Cataloging-in-Publication Data

Political learning and redemocratization in Latin America: do politicians learn from political crises? / edited by Jennifer L. McCoy
    p.cm.
    Includes bibliographical references and index.
    ISBN 1-57454-063-7 (hc: alk.paper) — ISBN 1-57454-066-1 (pb: alk. paper)
    1. South America—Politics and government—20th century. 2. Democracy—South America. 3. Organizational learning—South America. I. McCoy, Jennifer.
    JL1860.P64 1999   99-047546
    320.98—dc21   CIP

Printed in the United States of America/TS

The paper used in this publication meets the requirements of the American National Standards for Permanence of Paper for Printed Library Materials.

04 03 02 01 00 99 7 6 5 4 3 2 1

Contents

Preface and Acknowledgments i
    Jennifer L. McCoy

Chapter 1
The Learning Process 1
    Jennifer L. McCoy

Chapter 2
Argentina: Lost Opportunities and Ongoing Learning 15
    Marcelo Cavarozzi

Chapter 3
Chile: Political Learning and the Reconstruction of Democracy 37
    Manuel Antonio Garretón and Malva Espinosa

Chapter 4
Uruguay: Democratic Learning and Its Limits 73
    Luis Costa Bonino

Chapter 5
Venezuela: Old Successes, New Constraints on Learning 99
    Francine Jácome

Chapter 6
Comparative Lessons 131
    Jennifer L. McCoy

Contributors 149

Index 151

Preface and Acknowledgments

JENNIFER L. MCCOY

This study began with a conversation Luis Costa Bonino and I had while I was on a Fulbright award in 1991. We found that in the prolific writing on democratization in Latin America, there was little research about how political actors change attitudes and behaviors and internalize the norms associated with liberal democracy, such as compromise, tolerance, and negotiation. Instead, much of the literature had moved beyond the processes of transition to focus on institutions and rules during democratic consolidation. Luis Costa and I still wanted to know how societies come to adopt new norms and behaviors; specifically, how do societies with little experience or with interrupted experiences learn the practices of democratic politics?

I then contacted Manuel Antonio Garretón in Chile, Marcelo Cavarozzi in Argentina, and Francine Jácome in Venezuela to discuss a joint project on political learning and democracy. Luis Costa had agreed to write a chapter on Uruguay. We decided to start with these four country cases, as they had significant experience in democracy. Though we maintain an interest in how learning occurs in new democracies, we felt that the processes would be sufficiently distinct that we should begin our exploration with similar cases. We added Venezuela to the Southern Cone cases because of its status as a more established democracy, so that we could see what happens over time and whether the learning process changes as democracies mature. The political developments in 1999 in Venezuela dramatize the failures of learning, foreseen in that chapter.

The learning literature is rather disjointed, with several strands from cognitive psychology to organization theory and social learning. We decided to focus on an intermediate level of analysis — political actors or groups — and to examine a particular type of learning — learning about democracy. Thus, we have concentrated on crises of democracy, both the lessons learned from earlier breakdowns and from new tensions or crises, and the ongoing processes of democratization in less crisis-prone situations.

We very much consider this an exploratory study in political learning, since very little work has been done on this topic in the Latin American politics field. We ourselves have learned a great deal in the process of this project, including how to work together as a research team. We hoped to generate ideas and an analytical framework for future research on the topic that may be expanded to other types of actors and different types of cases.

Much of the research was funded by a grant from the North-South Center at the University of Miami. This grant financed two team meetings in Atlanta in August 1993 and March 1994. Between these two meetings, the four country authors carried out intensive interviews of political leaders and "insiders" in their countries to gain a subjective view of the process of learning in political parties and other groups. The authors then supplemented this subjective information with objective data, tracing the behavior of the groups to determine the effects of learning.

Our last team meeting was held in August 1995 in Bellagio, Italy, at the Rockefeller Foundation's Retreat and Conference Center. Here we commented on initial drafts of each chapter and on our conclusions. In addition to the North-South Center and the Rockefeller Foundation, I would like to thank the Policy Research Center at Georgia State University for providing research time for the writing of my chapter and the Center for Latin American and Hispanic Studies at Georgia State for providing assistance for editing the chapters. My research assistants, Cindy Wilson and Katherine Rozei, have provided invaluable assistance with bibliographic searches and editing. Kathleen Hamman, editorial director, and her team at the North-South Center Press, including Karen Payne, free-lance editor; Michelle Perez, proofreader; and José Grave de Peralta, senior editor; were patient and careful editors, encouraging us all along the way. We also appreciate Mary M. Mapes' cover design and Susan K. Holler's graphic design of the text and creation of the index. Finally, Francine Jácome, Marcelo Cavarozzi, and I thank Nancy Bermeo for her helpful comments on our draft chapters presented at the Latin American Studies Association Congress in September 1995.

CHAPTER ONE

The Learning Process

JENNIFER L. MCCOY

THE PROBLEM

How does democratic political change occur? How do societies come to adopt norms, institutions, and rules generally associated with liberal democracy? We found existing theories of democracy and democratization to be wanting in answering these questions. Democratic theory focuses on the functioning and improvement of existing democracies. Democratization theories argue over which combination of political culture, values, economic and social conditions, institutional framework, and consensus on the rules of the game is necessary to achieve democratic governance.[1] Yet, neither body of literature satisfactorily addresses the question of how political actors reorient their behavior and attitudes in order to support, adapt, or acquiesce to political democracy.

We argue that an important source of democratic change is learning by political actors.[2] We are particularly interested in the survival of reemerging democracies — and in how to prevent the recurrence of democratic crises and avoid democratic breakdowns. We suggest that the internalization of new attitudes and behavior during and after the redemocratization process may be the result of a learning process based on the evaluation of experience or new knowledge acquired. We ask under what conditions political actors learn, what they learn, and whether they apply those lessons to improve the prospects for democratic governance in the future.

We examine four cases in which democracy has broken down and been reinstated: Argentina, Chile, Uruguay, and Venezuela. The Argentine case is one of a cyclical democracy alternating and intertwining with authoritarian periods. Chile and Uruguay represent stable democracies interrupted by authoritarian regimes in the 1970s and reinstated in the 1980s — Chile with new authoritarian enclaves, Uruguay with a return to pre-coup constitutional rules. In the case of Venezuela, a democratic transition in 1958 was sustained through mid-1999 (the time of this writing), but latent crises of the economy, political institutions, and legitimacy erupted in 1989 and called into question the very survival of the democratic regime. Venezuela thus provides an opportunity to examine the effects of early learning on later learning opportunities, some decades after a democratic transition, and to examine the ability of political actors to learn from new situations and crises that do not yet constitute a complete breakdown of the system.

instrumental

normative

We start from the premise that in all of our cases, political and social actors now support, acquiesce to, or have adapted to democratic politics either for instrumental reasons (they believe democracy best serves their private interests for the moment) or for normative reasons (they believe democracy will always be the best system for society as a whole). Although all of these (re)orientations toward democratic politics may be a product of learning, they have different implications for democratic governance.

LEARNING THEORY

Learning theory attempts to explain how and why individuals change beliefs and organizations change policies and routines. It can be traced to organizational, decision-making, and psychological theories of the 1960s and 1970s, exemplified by James March, Herbert Simon, and Karl Deutsch. In the 1980s and 1990s, theories of organizational and social learning have been increasingly applied to government policymaking in the comparative politics and foreign policy literature[3] and to international negotiation and cooperation in the international relations literature.[4] Thus, three major branches of political learning have evolved — psychological theories of cognitive change within decisionmakers, organizational theories of bureaucratic or corporate behavioral change, and social learning theories of policy change. In addition, socialization theory seeks to explain the imparting of values and the acquisition of political attitudes and orientations at the mass level (Conover and Searing 1994).

Branches of pol. learning

Defin - learning

The most prevalent definition of learning involves a cognitive change involving changes in beliefs and perceptions. According to arguments derived from this definition, the interpretation of experience or new information alters prior beliefs about how the world works. This cognitive change in turn may produce changes in goals or tactics (the means to reach those goals), or in both. Different types of learning have different results; for example, simple learning produces changes in means, whereas complex learning leads to changes in priorities and underlying goals (Deutsch 1963; Nye 1987).

Learning theory assumes that learning is a deliberative or conscious process of reevaluating causal relationships in response to new information. Such a concept of learning implies rationality in the assessment of means and ends. Yet, an affective dimension to learning exists as well, in that prior beliefs and experiences shape the processing of new information. Indeed, strong beliefs, rather than be altered by learning, may block or distort new information and result in no learning or negative learning (Nye 1987, 379). Or, individuals may learn different lessons from the same event since each person interprets history from his or her own worldview or frame, creating a process of divergent learning.

The methodological dilemma of moving from individual to group learning is addressed in various ways. Some analysts simply reify the organization or state as a single, unitary actor (Reiter 1994). Organizational theory, on the other hand, investigates how individual cognitive change and interpretations of history are embedded or internalized in the organization's memory and procedures, and how organizations develop new routines and procedures through trial-and-error experimentation or the search for alternative processes.[5] Analysts of epistemic communities examine how ideas are transferred from the scientific community to the policy community to form the basis for "consensual knowledge."[6]

Nevertheless, the dynamics of learning by a group is still underspecified in learning theory. A small, but growing, literature on political learning gives us some clues about the process and constraints of collective learning.[7] Individual learning is usually considered a necessary, but not sufficient, condition of collective learning. Instead, the nature and extent of collective learning is also posited to be a function of group dynamics, power relationships, and the level of uncertainty surrounding issues. Emanuel Adler and Ernst Haas (1992) argue, for example, that the greater the uncertainty about an issue, the more room there is for new ideas and the higher the chances for learning.

Jack S. Levy (1994) and Joseph Nye (1987) examine the relationship between politics and learning, arguing that political struggles within and between groups will determine whose learning counts and that political or bureaucratic constraints may impede the implementation of some lessons learned. Richard Anderson (1991) extends Haas' argument (1990) to conclude that learning by public organizations must originate outside politics, since it is political competition among rival decisionmakers that determines changes in policy, rather than a learning process leading to improved evaluation of situations. In other words, for new ideas politicians rely on scientists, who work in institutional settings different from those of competitive politics.

Actors may also use knowledge instrumentally to promote their own strategic interests. Similar to Anderson's political competition model, James Clay Moltz (1993) argues that individual Soviet leaders adopted ("borrowed") those economic ideas from abroad that would advance their own strategic political positions, creating a form of divergent learning within groups. Levy (1994, 302) and George Breslauer (1987) argue that the instrumental adoption of ideas for political purposes does not in itself constitute learning, but politics can motivate learning in the search for the best means to reach one's goals or in the reevaluation of assumptions and goals.

THE PROJECT

Although we draw on the literature of learning theory, our task is different. Rather than explain policy change, we focus on political change. Rather than focus on individual psychologies or organizational/governmental bureaucracies, we focus on a middle level of analysis — political groups. Political parties and factions typically are more influenced by individuals than are large bureaucracies, but they involve a group dynamic that goes beyond the learning of key individuals.

We define learning as "a process of reflection on experience or new information that affects orientations and behavior." In other words, learning includes both a cognitive process and a practical application. We are especially interested in *democratic* learning — the acquisition of attitudes and practices that contribute to democratic governance, that is, resolution of collective problems in a given democratic context. But we also analyze nondemocratic learning, that is, learning that does not contribute in a positive way to democratic practice.

Nancy Bermeo (1992) has examined the concept of learning in democratic transitions, arguing that this is the stage of democratization at which learning matters most. We argue that learning is an ongoing process that is also vital in explaining how a democratic system matures, deepens, weathers crises, and manages systemic changes.

In our conceptualization, learning may reinforce existing orientations and therefore be manifested in continuity of strategies and behavior, or it may cause a change in orientations, assumptions, goals, and the means to achieve goals. It does not require that actors gain an improved or more realistic understanding of a situation from their experience (the accuracy criterion). Indeed, one of the lessons of our analysis is that actors can have good (accurate), bad (inaccurate or negative), or incomplete learning.

Neither does our definition require that actors be more capable of achieving their new goals or be successful in their new strategies (the efficiency or effectiveness criterion of learning), but it does imply that they behave in a way that manifests the lessons they have drawn.[8] Likewise, political learning can have both positive and negative implications for democratic governance, as our case studies so clearly point out. In analyzing the consequences for democratic stability, governability, and participation, we engage in an admittedly normative exercise as we impart negative and positive connotations to each learning experience. However, in each case, the authors explain the criteria and rationale for analysis of the implications for democratic functioning.

The four case studies analyze learning by political actors. We focus primarily on groups of political and social elites, arguing that their consensus on and respect for the rules of the democratic game are crucial to the process of democratic consolidation and governability. This is not to say that societal orientations are not important or that they may not stimulate a change in elite orientations. Indeed, mass-level orientations may follow elite attitudes, change simultaneously, or even precede a change in elite orientations. The interaction between the two levels will vary from country to country. But we consider changes in societal attitudes in this project only to the extent that they are a source of learning for political elites.

For each case, we ask five sets of questions:

1. *What* did political actors learn from their experiences with democratic breakdown, renewal, and governance?

2. *How* did they learn? What are the sources and processes of learning?

3. What were the *effects* of learning on behavior? In particular, did groups take action to forestall a recurrence of democratic crisis and breakdown or to improve democratic governance? In other words, how have political actors applied the lessons learned?

4. *How well* did they learn? Do the lessons learned have positive or negative implications for the functioning of democratic politics in each case?

5. What are the *limits* to learning? How do we explain, for example, instances in which learning appears to have negative consequences for democratic governance or in which political groups appear to repeat old mistakes and not learn at all?

Dimensions of Dem. learning.

The first question concerns the content of learning. Since we are interested in the learning by political actors that contributes to or subtracts from effective democratic practice, we identified five dimensions of democratic learning: 1) Have political actors modified their *political discourse* to minimize demagogic appeals to the populace, intolerant and slanderous discrediting of opponents, and polarization of dogmatic debates? 2) Do *political projects* reflect the value of the democratic regime? 3) Do actors respect the *rules of the democratic game* for normative or instrumental reasons? 4) In their *relations with others,* have actors expanded the range of potential coalition partners? Do actors treat opponents as an enemy to eliminate, as an adversary to weaken or coopt, as an opponent to beat in a fair competition or negotiate with for a compromise solution, or as a potential coalition partner? 5) Does the process of agenda setting and problem solving in public *decisionmaking* include bargaining and consultation with political or social actors, or is it limited to technocratic or imposition (*decretismo*) styles?

We have defined learning as a process of reflection on experience and new information. Both cognitive psychology and organizational theory predict that crisis or trauma is more likely to produce learning than a gradual accumulation of knowledge; that failure stimulates reevaluation of beliefs and, thus, aids learning more than does success; and that direct experience produces more learning than does vicarious experience.[9]

The rationale for these predictions lies in the entrenched belief systems of individuals and the collective myths of organizations, both of which are expected to be very resistant to change. Success may lead to a search for improvements in tactics (simple learning), but it is also likely to produce complacency and a "competency trap."[10] The rarer complex learning (change in goals and assumptions) may require a "formative" event or a crisis that threatens an organization's goals (Reiter 1994), or repeated strategic failures accompanied by massive personnel shifts (Levy 1994).

We posit that the sources of learning include both experience and new information. Unlike Levy, we expect that complex learning may occur from a single traumatic experience, without a shift in personnel. The trauma of repression or economic crisis, for example, can lead actors to reevaluate their goals and assumptions. On the other hand, repeated, non-traumatic experiences, such as political defeats and victories, may lead actors to evaluate the most effective strategies and tactics to achieve goals. New information regarding democratization processes may come from study or exile abroad, from comparison with other countries' experiences, or from scientific communities within the country.[11]

The methods or means of learning include interaction, reflection, and personnel change.[12] Interaction with other domestic groups may contribute to learning through, for example, negotiations with the military, other political parties, or former adversaries during the transition, thus contributing to improved mutual understanding. Interaction with external groups may lead to learning through the provision of new information or through a demonstration effect. For example, international party foundations such as the Friederich Ebert Foundation or the National Democratic Institute provide technical assistance, while party leaders from other countries may relate successful and unsuccessful experiences in carrying out democratic transitions and handling post-transition crises.

Reflection is the conscious attempt by a group to deliberate on and evaluate the causes of past crises or the relative success of various strategies and tactics used to achieve group goals. It may lead to a change in strategies and behavior, or it may reaffirm winning strategies and tactics. Reflection will be most readily evidenced by internal debates and self-criticism.

Finally, the renewal, rotation, or addition of personnel may bring in new ideas, attitudes, and experiences that contribute indirectly to the learning of the group as a whole. The group's collective memory may be changed by the entry of new personnel with new experiences, or by the departure of members. Although personnel change may be caused by external factors, such as political defeat, the process of changing personnel itself is often a result of learning at some level, whether by voters who oust an incumbent, by supporters of a military coup, or by group members who change their leadership.

The authors of the four case studies used a combination of subjective and objective analysis to examine the learning process of political actors. In-depth interviews with key political leaders and insiders provided access to the perceptions of those leaders about the content and process of learning within their own groups and other groups. Empirical analysis of the behavior of political actors revealed the extent to which declared lessons resulted in changes in behavior and rules. Each author then evaluated the declared lessons and the resulting behavior to determine the nature and extent of learning and its implications for democratic governance.

THE CASES: STRUCTURAL CONTEXT AND CORE PROBLEMS

A core problem or challenge for democratic learning was identified for each country. These core problems derive from the crises and changes of political regimes in some cases and from new tensions and crises in others, thus tending to correspond with changes in social-political-economic models or matrices in each country.[13] In different ways, all four countries have been or are in the midst of a transition from one model of state-society relations to another.

Argentina

In Argentina, the core problem for democratic learning has been not so much how to oust a failed dictatorship, but rather how to break a historical cycle in which democracy and authoritarianism have intertwined in a hybrid political formula. In Chapter Two, Marcelo Cavarozzi argues that the transformation of a state-centric matrix in Argentina did not correspond neatly with the shift in political regimes, but rather has occurred throughout a cycle of changes of political regime. From the 1940s to the 1970s, the alternation of semi-democratic and autocratic regimes succeeded in maintaining a relative equilibrium even without a stable institutional framework.

By the 1970s, however, the implicit norms that had sustained equilibrium and avoided a cataclysmic social breakdown — a fiscal pact among workers, capitalists, and the state tolerating significant but controlled inflation; and the rejection of political violence — dissolved, leading to a particularly repressive military regime and the unraveling of the state-centric matrix. Only in the early 1980s, when the costs of this hybrid political formula became unsustainable in terms of economic instability and political violence, did the conditions become ripe for democratic learning. At that point, the economic and political costs of authoritarian methods became clear, and the authoritarian component of the hybrid component was vacated in favor of a revalued democratic component.

One of the principal elements of the state-centric matrix in Argentina was a statist management of the economy that permanently expanded the range of issues managed by the state while simultaneously weakening parliamentary institutions and state capacity to resolve those issues. Thus, another of the core problems of Argentine political actors during the 1980s and 1990s has been to redefine not only the functions and responsibilities of the state and representative institutions, but also the very meaning of politics. Cavarozzi concludes that both political parties and the military learned the value of restructuring civil-military relations, whereas learning from economic crisis varied among the key actors — the business class, labor sector, and political parties.

Chile

In Chapter Three, Manuel Antonio Garretón and Malva Espinosa argue that in the decades preceding the 1973 military coup in Chile, the political parties, acting as class representatives with distinct ideological political programs, mediated relations between a socially and politically active state and the society. Political polarization and the inability of any single party to form a majority government or to enact projects on its own led to the collapse of the democratic system with the military coup of 1973. The change in political regime coincided with and stimulated a fundamental transformation of the larger matrix of state-society relations in which the political parties became technical governmental administrators, the state began to act "above" politics to ensure economic and political stability, and civil society became more concerned with individual access to the economic and political market than with collective action to achieve social demands and goals.

The tensions in the political-social model that culminated in the democratic rupture opened the door to a series of transformations, beginning with a radical restructuring of the economic model and the subsequent reorientation of the political and social order. The military regime also modified the substantive rules of the political game in the 1980 constitution, ensuring the political right a disproportionate voice in decisionmaking after the transition through electoral, legislative, judicial, and military rule changes.

The core problem for the restoration of democratic politics in Chile, then, became how to ensure majority governing coalitions that would facilitate governability and avoid the kind of ideological and political polarization that preceded the democratic breakdown. Specifically, political actors had to learn how to operate within the political rules imposed by the dictatorship. They also needed to learn how to eliminate the authoritarian enclaves that were the legacy of the Augusto Pinochet government's constitutional manipulation. Garretón concludes that the principal learning experience occurred in parties opposing the dictatorship, which learned to form alliances both to oust the military and to govern subsequently.

Uruguay

Among our cases, Uruguay has had the most extensive democratic experience in this century. Its twentieth-century model of state-society relations, characterized by a well-developed welfare state and functioning representative political system, continues to operate with only incipient signs of its transformation. The interruption of the democratic system appeared to be exactly that, a 12-year break after which the constitutional rules were wholly reinstated in 1985, when the same actors reappeared on the scene and the same model of state-society relations continued. Nevertheless, underlying tensions emerging in the 1950s and contributing to the 1973 military coup suggested a need for modification of the larger model; those tensions included a declining economic base following the collapse of the beef and wool market in the mid-1950s, a corresponding deterioration of state capacity to solve collective problems and provide social services, and a realignment of the Uruguayan electorate beginning in 1971.

In Chapter Four, Luis Costa Bonino describes a two-fold core political problem for Uruguayan political actors after the 1985 democratic restoration: 1) how to construct rules of the game to achieve both governability and representation in the context of a shift from a two-party to a multiparty system, and 2) how to avert the threat of reemerging social and political violence led by the radical left and drawn from the growing marginal sectors of the society. Costa concludes that Uruguayan political actors clearly learned from past mistakes. The question now is whether they can learn from new mistakes in a noncrisis atmosphere and whether the society can learn to process and manage the tensions in the Uruguayan model of state-society relations.

Venezuela

The unraveling of a statist model in Venezuela became evident much later than in other cases. In Chapter Five, Francine Jácome argues that, cushioned by petrodollars and mediated by an unusually well-organized party system, the tensions of the post-1958 political-social-economic model were first evident in the devaluation in 1983, then deepened with the 1989 *Caracazo,* the 1992 military coup attempts, and the 1994 banking failure. Within the political system, elite consensus-building and decisionmaking achieved the core goal of democratic stability but at the expense of representation, participation, and legitimacy.

Unlike the first two cases, the core problem for the Venezuelan political elite was to manage the transformation of the socio-economic-political model within the context of the existing political regime while avoiding its rupture or collapse. With the inauguration of the Rafael Caldera administration in 1994, Venezuela's tentative movement toward a new matrix was placed in doubt, and fundamental debates about the nature of Venezuelan democracy and economy were brought to the forefront. The election of Hugo Chávez Frías in 1998 brought an even greater level of uncertainty about the future nature of Venezuelan democracy and economy.

In Jácome's view, the basic questions are whether Venezuela will make a transition from a state-centered to a market-centered economic model and from a delegative/authoritarian to a participatory/democratic political culture. She concludes that the superb learning from the 1958 transition was transformed into a type of overlearning as political elites repeatedly strove to implement a pact-making strategy. She is less than sanguine about the prospects for a smooth transition to a new economic/political model.

The following chapters present the case studies and analyses of learning in each country. The final chapter compares those learning experiences, analyzing the nature and content of learning and the consequences for democratic governance.

Notes

1. Scholars have produced a long list of preconditions or facilitating conditions hypothesized to be necessary (though usually not sufficient) for democratic development (see Pinkney 1994 and Dahl 1989). The literature also boasts a number of explanations of the process of democratic development, some more deterministic than others. Modernization theory posits that economic development is both a necessary and sufficient condition for democratic development. Once a certain level of education, standard of living, and institutional capacity is attained, democratic government is likely to follow naturally (Lipset 1959). More recent variants posit a threshold of transition (Huntington 1984). Sociological theories argue that the dynamics of class development and interaction have produced historical transitions to democratic governance (for example, Moore 1966 and Rueschemeyer, Stephens, and Stephens 1992). Cultural approaches variously claim that only some cultures are amenable to liberal democracy, while socialization theory explains the long-term process of inculcating certain values at the mass level (for example, Huntington 1991 and Parekh 1993).

Institutional approaches have generated a long debate over the best form of government and electoral system for developing democracies. (See, for example, the special issues of *Journal of Democracy,* Fall 1990 and Summer 1991, with all the articles devoted to these matters.) More voluntarist approaches include elite theory, which suggests that elite unity is a prerequisite to democratic change and consolidation (Higley and Burton 1989).

2. The set of relevant political actors will vary from country to country, but may include, in addition to political parties and public officials, the military, organized labor, the church, business organizations, and intellectuals.

3. See, for example, Heclo (1974), Etheredge (1985), Moltz (1993), Hall (1993), and Breslauer and Tetlock (1991).

4. See, for example, E. Haas (1990), E. Haas (1991), Nye (1987), and Mann (1991).

5. See reviews of organizational theory by Levitt and March (1988) and Levy (1994).

6. See, for example, E. Haas (1991), P. Haas (1992), and Goldstein (1989).

7. See excellent reviews by Tetlock (1991) and Levy (1994).

8. Levy (1994) criticizes both the effectiveness and the accuracy criteria, respectively, arguing that political and bureaucratic constraints may impede implementation — and thus the manifest evidence — of learning and that the evaluation of the goodness or accuracy of learning is a normative evaluation by the researcher, which should be avoided. We agree with his criticisms but argue that learning must be manifested in at least an attempt to implement lessons learned, i.e., it must affect behavior by either reinforcing it or changing it, in order to be included in our analysis. Otherwise, learning is reduced to an individual cognitive phenomenon requiring a psychological analysis, which is not our intent here.

9. Decision-making theory indicates that during crisis, elites search for new information and alternatives to existing norms that have been discredited by events. See Moltz (1993, 301). Bermeo (1992) also posits that crisis, frustration, and dramatic changes in environment

lead to political learning. Gregory Bateson (1972) asserts that only when it becomes impossible to avoid the awareness that the world no longer makes sense can the mind consider radically different ideas and perceptions. This implies that some event or experience must convince the mind that the old beliefs are no longer sufficient to explain the reality.

10. A competency trap occurs when an inferior procedure produces favorable performance so that the organization becomes more adept and specialized with that procedure but fails to consider superior procedures (Levitt and March 1988).

11. The acquisition of knowledge is central to the concept of learning. An emerging body of literature on epistemic communities explains how ideas are generated among experts and how they are transmitted to decisionmakers. This work emphasizes the development and diffusion of consensual knowledge among experts leading to new collective understanding and behavior within organizations, both for domestic policymakers and for international organizations and regimes (E. Haas 1990; Adler and P. Haas 1992).

12. Bermeo (1992) posits that individual learning during democratic transitions occurs through interaction (internally and abroad) and comparison (with prior national experiences or with other countries' experiences). We expand her analysis to include processes of group learning.

13. Several authors use the concept of matrix to describe the change in state-society relations. Each author defines the concept as used in his or her case. Here, I refer generally to broad changes in the social, political, and economic bases of the relations between the state and civil society, which are widespread not only in Latin America, but globally.

References

Adler, Emanuel, and Peter M. Haas. 1992. "Conclusion: Epistemic Communities, World Order, and the Creation of a Reflective Research Program." *International Organization* 46 (Winter): 367-390.

Anderson, Richard. 1991. "Why Competitive Politics Inhibits Learning in Soviet Foreign Policy." In *Learning in U.S. and Soviet Foreign Policy*, eds. George Breslauer and Philip Tetlock. Boulder, Colo.: Westview Press.

Bateson, Gregory. 1972. *Steps to an Ecology of Mind: Collected Essays in Anthropology, Psychiatry, Evolution, and Epistemology*. San Francisco: Chandler Publishers.

Bermeo, Nancy. 1992. "Democracy and the Lessons of Dictatorship." *Comparative Politics* 24 (April): 273-291.

Breslauer, George. 1987. "Ideology and Learning in Soviet Third World: Review Article." *World Politics* 39: 429-448.

Breslauer, George, and Philip Tetlock, eds. 1991. *Learning in U.S. and Soviet Foreign Policy*. Boulder, Colo.: Westview Press.

Conover, Pamela Johnston, and Donald Searing. 1994. "Democracy, Citizenship and the Study of Political Socialization." In *Developing Democracy*, eds. Ian Budge and David McKay. New York: Sage.

Dahl, Robert. 1989. *Democracy and Its Critics*. New Haven, Conn.: Yale University Press.

Deutsch, Karl. 1963. *The Nerves of Government*. New York: Free Press.

Etheredge, Lloyd S. 1985. *Can Governments Learn? American Foreign Policy and Central American Revolutions*. New York: Pergamon Press.

Goldstein, Judith. 1989. "The Impact of Ideas on Trade Policy." *International Organization* 42 (1): 31-71.

González, Luis Eduardo. 1992. *Political Structures and Democracy in Uruguay*. South Bend, Ind.: University of Notre Dame Press.

Haas, Ernst. 1990. *When Knowledge Is Power: Three Models of Change in International Organizations*. Berkeley and Los Angeles: University of California Press.

Haas, Ernst. 1991. "Collective Learning: Some Theoretical Speculations." In *Learning in U.S. and Soviet Foreign Policy*, eds. George Breslauer and Philip Tetlock. Boulder, Colo.: Westview Press.

Haas, Peter M. 1992. "Introduction: Epistemic Communities and International Policy Coordination." *International Organization* 46 (1): 1-35.

Hall, Peter A. 1993. "Policy Paradigms, Social Learning, and the State: The Case of Economic Policymaking in Britain." *Comparative Politics* 25 (April): 275-296.

Harrison, Lawrence E. 1985. *Underdevelopment Is a State of Mind*. Lanham, Md.: Center for International Affairs, Harvard University, and University Press of America.

Heclo, Hugh. 1974. *Modern Social Politics in Britain and Sweden*. New Haven, Conn.: Yale University Press.

Higley, John, and Michael G. Burton. 1989. "The Elite Variable in Democratic Transitions and Breakdowns." *American Sociological Review* 54 (February): 17-32.

Huntington, Samuel. 1984. "Will More Countries Become Democratic?" *Political Science Quarterly* 99 (Summer).

Huntington, Samuel. 1991. *The Third Wave: Democratization in the Late Twentieth Century.* Norman, Okla.: University of Oklahoma Press.

Ikenberry, G. John, and Charles Kupchan. 1990. "Socialization and Hegemonic Power." *International Organization* 48 (2): 279-312.

Jarosz, William W., with Joseph Nye, Jr. 1993. "The Shadows of the Past: Learning from History and National Security Decisionmaking." In *Behavior, Society, and International Conflict*, vol. 3, eds. Philip E. Tetlock, Jo L. Husbands, and Robert Jervis. New York City: Oxford University Press.

Levitt, Barbara, and James G. March. 1988. "Organizational Learning." *Annual Review of Sociology* 14:319-340.

Levy, Jack S. 1994. "Learning and Foreign Policy: Sweeping a Conceptual Minefield." *International Organization* 48 (2): 279-312.

Lipset, Seymour Martin. 1959. "Some Social Requisites of Democracy." *American Political Science Review* (March): 69-105.

Mann, Dean. 1991. "Environmental Learning in a Decentralized Political World." *Journal of International Affairs* 444 (Winter): 301-337.

McCoy, Jennifer, and Luis Costa Bonino. 1992. "Political Learning in Reemerging Democracies: Framework for Analysis and Illustrations from Uruguay." Presented at the Congress of Latin American Studies Association in Los Angeles, September.

Moltz, James Clay. 1993. "Divergent Learning and the Failed Politics of Soviet Economic Reform." *World Politics* 45 (January): 301-325.

Moore, Barrington. 1966. *Social Origins of Dictatorship.* Boston: Beacon Press.

Nye, Joseph S. 1987. "Nuclear Learning and the United States: Soviet Security Regimes." *International Organization* 41 (Summer).

Parekh, Bhikhu. 1993. "The Cultural Particularity of Liberal Democracy." In *Prospects for Democracy: North, South, East, West*, ed. David Held. Stanford, Calif.: Stanford University Press.

Pinkney, Robert. 1994. *Democracy in the Third World.* Boulder, Colo: Lynne Rienner Publishers, Inc.

Reiter, Dan. 1994. "Learning, Realism, and Alliances: The Weight of the Shadow of the Past." *World Politics* 46 (July): 490-526.

Rueschemeyer, Dietrich, Evelyne Stephens, and John Stephens. 1992. *Capitalist Development and Democracy.* Chicago: University of Chicago Press.

Tetlock, Philip. 1991. "In Search of an Elusive Concept." In *Learning in U.S. and Soviet Foreign Policy*, eds. George Breslauer and Philip Tetlock. Boulder, Colo: Westview Press.

CHAPTER TWO

Argentina: Lost Opportunities and Ongoing Learning

MARCELO CAVAROZZI[1]

POLITICAL TRANSITION AND THE DECLINE OF THE STATE-CENTRIC MATRIX

In 1983, a new political era began in Argentina — a sharp departure from the previous five decades, which had been fraught with political instability. Between 1930 and 1983, six successful coups d'état had set a pattern of military intervention that precluded any real possibility of consolidating a democratic system of governance. However, the military dictatorships were unable to consolidate their hold on power. The result was a complex, hybrid political formula of democratic and authoritarian regimes, which I will discuss in depth in the following sections.

Since 1983, in contrast, free and competitive elections have become the norm, and the threat of institutional breakdowns has been reduced to a minimum. Who governs Argentina is determined by a competition between party platforms, resolved through periodic popular elections. Likewise, stabilization of electoral procedures has helped to ensure that different political parties have access to executive and legislative powers at the national, state, and local levels. This chapter argues that the transition from the previous period and the consolidation of a democratic system of governance are positive results, garnered from the process of political learning that has been taking place in Argentina since the early 1980s.

This learning, however, has also included a negative component that erodes the process of institutionalization and could compromise the stability of democratic governance in the long run. Large sectors of the population no longer seem to pay much attention to controversies within or among the various political parties, nor to the nature of the political regime itself. In short, these segments have "learned" that the political system, whether democratic or authoritarian, has lost relevance as a mechanism for sorting out economic and social controversies.[2] Therefore, an important question is how this negative component has played into the overall political learning process.

A gap exists between, on the one hand, issues pertaining to parties and political institutions and, on the other, most of the issues that affect the population on a daily basis (particularly those having to do with economic problems and survival) and the political mechanisms for resolving them. This suggests that the changes that have taken place since 1983 are not limited to the process of democratic consolidation but also include other dimensions of Argentina's social and political organization. These changes could redefine the significance of the country's return to democracy by minimizing or altering its possible repercussions. The outcome remains undefined, but this negative learning is an integral part of the political transition that has been taking place since the 1980s.

The year 1983 was defined by the catastrophic collapse of a military regime that had set out to transform Argentine society radically and by the installation of democratic institutions that, in time, proved to be more solid than the previous ones. This turning point implied changes in politics, which in turn displaced the import of politics for society at large. Not only was the political regime transformed, but the functions of politics in the marketplace and in civil society were transformed as well. In this latter sense, what changed was *what* and *how much* could be resolved through politics in these spheres. More specifically, the hybrid political formula that had predominated since the 1930s was replaced by a stable system based on democratic political rules and principles, and the manner in which the political system was "present" in the marketplace and civil society was substantially redefined.

Within the framework of the state-centric matrix (SCM) that prevailed for five decades after 1930, state arenas were the preferred venue in which distributive conflicts and disputes related to potential areas of equality in civil society were settled. These areas included political citizenship, the workplace, and the access to public education and common urban spaces. In a paper analyzing this framework in depth, I defined it as "statist hyperpoliticization" (Cavarozzi 1994). Within the SCM framework, the contents and dimensions of conflicts and disputes were profiled in a relatively clear way, even though the rules for resolving them tended to be discretionary and unstable.

By definition, the exhaustion of the SCM model implied that the state lost its centrality. In turn, this meant that there would be fewer areas for political resolution in the marketplace and civil society. Although this phenomenon had its positive effects, especially a reduction in the levels of conflict and drama in Argentine politics, it is associated, nonetheless, with the danger that politics would become irrelevant.

A stable alternative societal matrix has not yet emerged in Argentina to define a pattern of interactions among politics, the marketplace, and civil society. The same factor that was at the root of conflict in the state-centric model — namely, the unequal distribution of material and symbolic resources — underlies the current scenario; in fact, it has even worsened. The signs of this inequality, however, have been overshadowed by new patterns of social behavior that have emerged. Some of these behaviors have been defensive in nature, reactions against the dissolution of the previous matrix. This is evidenced by the extreme economic instability and the destruction of the networks of collective reciprocity: for example, the decrease in private investment (traditionally induced by public spending and investment, which at present has been substantially reduced) and the weakening of popular organizations, such as neighborhood associations and labor unions, which had been state-promoted.

Other behaviors, such as the business sector's search for new ties with international markets, have been more innovative. These behaviors have led to technological innovations and to a new emphasis on strategies designed to take advantage of the quality of human resources in settings where rent-seeking possibilities from the state have been drastically reduced.

It is important to note, however, that both types of behaviors — defensive and innovative — have contributed to the erosion of the state's scope of action. The former did so by eroding the "implicit fiscal pact" (a term coined by Ricardo Carciofi), upon which the viability of state policies was based under the SCM model (Carciofi 1990). This pact had established two mechanisms for putting into effect the implicit agreements among relevant actors: one, the persistence of an annual inflation rate averaging 30 to 50 percent; and two, the generation of moderate public deficits. The indicator of a crisis in the fiscal pact was the onset of the first episode of high inflation in 1975. During the following 17 years, the inflation rate remained above 100 percent per year. In 1989 and 1990, hyperinflationary levels were reached. However, innovative behaviors also weakened the state because they were equated with a systematic perception of the state as a source of inefficiency and rent seeking.

Therefore, the new setting for players in the transition process, particularly for the political parties, cannot be defined merely by the stabilization of democratic institutions. The changes occurring in Argentina have affected and redefined the meaning of politics itself, as well as the very nature of the country's governmental mechanisms.

The second part of this chapter describes the characteristics of politics in Argentina for the half century following the 1930 crisis, a period in which institutional learning failed over and over again. The third part of this chapter analyzes the decade that began with the democratic transition of 1983. I conclude that contemporary Argentine politics has been characterized by a contradictory combination. A positive learning process in which various social groups and the elites have been the leading players has resulted in a renewed valuation of democratic institutions and rules. However, a negative learning process associated with the alienation from politics of large segments of the population could compromise the stability of democratic governance over the long term.

WASTED OPPORTUNITIES FOR LEARNING (1930-1983)

During the half century preceding World War I, Argentina attained high levels of economic and sociocultural development, but in the period between World War I and World War II, the country's growth rate gradually diminished, and its economy never again recovered the dynamism of the *belle époque*. Resorting to the now-discredited Rostowian image, Argentina could be characterized as a country whose flight was canceled just before take-off. Nevertheless, the country managed to elude political and economic catastrophes for several decades. Argentina's economy continued to grow, although at a much more modest rate than those of Australia and Canada, countries it had been compared to until the beginning of

World War II. Argentine society also managed to maintain its integrative character while incorporating the majority of the population into the political process.

The most important players — capitalists, labor unions, and the military — refrained from the sort of behavior aimed at the annihilation of social and political enemies or at the abandonment of the implicit accords that underlay the very functioning of the economy. The most important of these accords were compliance with fiscal obligations and negotiation of mutual restrictions on the change of relative prices. The military, in turn, abstained from implementing extremely repressive policies until the early 1970s.

Thanks to these self-imposed restrictions, for many decades Argentina did not explode, nor did its social and economic organization fall apart. However, recurrent cycles of political instability and the stop-and-go economy resulted in the accumulation of unresolved dilemmas and conflicts. The conclusion of the first democratic experience in 1930 and the failed attempts at reconciliation between the Radicals and the Conservatives at the end of that same decade sealed the schism between the party system as a whole and the capitalist sectors of agriculture, finance, commerce, and industry.[3] This schism became entrenched, either openly or behind the scenes, as an unresolved problem of Argentine politics.

The early Peronism of the 1940s was, among other things, a reaction to the blockage of channels of popular representation. However, the unfolding of the Peronist formula did not allow the practices of representative democracy to develop, either. Tulio Halperín Donghi (1994) skillfully analyzes how, during his early years, Juan Perón lost an opportunity to re-legitimize Argentinean politics on the basis of the universal right to vote. Despite the fact that Peronism won up to two thirds of the votes during the decades preceding 1955, Perón had the tendency to interpret these votes simply as a manifestation of acquiescence toward his leadership. This was aggravated by his reluctance to institutionalize political procedures, which ensured that "the only indisputable authority would be his own" (Donghi 1994, 26). For this reason, when Perón fell in 1955, the disarticulation of his plebiscitary personalism did nothing more than bring to the fore once again the difficulties of establishing a political democracy in Argentina.

Until 1955, the armed forces rarely became involved in the legitimization of political regimes in cases of conflict because both the officials of the conservative restoration period (1930-1943) and Perón himself succeeded in keeping the military on the periphery of everyday politics. Between 1955 and the beginning of the 1970s, however, a progressive militarization of politics ensued, with the military taking direct control in 1955, 1962, and 1966.

Learning from the Militarization of Politics

At the end of 1969, the leaders of the two major parties — Juan Perón and Radical Ricardo Balbín — signed a pact of reconciliation known as the Hora del Pueblo (Hour of the People), to which smaller parties also subscribed. This pact remained in effect between 1970 and 1973, for the duration of the liberalization process. In 1973, the first free elections in Argentina in two decades put Peronists back in power. More important, these elections facilitated the legitimization of electoral and parliamentary institutions by all parties. Thus, one of the most serious shortcomings ailing Argentine politics since 1930 was remedied.

The 1969 party pact, however, had a couple of serious flaws that eventually frustrated the process of democratization. The first was that Perón thought he would be able to control the Peronist guerrillas once the institutional restoration was concluded.[4] He was proved wrong by the Montoneros (guerrilla movement), who resorted to violence when they were dismissed from the government positions they had reached in May 1973.[5] The second flaw was that noncompliance with institutional rules and the law of the land extended beyond the Peronist guerrillas to include other sectors vying for power within the chaotic universe of Peronism in the 1970s. Then, following Perón's death a mere eight months after he assumed power, an all-out war within the Peronist Party quickly permeated the different spheres of government, drastically undermining its ability to govern the Argentine society.

Despite these conditions, the failed transition to democracy between 1973 and 1976 handed down a positive legacy in terms of political learning: The parties, which had been at loggerheads during the previous four decades, learned that the success of any process of democratization would require the inclusion of all significant political actors. Perón and Balbín learned this lesson through trial and error. Ever since 1952, when they first ran against each other as presidential candidates for their parties, they had been the main players in a repetitive and perverse political game in which exclusion of the adversary by transgressing the rules produced pyrrhic victories. The temporary fall of the adversary would be followed by a coup d'état, and the coups d'état ousted both Peronists and Radicals from the center of the political arena. By the 1980s, leaders of both parties would demonstrate that they had learned the lesson of more inclusive politics.

The all-out war between the armed forces and the guerrillas, most of whose casualties did not belong to either faction, signified the exhaustion of the political modus operandi that had prevailed since the 1930s. During the 1970s, the implicit norms that had helped to avoid great debacles within Argentina's state-centric formula were permanently dissolved. During the first half of the decade, the self-imposed restrictions that players had placed on their own economic and political behavior vanished. The "fiscal agreement" that had successively been built and then torn down since the end of World War II burst apart in 1975. The business sector and labor unions abandoned all the relative restrictions they had previously imposed on their own economic behavior, and price rises as well as demands for wage increases became their standard operating procedure. This lack of restraint in 1975 led to the first episode of hyperinflation in the twentieth century's monetary history, and the ensuing generalization of mechanisms such as indexing and dollarization seriously curtailed the ability of the state to implement effective economic policies. In turn, a weakened state furthered the downward spiral of public confidence and fueled the reluctance of the business sector to meet its fiscal responsibilities.

Beginning in 1970, the level of political violence increased; assassinations, kidnappings, and disappearances became the rule of the day. At the same time, some military and para-police units became the main transgressors of judicial norms.[6] The repressive forces initiated a perverse cat-and-mouse game with the guerrilla groups.[7]

Out-of-control inflation, worsening instability, political violence, and government terrorism marked the end of the 1973-1976 interim period. Yet, despite having repeatedly failed to build a stable institutional framework, Argentine society nonetheless managed to continue functioning.

The military government that was installed in 1976 clearly aimed at replacing the SCM model with an alternative economic and political model. The core diagnosis of society's ills made by the authoritarian regime was a criticism of the centralized role that the state had assumed from 1930 to 1973. The ideologues, led by Secretary of the Economy, José M. Martínez de Hoz, concluded that government interventionist policies not only had generated permanent political conflicts, but also had contributed decisively to deforming the behavior of social players, particularly workers and businessmen.

The military failed both in implementing its projects for economic reform and in stabilizing an authoritarian order. The main objectives of the orthodox policies applied from 1978 on — rebuilding capital markets and disciplining national producers — were not fulfilled. The military government failed in its attempt to reorient economic behavior partly because of inconsistencies in the implementation of its economic reform program and partly because of errors in the premises upon which it based its anti-inflationary policy.

The unfolding of these "neoliberal" policies was aggravated by the government's irresponsible handling of foreign credit and by an exorbitant increase in military spending.[8] The set of policies applied by the military completely sank the old model of political management of capital, which had been eroding since 1974. This precipitated the chaotic economic adjustment that began in Argentina in 1982.[9]

Even while failing to achieve its economic reforms, the authoritarian project weighed heavily in the definitive exhaustion of the economic formula of the SCM model. Its political failures helped to upset the unstable balance between the semi-democratic and autocratic regimes, which had constituted the base of the Argentinean state-centric political formula. The armed forces' loss of credibility and the calamities they triggered thus produced effects that would outlast the 1976-1983 military dictatorship. The long-term effect was the nullification of the authoritarian component of the hybrid formula that had prevailed in Argentina since the 1930s. This, in turn, caused Argentine society to revalue democracy as a system of government.

The last straw for the military government between 1980 and 1982 was a combination of internal discord and the most wanton military adventurism.[10] Once again, in light of the completely pulverized military government, important sectors of Argentina's population began to discover and eventually condemn the faults that many had previously chosen to tolerate or ignore. The settling of accounts with the military government during the first half of the 1980s, however, swung even further than the traditional pendulum of past decades. In contrast with the results of previous political cycles, condemnation of the military regime was not limited to censuring the (substantial) failure of its policies but also included censuring its methods, which were obviously authoritarian in nature.

These condemnations, of course, focused first on the more perverse aspects of the military government: the methods used for illegal repression, the disappearances, and the total disregard of human rights. Such aberrations were seen as the most extreme manifestation of the intrinsic arbitrariness of authoritarianism. There was a similar reaction with regard to economic policies. Important business-community sectors that previously had proclaimed the military government as their own started by rejecting foreign exchange and monetary policies that had harmed their interests, and, later, they went much further. In contrast to what had happened under past military dictatorships, the business sector attributed the impossibility of negotiating and correcting mistaken policies to the arbitrariness and isolation of authoritarian government. Even more, they associated the authoritarian government's arbitrariness and despotism with a pattern of politics typical of a centralized state.

Among large capitalists, the perception of a link between authoritarianism and state centralism helped to lessen the schizophrenia that had characterized business behavior for several decades. The business sector had criticized the state's excessive economic regulations; yet, it had favored the installation of authoritarian governments. Thus, the business sector fed a process that it claimed to reject. The military regime, by making policy in a despotic manner, failed in its goal of dismantling the strong state but paradoxically succeeded in reinforcing the statism of the political process.

During the 1980s, a clear destatization of the economy occurred when regulatory mechanisms accumulating since the 1930s weakened and broke down in a chaotic manner. At the same time, a process of political destatization was also taking place, although in a less apparent way than the economic destatization. Under the SCM model, the Argentine people, both individually and collectively, had gradually built up behavior patterns by which the government and, by extension, the state helped to maintain acceptable levels of order and cohesion through function "overload." At the same time, this "overload" allowed the players to unload their own responsibilities onto governmental agencies.

While it was a negative collective norm, the unloading onto the government was also a powerful social bond, which was maintained as long as the players nurtured expectations that the state effectively could take charge, at least partially, of the responsibilities that were being transferred to it.

The political economy of the SCM yielded some gains and some losses. What the state could do — which included maintaining a relative, albeit precarious, economic stability — contributed to reducing the autonomy of private players in the marketplace and in civil society. At the same time, the government became a sort of crutch by providing mechanisms that made up for the deficiencies of these players. On their own, the players proved to be unable to abide by any rule, whether it responded to market mechanism or to a principle of collective solidarity.

RISE OF DEMOCRACY AND POLITICAL LEARNING

The demise of authoritarianism and the consolidation of democracy implied a multi-round learning process (which is still ongoing) concerning the complex and multi-dimensional characteristics of statism and its ambivalent effects on the workings of society. The 15 years since 1983 have witnessed three such rounds:

1. Round One was the transition period in the strict sense of the word, for example, the downfall of the military dictatorship and the first 18 months of the Radical Party's government headed by Raúl Alfonsín. During that time, it became apparent that governmental hyperpoliticization was again being fed by authoritarianism. The transition repeated a pattern of social action that implied constantly walking on the edge, since the risk of violence and loss of monetary control still loomed over the horizon. In this sense, the statist crutch, exacerbated by authoritarianism, posed an obstacle that made it difficult for any sort of autonomous and responsible behavior to come forth that might minimize the risk of economic (and political) chaos. The fact that this crutch had also provided support was not perceived, even though it continued to sustain the society, albeit in an ever more precarious way, given its accelerated exhaustion. This support prevented society from disintegrating on the verge of crisis and chaos stemming from weak social bonds. During this first phase, capitalists were the lead players in the more significant learning processes.

2. Round Two, which coincided with the last four years of Alfonsín's government, involved the irreversible crisis of the SCM model, in particular the breakdown of the implicit and explicit inflationary mechanisms that were the bases of the predictability of economic transactions. The main episodes of this period were the failure of the Austral Plan and the outbreak of hyperinflation in 1989. During these years, Peronist politicians in particular completed a learning process whereby they came fully to accept the possibility of suffering definitive electoral defeat. This novel train of thought within the Peronist Party was brought about by the electoral defeats they suffered during the first half of the Radical administration.

3. Finally, during Round Three — which has extended through Carlos Menem's presidency — the vast majority of the Argentine population interpreted the 1989-1990 outbreak of hyperinflation as a definitive sign of the irreversibility of the SCM crisis. This transformation served as an indispensable foundation for the implementation of the drastic economic reforms promoted by the capitalist sectors and the Peronist Party, as redefined by President Menem's leadership. These reforms have redesigned the economic model by privatizing the vast majority of public companies and services provided by the government and by deregulating many areas of economic activity. In contrast with leaders of the 1960s and 1970s, these players have forged ahead with the restructuring of the economy within the framework of a political democracy. At this stage, the armed forces also underwent an unprecedented learning process. For the first time in the political history of the twentieth century, the higher echelons of the armed forces suppressed a military uprising against democratically elected authorities. The squelching of this revolt implied support of democracy and democratic rules by the majority within the military institution, in clear contrast to the practices that prevailed between 1930 and 1989.

The following sections analyze in greater detail the aforementioned rounds.

Round One: Aversion to Authoritarianism and Enchantment with Democracy (1982-1984)

The downfall of the SCM model left a threefold legacy: The authoritarian regimes lost their legitimacy; economic instability was exacerbated; and there was a general crisis of the state. Raúl Alfonsín's success in the presidential elections of October 1983 was based first on the Radical candidate's ability to embody, in a believable way, the society's generalized rejection of the military dictatorship in power since 1976. Alfonsín made a frontal attack on military officials when he refused to accept the amnesty that they had mandated for themselves. He also denounced an alleged pact between the military and the unions, thus convincing many voters that his Peronist adversaries were leaning toward an agreement with the armed forces. The idea of this pact was credible, since the Peronists, more than the Radicals, supported legislation that blocked any possibility of punishing the transgressions of constitutional standards and the violations of human rights perpetrated by the armed forces.[11] But the effectiveness of the Radical candidate's message ultimately rested on the convincing dissemination of the idea that a Peronist victory would risk a return to the disorder and political violence of the 1970s. Both the internal disputes of the Peronists, which were more blatant during the electoral campaign, and the disregard they repeatedly manifested in 1983 for the rule of law gave credence to the Radical Party's allegations.

Another argument the Radicals wielded very effectively during the electoral campaign was that the serious economic crisis affecting Argentina since 1981 was the result of the orthodox policies applied during the five years of General Jorge Rafael Videla's administration (1976-1981). Authoritarianism thus came to be closely associated with the economic crisis. Alfonsín postulated that democracy and economic recovery would feed off each other and that democracy would become the guarantee of "fair wages, food, education, and housing" for the majority of the population.

When Alfonsín and his associates assumed power, their central focus was on political and moral rejection of the military governments. Radical politician Federico Storani stated in an interview for this project, "I believe that this first stage was tinted by the euphoria of doing away with authoritarianism and the dictatorship, and the quasi-militant [popular] participation was for the reestablishment of democratic values and rules, without a clear course of action beyond that, which is why it was so short-lived."[12] In the end, the new democratic government even denied the very existence of the crisis the Argentine state was undergoing at the time.

Alfonsín, and to a greater extent the members of his party, became political and psychological hostages of the SCM model. They failed to perceive that state-centric policies were becoming totally counterproductive in this new setting and that populist reflexes were losing their usefulness. As I have indicated, an additional problem was that the expectations of the majority of the population were not realistic either, as they believed that democracy would correct economic difficulties without an excessive cost and that it also would compensate the losses incurred during the authoritarian period.

In the economic sphere, then, the Radical government started with the premise that it was possible to return to a situation of "politics as usual." Alfonsín named to the economic cabinet a group of traditional Radical politicians who had carried out similar functions some 20 years before in the short-lived government of Arturo Illía.[13] Headed by Bernardo Grinspun at the Department of the Economy and Alfredo Concepción, president of the Central Bank, this group espoused the idea that the solution to the crisis was to repeat the income policies and Keynesian recipes that had "worked" (despite ups and downs) between 1946 and 1975.

Even if the Radicals thought it was possible to avoid introducing any innovations in the economic sphere, their initiatives in the political sphere were extraordinarily daring. After failing in its attempts to persuade the armed forces to use the military justice system to punish the perpetrators of the 1976 military coup and the human rights violations, the government decided to file an action against the juntas that had presided over the authoritarian regimes until 1982. It further decided to let the ordinary justice system try cases about disappearances and tortures brought by individuals against individual officers and sergeants major.

During the first year of Alfonsín's government, the economic crisis and the ineffectiveness of governmental policies in overcoming it became the issues of greatest concern. Hope that foreign debt negotiations would be facilitated by a political decision by the U.S. government to support the new democracy was quickly dashed, and both inflation and the fiscal deficit continued to soar each month. The exhaustion of the SCM model's stabilizing mechanisms, together with the country's external vulnerability, created a situation in which the impact of any disequilibrium was amplified in the economy.

Round Two: Rise and Fall of "Alfonsinism" (1985-1989)

This context of serious economic deterioration already was foretelling the plunge into hyperinflation by the end of 1984. During the first few months of 1985, Alfonsín realized the seriousness of the situation and changed the members of his economic cabinet, with the exception of Alfredo Concepción, president of the Central Bank. The new officials, whose most prominent figure was Juan Sourrouille, secretary of the economy, were a group of economists who enjoyed tremendous academic prestige but were practically unknown to the public. In addition, the Radical lineage of most of them was at best questionable, and they did not enjoy much sympathy from the business community.

The new stabilizing measures — the so-called Austral Plan — achieved some success in the beginning. In only a few months' time, inflation rates and the fiscal deficit were significantly reduced, and the Radical Party achieved a spectacular victory in the parliamentary elections of 1985.

This success, however, was short-lived. Blinded by the temporary achievements of the Austral Plan, Alfonsín overestimated the pliancy of the economy. He thought he would be able to subordinate the rhythm and content of his economic reforms to his political objectives. During 1986, Alfonsín and his closest associates — in particular, Enrique Nosiglia and Leopoldo Moreau — targeted a faction of the Peronist Party to join a "Third Historic Movement" that presumably would consolidate the Radical Party's electoral supremacy as the Peronist Party had done in the 1945-1946 period.[14] Already by 1987, less than two years after the Austral Plan was launched, signs of its failure were evident. Inflation rates had returned to the high 1983-1985 levels; the national economic authorities once again had lost control of the fiscal deficit. These authorities found themselves in a trap, just as their predecessors had, when they implemented successive, short-term emergency measures that quickly became outdated. In the 1987 mid-term elections, the Radicals lost most of the governorships at play, including the decisive province of Buenos Aires. The defeated Buenos Aires candidate, Juan Manuel Casella, had been Alfonsín's favorite for the upcoming presidential election. From then on, the government became a lame duck even in areas where its initiative once had been clear.

In February 1989, Argentina underwent what some analysts call a "market coup." Faced with the assumption, finally confirmed by fact, that the U.S. government would not continue to back the exchange stabilization policy of Alfonsín's government, a group of the most important financiers "ran" to the dollar, thereby applying unendurable pressure on the *austral* — which was the name given to the monetary unit created in 1985, also used to identify the anti-inflationary plan implemented that year. The effect of this "market coup" was the complete collapse of any semblance of stability.

Yet, the collapse of the heterodox stabilization measures fail to produce another institutional breakdown like those that have abounded in contemporary Argentina — even in crisis settings of lesser magnitude than that of the 1989 crisis. Why? The responses to this question can help us evaluate the nature of the processes of political learning since 1983.

The errors of the Radicals turned out to be dramatically costly for them, first in regard to their ability to maintain political power in 1987 and 1989, and later in terms of the erosion of their electoral appeal until the mid-1990s. The main party adversaries, in particular the second democratic president, Carlos Menem, took advantage of Unión Cívica Radical's negative experience. In contrast with the past, however, in which the goal of attaining power had not been linked to a concern for institutional stability, the Peronists now attacked the government while defending the political system. Neither the elites nor the majority of the population believed that a military coup could solve the problem of instability. Instead, it was the other way around: The polls became the recourse used to reject the government and its Radical candidates. The Peronists were way ahead in the presidential elections of May 1989, and the reins of power were turned over several months ahead of time to avoid prolonging an extreme situation of ungovernability.

Round Three: Menem and Hyperinflation and Its Effects: Achievements and Risks (1990-1994)

The election that cemented the victory of the Peronist candidate — which was held in May 1989 in the midst of hyperinflation's upward climb — involved something more than a simple changing of the guard. The replacement of the Radical Civic Union (Unión Cívica Radical — UCR) by Peronism coincided with a fundamental change in the way most people related to politics. By helping to destroy the routines of everyday life, the successive failures of the 1976 military government and the first democratic civilian government nourished a general disillusionment with the solutions proposed by those in power. In other words, there was a collective devaluation of politics.

This withdrawal from politics had ambiguous effects: while it paved the way for the people's acceptance of policies aimed at drastically shrinking the spheres of governmental action and regulation, this retreat also weakened the informal rules and, in an even broader sense, the moral consensus that form the basis of government and society. Therefore, the depoliticization of the second half of the 1980s meant a reversal of the pattern of statist politicization that had prevailed in Argentina for several decades. Political space was opened to form a new matrix that combined "less government" with "more market," facilitated by the fear of reverting to an extremely unstable situation.

Interviews for this project with leaders from across the political spectrum confirm this interpretation. In this regard, the right-wing politician Federico Zamora, when asked what prompted society to accept the transformation, responded, "Of course, hyperinflation and its effect in disintegrating social and economic structures." The FREPASO left-wing politician Carlos "Chacho" Alvarez remarked, "The topic of hyperinflation is a frontier of sorts. In politics there is a before and an after hyperinflation. How much Menem has gotten away with has to do with this, and it is something the left simply does not understand." Radical politician Federico Storani expressed the opinion that ". . . in the case of Argentina, the collective memory of hyperinflation gives a broad margin to maneuver with stabilization plans such as the one being implemented." Finally, business leader Jorge Born's response was, "The tremendous hardship and fear generated by hyperinflation, that everything would go up in flames, played a decisive role. But also the fact that for many years people could see it coming. We went through a civil war, through the 'Malvinas' (Falkland Islands) war, one failure after the next, and I believe that had an influence on the situation."[15]

The electoral victory of 1989 also contributed to the consolidation of a trend that had begun in 1987, as a result of which the Peronists gradually won back the electoral favor they had enjoyed from 1946 to 1975. But in contrast with the post-1955 period — when the attractiveness of the Peronists had been based on their ability to express the majority's rejection of the governments in power — Menem's success starting in 1989 depended on showing his effectiveness in recovering stability by reconstructing the principle of political authority.

Menem's strategy included important innovations. During the campaign, he did not depart from the staunchest Peronist style: He criticized the Radicals and their candidate, Eduardo Angeloz, for their neoliberal policies and promised to implement a "wage boost" upon assuming power. However, as soon as he was elected, he made it very clear that his main objective was to stabilize the economy and that his program would abandon the postulates of nationalism and statism his party had traditionally supported. This position was announced even before he took office, and it was soon confirmed by the policies implemented starting in December 1989, when the new president was forced to replace his first economic team due to a relapse into hyperinflation. During 1990, and particularly when Domingo Cavallo accepted the office of secretary of the economy at the beginning of 1991, Menem's administration adopted a free-market strategy that led to sudden cuts in services and government subsidies and to the privatization of practically all publicly owned companies. The steadfastness with which privatization policies were applied and public spending was reduced helped Menem win and retain support from large business groups based in Argentina and from international financial circles. The seven largest financial groups in Argentina, along with foreign investors (mainly from the United States, Spain, and France), were the main beneficiaries of these privatizations, many of which were brazenly corrupt.

Menem, however, did not limit himself merely to implementing measures with greater consistency than his half-hearted predecessors. He also used the same level of energy he had applied to policies for stabilization and privatization to reaffirm his political decision-making power. Turning the economic policies adopted since 1990 into a positive symbol of his political style did not come easily or automatically. But even though his stabilization policies drastically affected the standard of living of both the population's poorer sectors and the middle classes — who directly or indirectly depended on public spending — Menem took advantage of the circumstances to present these policies as the only way out of an even worse alternative: deeper economic instability and disorder.

Menem's next move was to convince the public that the effectiveness of his stabilization and economic reform measures required the exercise and reestablishment of a strong political authority[16] with two clearly distinguishable dimensions. It implied a partial recovery by the government of its ability to induce social players and individuals, through sanctions and rewards, to subject their behavior to rules.[17] One of the more significant aspects of this process was to revitalize the government's negotiating power vis-à-vis the business community. The margin for maneuvering that the government enjoyed when dealing with the business community during the initial phase of the Austral Plan from 1985-1986 was destroyed later on. The Peronists received a defenseless government, one in which the tools of economic policies had lost all of their effectiveness. Furthermore, the government adopted measures deemed harmful by a large number of businesspeople — in particular, the increased tax load and the accelerated opening of markets.[18] Obviously, the plausibility of enforcing fiscal legislation and trade policy depended on the credibility of the government, and this credibility increased with Domingo Cavallo's arrival at the Department of the Economy.

The second dimension of the strengthening of political authority under Menem was directly linked to a process of "representialization" in the Argentine political system and to an intensification of anti-politics postures. Both phenomena have had negative connotations from the perspective of the functioning of democratic institutions. One factor upon which Menem based his 1989 electoral victory, which he continued to use afterward, was his skillful exploitation of the generalized rejection by the great majority of Argentines of the political class since the end of the 1980s. These attitudes became more acute with the successive failed attempts at economic stabilization by Alfonsín's government and the ensuing hyperinflation. Faced with this phenomenon, and cultivating a political style not entirely foreign to the traditions of his party, starting with Perón himself, Menem positioned himself as a political "outsider." He minimized the importance of the word as carrier of a political message and resorted to promoting his figure as someone accustomed to circulating outside the political arena, in the world of sports, television, and show business.[19]

The success of Menem's anti-politics style was a factor that contributed to the system's return to a strong presidency. His criticism of the traditional mechanisms of political and parliamentarian negotiation (which had never worked effectively in Argentina in the first place) rested on the premise that these procedures were not particularly useful and could even be dispensed with in case of an economic emergency. Menem correctly grasped the political climate at the end of the 1980s and thus was able to displace the legislative power further, as well as to impose severe restrictions on the autonomy of the judicial power. The judicial power, in particular, had gained unprecedented ground under the previous Radical government.

Two forces came into play to the benefit of the new holder of the presidency: an increased imbalance of power between the branches of government with a concentration of power in the executive, and the splitting of political parties into increasingly numerous factions, which led to their loss of prestige in the eyes of the public. This particularly affected the Radical Party; fighting between various Radical factions, the so-called "internal fights," became highly visible by the end of Alfonsín's government and became outright ruthless during the 1990s. In spite of its defeat, the Radical Party was not excessively damaged by the 1989 presidential election. The party won one third of the votes, and even its presidential candidate, Eduardo Angeloz, came close to getting 40 percent of the total vote. The election, therefore, was not lacking in competition, since Menem did not get an absolute majority of the votes. But in the legislative elections of 1991 and 1993, the Radical Party continued to lose electoral ground, and its representation in Parliament gradually began to diminish, particularly in the national Senate. At the same time, the loss of institutional positions at the national, regional, and local levels exacerbated struggles among the factions. In the eyes of the public, this looked like an ugly contest for public office and for the control of governmental resources that were becoming more scarce.

Another factor sapping the appeal of the Radical Party was ex-President Alfonsín's reticence to give up his leading role within the party and on the political scene. In spite of advances made in the process of institutionalization, Alfonsín did not come to grips with the fact that his presidency had been marked permanently by his forced resignation in the midst of the hyperinflationary period. After he left power, his mere image evoked the opposite of the monetary and economic stability that became so valued in the eyes of the Argentine people from 1989 on. As Radical politician Federico Storani explained, "Alfonsín's leadership, unlike other styles of leadership, was rationally formulated — and the idea was to distinguish this from the old-style leadership based on charisma. It nonetheless had a high level of wishful thinking, for even the staunchest militants of the Radical Party, when there were no clear solutions at hand, would say, 'Well, Alfonsín will soon pull something out of his sleeve.' And Alfonsín fostered that sentiment, and continues to do so, because he loves to play on mystery and magical solutions. I remember many instances in which this myth was fed; for example, when he came up with the Beagle plebiscite, the Austral Plan, it was all concocted in secret. Perhaps the last straw was when he proposed, without warning, to move the national capital and begin constitutional reform. I think that at this point he misread the demands of the Argentine people, and the bubble burst."

The Radical Party's decline was reinforced toward the end of 1993, when Alfonsín, having again assumed the party's presidency, drastically redefined the Radical Civic Union's (Unión Cívica Radical — UCR) strategy toward government. Alfonsín abandoned the hard-line opposition stance he had maintained since the beginning of Menem's government and instead agreed that his party would provide the legislative consensus required to reform the Constitution and finally open the doors to the prospect of presidential reelection. The Peronist-Radical agreement, known as the Pacto de Olivos (Olivos Pact), was cause for the UCR's complete breakdown during the Constitutional Reform elections (Convencionales Constituyentes) in 1994. Its electoral constituency was reduced to around 20 percent of the vote, and it was upstaged in several districts by the newly formed left-wing coalition called Frente Grande (Grand Front).

The decline of the Radicals was further accelerated in the 1995 presidential elections, in which the combination of a weak presidential candidate — the ex-governor of Río Negro, Horacio Masacesi — and a misguided campaign yielded only 17 percent of the votes, which was surpassed by the Peronists and the center-left coalition renamed National Solidarity Front (Frente del País Solidario — FREPASO).

The setting in which the Radical Party's crisis unfolded illustrates the advance in the democratic learning process stemming from the recent transition from authoritarianism in Argentina, as well as the deficiencies and pitfalls that assail it. Democracy has resisted the unprecedented crisis of the 1980s. But at the same time, the political parties — the central institutions of representative democracy — have been weakened and have lost relevance as channels for the citizenry to express their positions and demands. The defeats of Menem's Peronist Party in the mid-term 1997 congressional election and in the 1999 presidential election have not been associated with a renewed appeal of the UCR and the FREPASO. The two opposition parties joined in a coalition, the Alliance (Alianza), which succeeded in blocking Menem's bid for reelection and in electing Fernando de la Rúa as his successor in October 1999. However, party politicians are not favorably perceived by public opinion, and opinion polls strongly suggest that the citizenry does not trust that they would be capable of answering the mounting demands for more jobs and improved urban security.

The legislative and judicial powers also witnessed a reduction in their power and prestige. The devaluation of politics reduced the prospect that Argentines would rely on institutional rules and on negotiation as the mechanisms best suited for overcoming the problems that beset their society.

UNEVEN LEARNING AND ITS CONSEQUENCES

The political learning that facilitated the consolidation of democratic governance in Argentina starting in 1983 was a gradual process, from the points of view of the four principal political actors referred to in this chapter — business leaders, the military, the Peronists, and the Radicals — and of the population at large.

The two hypotheses advanced here attempt to explain why the democratization process in Argentina was gradual. First, the transition to a stable democracy was the result not so much of dislodging a dictatorship that had successfully become entrenched in power, but rather of breaking a cycle in which democracy and authoritarianism intertwined in a complex, hybrid political formula. This hybrid formula was in place for several decades, from the beginning of the 1930s to the end of the 1960s, and it succeeded in maintaining a relative equilibrium without generating costly explosions for the actors involved or for the population at large. One of the main components of this formula was statist management of the economy, which continually expanded, simultaneously weakening the institutional framework.

In part, this explains why the aforementioned state-centric matrix had to unfold in several rounds, until the effects of its functioning became apparent. After repeated failures of this matrix, the actors finally came to realize not only the costs of authoritarian regimes (and the risks involved in supporting them) but also the limitations of democratic regimes (and the solutions that could reasonably be expected of them). Only when the costs of this hybrid political formula became unsustainable in terms of economic instability and political violence did the conditions become ripe for the type of learning that facilitated the process of democratization.[20]

Second, learning did not occur simultaneously for the various actors, nor did the learning imply that its substance or the mechanisms at work were always the same. This meant that the actors learned different things at different times and through different mechanisms. Our general premise is that any substantively defined process of political learning — for example, learning that leads to the consolidation of democratic governance — implies that the different actors "must" learn different things as "the areas in which they are lacking" also tend to differ.

In synthesis, this chapter proposes the following sequence: The Radical Party was the first to change its orientation and behavior, in terms of deliberately assessing its experiences in the country's political cycles between 1955 and 1973. The main manifestation of this learning was the party's new willingness to accept and even promote pacts with its traditional political enemy, Peronism, and to facilitate a party system that would legitimate all parties after 1969. (It should be noted that Perón himself underwent this process with the Radicals, but his premature death in 1974, when he was still president, was one of the reasons Peronists were slower than Radicals to learn lessons that would contribute to democratic governance.) Nevertheless, for an entire decade (1970-1980), the Radicals' complete acceptance of democratic rules was inhibited by a hesitance to pursue the possibility of electorally defeating their main political adversary, the Peronist Party. The Radicals essentially believed that their party's role was one of resigned opposition within a party system dominated by Peronist hegemony. The final step of the Radical Party's journey was taken by Alfonsín in 1983, when he set out to defeat the Peronists in that year's presidential elections and actually take the reins of government. As the Radical politician Jesús Rodríguez stated, "Not settling on merely being a control force, a minority . . . I believe *that* was the big change that Alfonsín incorporated in Radicalism: the push to become a majority."[21]

Ten years later, large capitalists would assume a crucial role in the learning process with decisive results. Negatively affected by the economic policies of a government they had called their own (the military regime that took power in 1976), not only did they start to criticize openly the authoritarian regime they had once found attractive, but also, upon evaluating its policy-making style, they concluded that it was arbitrary and discretionary and that it lacked flexibility in the design and implementation of policies. Business leaders, however, were not ready to support the transition to a democratic system until they realized that the crisis of 1982 was forcing a process of depoliticization of the economy, thus divorcing government policies from the economy's internal dynamics. Reverting to what business leaders traditionally had maintained, business leader Jorge Born expressed the following opinion, "Nothing can be done without the support of the majority of the population. This is absolutely essential; otherwise, nothing can be attained. You may have an excellent technocracy managing things for a while — I visited Brazil during the military regime, when the economic teams in place were performing superbly (the so-called 'Brazilian miracle') — but the populace had nothing to do with it and didn't have the foggiest idea what was going on. The military left and everything went down the drain. . . ."[22] The shift in orientation of large capitalists as a group, then, became decisive in the process of democratic consolidation in the 1980s.

Peronists, however, were slower in learning these lessons. They arrived at the 1983 transitional elections still permeated by their tendency to discredit the role of institutions and the importance of peacefully resolving their internal conflicts. This inadequacy, which partially accounts for their failure in government during the period between 1973 and 1976, was noticed by important sectors of the Argentine population, including many people who had previously supported Peronism. It appeared to these people that the Peronist Party of 1983-1984 was a carryover from a past they wanted to leave behind. Therefore, they felt more attracted to Alfonsín's discourse about democratic revival, which offered a greater likelihood of avoiding the risk of reverting to the past.

After 1985, a process of reform was launched by a minority faction of the Peronist Party known as Renovación, which became strategically visible in 1987 by playing an important role in the party's denunciation of the "Carapintada"[23] military uprisings and by leading the party to victories in mid-term parliamentary and provincial elections. The Peronist Antonio Cafiero stated, "We learned that the authoritarian, gangster-like, and violent system of some Peronist elites, which did with the party whatever they pleased, no longer inspired credibility. This is why the Argentine society rejected it. We learned how convenient, or how necessary, it was to extend onto Peronism the environment and value of democracy, and even a certain intraparty pluralism that was an absolute novelty for those of us educated for decades in a vertical structure. This is what was called the Peronist Renovación, which posited those issues within the party and subjected them to debate. Thanks to this process of renovation, we find ourselves once more in power. Otherwise, it would have never happened again."[24]

These Peronist electoral victories, in turn, forecast the party's return to power in the 1989 presidential elections, despite the fact that Menem's representation of the Renovación faction was questionable. Although he had been part of Renovación at its inception, he withdrew from its ranks when he had to compete against Cafiero in the party's internal process of presidential candidate selection. It should be noted that in the case of Renovación, the international contact of its principal leaders — Antonio Cafiero, José Luis Manzano, Juan Manuel de la Sota, José O. Bordón, and others — during the period between 1982 and 1987 played a decisive role in refurbishing the Peronist Party.

The military clearly was lagging behind in democratic learning. For seven or eight years, until the end of the 1980s, military leaders staunchly defended military officers' rights not to be tried for human rights violations perpetrated in the previous period (1976-1983). As a result, the behavior of the armed forces, particularly that of the army, had a negative impact on the stability of democratic institutions. After the Peronists returned to power, however, the military initiated a process of self-criticism that culminated in the army's chief of staff acknowledgment that officers and sergeant majors had been involved in disappearances of the 1970s. Simultaneously, a large group of officers undertook an evaluation of their tendency to become involved in government affairs, which led them to their awareness of the unfavorable effects of such involvement on institutional cohesiveness.

The dramatic learning process that most of the important actors in Argentinean politics underwent after 1989, which resulted in radically changed public opinion, was mainly a result of the economic trauma of hyperinflation experienced that year. The extreme uncertainty generated by this hyperinflation modified the attitudes of Argentines, making severe adjustment programs more acceptable to the populace and reducing the demands for high income levels and extensive public services. This lowering of expectations opened the door for the main actors — in particular, the Peronist Party in power — to implement anti-inflationary programs between 1989 and 1994.

It should be noted that the 1989 change in attitudes also has had a negative implication. The crisis of the old way of doing politics, hand in hand with the conduct of the SCM, reduced the people's expectations as to what they could expect or even demand to be solved through political processes. Their lowered expectations, in turn, led to less popular political involvement, greater disaffection, and a greater margin for government implementation of certain policies that in the past would have encountered insurmountable opposition.

This "withdrawal" of the Argentine society from politics made possible the success of stabilization programs implemented between 1989 and 1994. It also raised two questions, however: First, would these inclinations change once again as a result of the economic crises that beset Argentina during 1995 and again in 1998-1999? The growth rate during 1995 was practically nil, and it became negative in 1999. Outbreaks of public unrest in many provinces may have been an indicator that Argentines were "losing their patience" and starting to demand from the government more than stability in the value of their currency.

Second, would the prevailing disaffection become a dysfunctional factor in the implementation of a strategy to promote economic growth? The aforementioned "withdrawal" from politics made it possible for the Menem administration to implement adjustment programs paying little heed to the processes of parliamentary negotiations and partisan agreements. However, the return to satisfactory growth levels may require a negotiated political exchange in which the various actors use political institutions to reach agreement about the distribution of costs and benefits.

Notes

1. All of the interviews for this project were conducted by María Inés González in Buenos Aires. Ms. González also collaborated in the preparation of this article through discussions about its main ideas; I greatly appreciate her insights and patience. I would also like to extend my thanks to the other members of the team (Luis Costa Bonino, Manuel Antonio Garretón, Francine Jácome, and Jennifer McCoy) for their valuable feedback and suggestions.

2. This inference is derived from the analysis of public opinion surveys conducted by Edgardo Catterberg between 1982 and 1993.

3. The Radical Civic Union (Unión Cívica Radical — UCR) took power in 1916 as a result of the first elections in which the 1912 Sáenz Peña Law was applied. This law established guarantees for free and universal voting for adult Argentine males. The Conservative Party, which was truly a federation of provincial political oligarchies of different persuasions, broke apart in 1916 and never again recovered the ability to win a national election. The Conservatives, allied with an anti-Yrigoyen faction of the Radical Party, supported the 1930 coup d'état. Hipólito Yrigoyen, the historic leader of the UCR, was president between 1916 and 1922 and was reelected in 1928.

4. The two main guerrilla organizations at the time were the Montoneros, who had originally been Peronists, and the People's Revolutionary Army (Ejército Revolucionario del Pueblo — ERP), of Trotsky persuasion. The first was much more important than the second.

5. As a result of "arm wrestling" with the outgoing military president, General Alejandro Lanusse, Perón was not allowed to run as presidential candidate for his party in the March 1973 elections. Perón, therefore, named an old Peronist politician well known for his submissiveness, Hector Cámpora. Cámpora, however, upon assuming the presidency, behaved with unexpected autonomy. He favored the Peronist left and the Montoneros much more than Perón and the traditional sectors of the party — in particular, the unionists and the military — would have liked. After a brutal massacre of Montoneros supporters on the day Perón returned to the country, Cámpora and his vice president were forced to resign. The way was thus paved for a second election, wherein Perón won with 60 percent of the vote, to the great relief of the Peronist unionists and the very armed forces that had vetoed him only a year earlier.

6. The guerrilla groups became a true threat to public safety since they engaged in criminal assaults, kidnappings, and murders against the military, the police, union members, businessmen, and politicians. The Montoneros also managed to stir up significant support at the university level and in the outer urban sectors. The guerrilla threat acted as a detonator for extreme levels of violence and intolerance, and repressive illegal practices were unleashed, particularly from the government's end. The government used terrorism against the guerrillas and also against any person suspected of favoring leftist ideologies. The repression aimed at destroying the corpus delicti and used clandestine procedures to carry out its designs. In this sense, not only did the military government installed in 1976 engage in violating the previous institutions, but it also permanently infringed upon the rules it had set for itself at the moment of the coup. This particular style of lawlessness was partially a result

of a repressive methodology aimed at generating the maximum uncertainty among those labeled as subversive. But it was also a result of a lack of cohesion within the military, which was unable to set rules for its own government or for the administration of public resources.

7. In fact, the two guerrilla movements had already been practically disassembled before the military coup of March 1976. Nonetheless, as justification for the coup, the armed forces resorted to the argument of their need to be unfettered in carrying out the war against subversion.

8. As previously mentioned, the neoliberal rhetoric of Martínez de Hoz's program lost endorsement due to the policies that were actually applied by the economic team. Several of the people responsible for the program attributed the impossibility of restraining public expenditure and maintaining high rates of employment to pressures by the military.

9. In Cavarozzi (1991, 105-106), I defined the chaotic adjustment as a process to reduce external disequilibria through sudden decline in the levels of economic activity. This type of adjustment was the result of uncontrolled processes of deterioration, not the deliberate purpose of the policies themselves.

10. The most noteworthy episodes in the dissolution of the military government and of the armed forces were the support for the military putsch of Bolivian General García Meza in 1980; the ousting of President Viola by his colleague, General Galtieri, at the end of 1981; and the war against the United Kingdom in the South Atlantic.

11. During the campaign, the Peronist candidate, Ítalo Luder, declared that the self-amnesty legislation supported by the outgoing military government of General Bignone had an irreversible effect. This legislation established that human rights violations perpetrated by the military would go unpunished. By contrast, Alfonsín rejected its legitimacy and announced that he would not recognize it.

12. Interview with Federico Storani, Buenos Aires (see note 1).

13. Arturo Illía was in office as president from 1963 to 1966, at which point he was ousted by the military coup that put General Juan Carlos Onganía in power. During the 1960s, the Radical Party was divided into two different factions: the Unión Cívica Radical del Pueblo (People's Radical Civil Union) — Illía's roots, which would inherit the party's traditional name in 1971; and the Unión Cívica Radical Intransigente (Uncompromising Radical Civil Union), which had supported Arturo Frondizi's government. The military also deposed him from office in 1962, and this group gradually separated into factions and lost any importance in the polls.

14. In fact, the name "Third Historic Movement" itself alluded to the two forces that had previously attained absolute electoral majorities: Yrigoyen's Radicalism of the 1920s and the Peronism of the 1940s.

15. Interviews were conducted in Buenos Aires between October 1993 and January 1994.

16. According to business leader Jorge Born in an interview for this project in Buenos Aires, Alfonsín also had the opportunity to adopt significant measures, but he always lacked Menem's strength and determination to do so.

17. What is required for rules to work is the belief that the government has the ability to enforce them when they have been broken.

18. Nonetheless, there were sectors, such as the automotive industry, which were expressly excluded from the policies of opening.

19. We have analyzed this issue in Landi and Cavarozzi (1993).

20. Business leader Jorge Born acknowledged the following: "I would say that for me the greatest disappointment was the (military) government of Videla (1976-1981) — not only from a political point of view, but also because the time was ripe at that point to implement measures such as those taken by Menem, and it was not done. I don't know whether this was due to political or military reasons."

21. Jesús Rodríguez, interview, Buenos Aires, 1993.

22. Jorge Born, interview, Buenos Aires, 1993.

23. Barracks uprisings in 1987 led by mid-level military officers referred to as "painted faces" (Carapintada) for their camouflage paint.

24. Antonio Cafiero, interview, Buenos Aires, 1993.

References

Carciofi, Ricardo. 1990. "La desarticulación del pacto fiscal. Una interpretación sobre la evolución del sector público argentino en las últimas décadas." CEPAL: Document 6.

Cavarozzi, Marcelo. 1991. "Más allá de las transiciones a la Democracia." *Revista de Estudios Políticos*. 74:105-106.

Cavarozzi, Marcelo. 1994. "Politics: A Key for the Long Term in South America." In *Latin American Political Economy in the Age of Neoliberal Reform*, eds. Carlos Acuña, Eduardo Gamarra, and William Smith. Coral Gables, Fla.: North-South Center at the University of Miami.

Donghi, Tulio Halperín. 1994. *La agonía de la Argentina peronista*. Buenos Aires: Ariel.

Landi, Oscar, and Marcelo Cavarozzi. 1993. "Menem: The End of Peronism?" In *The New Democracy in Argentina,* ed. Edward Epstein. Westport, Conn.: Praeger.

CHAPTER THREE

Chile: Political Learning and the Reconstruction of Democracy

MANUEL ANTONIO GARRETÓN AND MALVA ESPINOSA

CONCEPTS AND HISTORICAL CONTEXT[1]

Concepts and Scope

This chapter investigates the extent to which learning about democracy has occurred within the Chilean political class. We consider the learning process as having developed during the military regime and the redemocratization process that encompassed the transition to democracy, beginning with the plebiscite of 1988 and the first three years of democratic government. The questions we ask vis-à-vis the learning process are, Who learns? What is learned, and how? How sound is this learning?

We also consider two analytical issues. The first issue is the distinction among three perceptions of learning: a) what is stated by the actor as to what has been learned, that is, *manifest* learning; b) the judgment of actors about what has been learned by another actor or *attributed* learning; and c) an "objective" or *latent* learning that is established by the observer or analyst, but not declared by the actor him/herself. None of these kinds of learning is "truer" than the others, and all of them should be considered in any study about specific learning processes.

The second analytical issue concerns the limits of the political learning process. These limits may come from learning defects, including overlearning or traumatic learning. The limits may also originate in vacuums or voids, that is, fields without learning or in non-permanent learning, that is, temporary lessons. The latter limit is especially relevant to collective actors because it raises a generational question: What kind of learning can be transmitted and which lessons must be directly acquired by personal experience?

Our analysis is based on in-depth interviews with members of the socioeconomic and political elite.[2] Three of the participants belong to the main parties of the Right; of these, two are from the Independent Democratic Union (Unión Demócrata Independiente — UDI), and one is from National Renovation (Renovación Nacional — RN). Two other participants are from the governing coalition, the Coalition of Parties for Democracy (Concertación de Partidos por la Democracia — CPD or 'Concertación'), formed by the Center's Christian Democracy (Democracia Cristiana — DC) and the Left's Socialist Party (Partido Socialista — PS) and Party for

Democracy (Partido por la Democracia — PPD). We also spoke with a representative of an alternative movement of the Left that supported the presidential candidacy in 1993 of Manfred Max-Neef, with a retired member of the armed forces, and with leaders from the business community and from the national labor union. Because the interviews were done at the end of 1993 and the beginning of 1994, we will refer only occasionally to developments after this time.[3]

Two methodological caveats must be addressed regarding the interpretation of information from these interviews. First, we are not seeking a representative sample, but rather, relevant or significant inside information. Each of the persons interviewed is or has been a leader of his/her respective sector, although they all speak personally and not in the name of their organizations.

The second caveat is more complex because it involves levels of analysis, for example, who learns. We are less concerned with individual actors in the learning process than with collective actors — social sectors or political organizations. Had it been possible to reduce social actors to aggregates of individuals, the problem of the representativeness of the interviewees would have been significant. However, since we assume that collective actors cannot be reduced to their atomistic components, our concern is not whom to interview; instead, we must ask how organizations and collective actors learn and whether the concepts of learning can be applied to collectives independent of the individual learning processes of their members. Our main assumption is that we can apply the concepts of political learning to collective actors. We are left, then, with the problem of explaining the transmission of experience from individuals to collective actors.

The remainder of this section and the next section describe the political context and evolution of learning from the breakdown of democracy in 1973 to the restored democracy of the Aylwin administration (1990-1994). The third and fourth sections address the content of the key interviews. In the third section, we analyze the critical elements of learning for each actor; in the fourth, we examine the effects of learning on the actors' political cultures and on their political identities and projects. In the final section, we present our conclusions about the consequences of learning for the future of democracy.

Political Context: The Construction of Democracy

Analysis of the political learning process should consider the context in which other kinds of processes are developing and are mutually influential. In Chile, the context of the case that we will analyze is the process of political redemocratization: the transition from authoritarian to democratic regimes and the consolidation of these new democracies.

The three main issues concerning political learning for redemocratization in the Chilean case are the crisis and breakdown of democracy in 1973, the nature of political struggle for either its preservation or its demise during the military regime, and the processes of transition and democratic consolidation subsequent to the 1988 plebiscite and the inauguration of the first elected government.

What is at stake is the means for constructing democracy and for ensuring that it will endure. The differences between the Right, the Center-Left in government, and the other parties or groups outside the Concertación derive precisely from their respective concepts about how to create or maintain stability and from the meanings they assign to the concept of governability. For the Right, governability is ensured by mechanisms established under the institutional framework created during the military government, within a scheme of restricted democracy. For the Concertación and the sectors to its Left, governability is attained through measures that broaden democracy.

Historical Trauma and the Dissolution of the Matrix. The concern for stability in Chilean politics has its origin in the shattering of the democratic system in 1973. More than two decades later, this experience is still the obligatory reference for any political act, making it the most significant event in Chilean political history, at least in the twentieth century. The reason for this impact is the "exceptionality" of the military intervention, which was an anomaly in the political culture dominant until 1973 and was aggravated by violence, repression, and violations of human rights. Beyond the dramatic content of these experiences, the breakdown had a long-lasting effect: it began to dissolve the sociopolitical matrix of Chilean society.

The year 1973 marked the end of a 30-year period that was characterized by a certain pattern of relations between the state and civil society, mediated by the political system. It was replaced with a period of military rule lasting 17 years, during which not only the actors changed (the state, parties and civil society), but also the meaning of politics and modes of interaction among actors within that matrix.[4] In the design established by the dictatorship for the Chilean political future, the state would be challenged in its role as the central social and political articulator for social actors, becoming instead an administrator of stability with increasing autonomy from the political parties and civil society (for example, a government above the parties, acting technically and not politically). Political parties, rather than serve as class representatives with competing political projects, would become governability administrators with a growing disregard for civil society (that is, parties with professional efficacy striving to obtain governmental positions while avoiding populist temptations). Finally, civil society would refer less to collective organization and action than to the development of individual insertion strategies in the market of material and symbolic goods (such as democratization through access to the market instead of through social demands and pressures).

Political Framework and the Legacy of Dictatorship. Substantive modifications to the political system — in particular, those codified in the Constitution written in 1980 under the military government — augmented the impact of the emergent social and political order. The reforms introduced with the 1988 plebiscite sprang from a political agreement about very specific issues[5] among representatives of the military government, the political Right, and the Concertación regarding the 1989 elections. Two other important reforms were implemented during the first government of the Concertación (1990-1994). First, the municipal regime was modified to permit the election of municipal councils and mayors. Second, leveraging this local enfranchisement, regional reform provided for the indirect election of regional councils by the municipal councils; these regional councils participate in some budget decisionmaking with the governor, who is still appointed by the executive.

The 1980 Constitution changed the traditional electoral system in several ways. First, it introduced a second round of voting if no presidential candidate won more than 50 percent in the first round of the presidential election. Thus, it forced parties to form coalitions in order to obtain an absolute majority in the first presidential vote. Second, the electoral system was structured to optimize the potential for minority party representation in Parliament by changing the proportional system to a binomial one (two seats per district). In this latter case, the party list that obtains an electoral majority in a given district wins the first of two seats. However, for the second seat, the majority list must double the number of votes of the next-most successful list in order to seat its second candidate. Failing this, the first candidate of the opposition will be seated, even if the second candidate of the majority list has more absolute votes than the first opposition candidate.[6] Another feature of the structure is that smaller parties are eliminated from legal existence if they enter an election independently and do not obtain more than 5 percent of the vote.

Binomiality, the regulation of absolute majorities, and the minimum vote requirement reconfigured the modes of contestation, resulting in the emergence of sectoral conglomerates with parties aligned in blocs. The new framework benefited the Right, which was over-represented in Parliament, and marginalized the traditional Left — outside the Concertación — in Parliament, the regions, and the municipalities. It also restricted the appearance of new Leftist parties or political groups opposed to the Concertación. Thus, discussion of alternatives within the coalitions lacked vigor because of the risk of breakdown and the lack of institutional incentives for alliances beyond the electoral ones.

A very important change in the present political landscape is the presence of Right, Center-Left, and traditional Left blocs, which have replaced the competition among high-profile individual parties that existed in the pre-authoritarian democratic situation. Bloc politics at the time of democratic reinstallation strengthened the position of the Right opposition (the only opposition bloc with representation in Parliament) in its negotiations for compromise with the Concertación, rendering uncertain the passage of constitutional reforms proposed by the executive. The Right attained a substantive veto over reforms affecting the judiciary, the institutional status of the armed forces in the organization of the state, and the electoral system; and it delayed consideration of other unresolved transition issues, such as human rights violations under the military regime. The Concertación policy of consensus and agreement with the Right moved legislative action toward "technical resolution" while avoiding substantive political agreements.

As suggested above, another consequence of bloc politics was the homogenization of the bloc in power, which limited the generation of alternative positions on issues and strengthened the hegemonic position of the majority party within a bloc. This phenomenon did not produce open conflict but was clearly demonstrated by the nomination of presidential candidates for the 1993 elections.

In 1993, the nomination of Ricardo Lagos as the pre-candidate for the Concertación, proclaimed separately by the PS and PPD without previous agreement of the coalition, foreshadowed the problem of internal hegemony. The Concertación lacked the mechanisms for inclusive debate on a common candidate.

The need for a formal alliance in order to attain a governmental majority forces dominant parties — which may also carry an electoral majority — to relinquish influence internally to their minoritarian partners. This was another matter not resolved during the transition.

Constructing Democracy: The New Challenges. The new challenges refer to two grand dimensions of democratic functioning: 1) the creation of the conditions for a democratic system that is more perfectible or more responsive to change and 2) the constitution of viable governments. How can democracy be broadened and deepened through substantive political reform within the current Chilean framework, which impedes majority governance by submitting it to the veto of the minority opposition? And how can majority governments thrive without sacrificing plurality?

The first challenge, expanding democracy, essentially requires the elimination of authoritarian enclaves.[7] The second challenge, forming majority governments that can govern while still representing ideological pluralism, is the subject of incipient debates in the country. It concerns, among other things, the presidential or parliamentary character of the government and the institutional incentives to configure political alliances for governing (for example, the internal problems related to hegemony within the Concertación).

POLITICAL EVOLUTION AND THE LEARNING PROCESS[8]

This section examines the evolution of political learning by the Chilean political class. We are mainly concerned with two critical learning periods: one during the military regime and the other during the transition after the 1988 plebiscite and the subsequent democratic period inaugurated in 1990.

Learning under Military Dictatorship

In other works, we indicate that the opposition to the military regime had undergone a triple process of learning and renewal of its thought. The first involved the causes of the military coup and the dictatorship. The second referred to the means of challenging and defeating the dictatorship. The third concerned the actors themselves, especially the unity of the opposition. In these three cases, learning was not evenly manifest but was dependent on the intellectual and practical background of the actors; this process incurred important costs in terms of identity and was not destined to evolve quickly. The Chilean political class was accustomed to governing and to opposing governments within a democratic context. It had neither historical experience with nor prior knowledge about political behavior under a dictatorship.

Differential Learning from the Democratic Breakdown (1973-1980). From the 1973 military coup until Augusto Pinochet's imposition of the 1980 Constitution on the Chilean people, the two dominant sectors of opposition to the dictatorship — the Center (Christian Democrats) and the Left (especially the socialists and the communists) — experienced the consequences of democratic breakdown very differently. The Center had to exorcise the guilt of having supported the coup implicitly, and it had the responsibility for restoring democracy. The Left sought to analyze its role in the breakdown and to ensure its own survival. The "Road to Damascus" of the Christian Democrats and the resistance and self-criticism of the Left constituted the initial phase of learning, prior to that of the political actors who ultimately constituted the opposition to military dictatorship. The unity of that opposition emerged not as a project of common action but from the need for cooperation in resistance and denunciation. In this early period, there was no link between learning from the causes of democratic breakdown and current or future political action. This probably stemmed from a misperception of the nature of the military regime as merely a catastrophic accident, a tragic moment that would end soon.

Pinochet's imposition of the Constitution in 1980, after a fraudulent plebiscite with no coherent opposition strategy, triggered assimilation of the new political reality by the opposition, whose members began to understand that they were facing a tenacious regime with a long-lasting political project. Yet, this realization produced only a simple unity among the opposition rather than an explicitly designed strategy.

The mechanisms of this initial learning, as analyzed in the next section, differ from one actor to another. In the wake of the 1973 defeat, the Left endured repression, forced clandestinity, and exile, which guided its political class at different levels to reflect on the nature of the Popular Unity (Unidad Popular — UP) experience. Several outcomes can be attributed to this complex and uneven self-criticism: reconstitution of political groups and study centers in Chile and abroad; generation of solidarity links with foreign organizations and similar political forces; rapprochement with the Catholic Church in Chile, which provided some shelter from repression; adaptation of political language toward a less ideological, more universal vision based on human rights doctrine; and establishment of new contacts with repressed and disarticulated social movements. These changes occurred within political organizations but also were evident in less organic formats such as intellectual and political seminars, conferences, meetings, journals, and international trials against the dictatorship.[9]

Three factors contributed to giving these activities the character of individual and collective learning. The first was the difficult, but effective maintenance of party structures and identities, along with greater flexibility in self-reflection and in the practices of party members. The second was the emergence of a segment of autonomous, mid-level militants whose activities linked party structures to activists or to leaders in organizations related to socioeconomic, cultural, local, and human rights issues. The last was the traditionally close link between the political and intellectual worlds, which facilitated permanent reflection and learning exchanges.

Among the Christian Democrats, learning was less explicit and dramatic than that of the Left. It was related to the confusion caused by the repressive character of the military; the critical stance toward the military by some of its leaders, especially the youth, concerning human rights violations; new contacts with the Church and the Left sectors regarding these issues; and, afterward, discussions with the Left about possibilities for common action against the regime. The content of this learning refers to the bad experience of alliance with the Right in opposing the Salvador Allende government and to the progressive recognition of a greater affinity with defeated Left sectors.[10] This occurred without abandoning the tradition of hege-mony, distrust of alliances, and monopoly of public leadership within the opposition.

Right-wing sectors dissolved their political organizations after the coup and participated in government activities individually or in groups but always subordi-nated to the military. Particularly important were the younger members' adoption of neoliberal economic ideas learned from Chilean and U.S. practitioners of the Chicago School and the participation of the so-called young *gremialista* (coming from the Rightist student movement of the Catholic University criticizing political parties and promoting corporatist action) sector as mayors or employees of the state working with mass fronts (youth, *pobladores*, and others). These sectors would later form one party of the Right, the UDI, and were the seed of what we will call the "Pinochetism" faction of the Right.

From Social to Political Opposition (1982-1988). From 1982 to 1988, the learning process and renovation of the opposition really took place. This period essentially marked the conversion from social and cultural protest to political opposition; the opposition was reborn as a protagonistic actor. At the beginning of the period, the socioeconomic model of the dictatorship partially collapsed, gener-ating a wave of protest and social mobilization that permitted the public appearance of opposition without the risk of a massacre. But this social protest movement did not find in political actors the capacity for linking itself to a political formula for getting rid of the dictatorship. Little by little, the hope that mobilizations or political alliances or any other formula would end the regime gave way to the perception that the only possibility for change was institutional. Trial and error was the main mechanism of political learning during this period.

However, this period also allowed for the partial recomposition of the regime, leaving the Constitution of 1980 and the plebiscite intact as the only mechanisms for political confrontation and opposition; any chance for a new democracy would be realized under this new institutional framework. The opposition found in this framework the answer to the question of how to put an end to the military regime. The regime used it to preserve the leadership of Pinochet and to change from a military to an authoritarian regime. Thus, the paradox of the plebiscite was that it institutionalized the authoritarian regime and legitimated Pinochet's leadership, but it also harbored the possibility of unleashing a democratic transition. Additionally, the opposition found that the problem of its unity was solved because no hegemony or programmatic debate was necessary to vote "No" in the plebiscite. This step was the basis for a more complex and profound learning process in the future.

There is no doubt that democratic transitions in other countries were crucial for this learning. The vehicles for the transference were the close links among intellectuals who analyzed these experiences and projected them for the Chilean situation and politicians who led the parties and proposed different political formulae. The key element was the understanding that, in the transitions model, regimes were not overthrown but were politically defeated, usually through their own institutional framework.

Learning from the experience of other dictatorships and transitions took place by the means mentioned above, but particularly through direct contact between Chileans and foreign leaders who had lived through those experiences. This contact, in turn, was facilitated by three other processes. One was the above-mentioned failure of various strategies tried by the opposition, coupled with the growing perception that insurrection would be futile. The second was the establishment of political and social encounters within the opposition, wherein the Christian Democrats took leadership without excluding the Left, and the Left did not confront this leadership. In this political convergence the Church played a special role, reaching to incorporate some sectors of the Right in the so-called Acuerdo Nacional para la Democracia Plena (National Accord for Complete Democracy). The third process was the renovation that occurred in the socialist sector, a very profound process that led it to abandon Marxism-Leninism and to distance itself from the orthodox Communist Party. This move favored an alliance with Christian Democrats and encouraged them to construct a political bloc that in 1998 became the Concertación de Partidos por el No. To participate in the 1988 plebiscite, the socialists created a legal party, the Party for Democracy (Partido por la Democracia), which later became an autonomous party. This renewal, which happened long before *perestroika* and the global crisis of the Socialist bloc, was similar in content to what happened in the Italian Communist Party (Garretón 1989).

From 1982 to 1988, the rightist sectors less directly linked to the government learned the necessity of autonomous political organization, in order not only to influence the regime, but also to forge space for a possible future "opening" of the regime. The *gremialista* sector had a natural or de facto organization, given its collective participation in the government. Therein was the origin of a dual phenomenon. It consisted of two factions on the Right with different projects for the future: one that envisioned itself as the heir to the military regime and became the UDI Party; the other, more oriented toward playing a democratic role in the future democracy, became the Center-Right party, National Renovation (Renovación Nacional — RN). However, both factions were penetrated by elements whose orientation was defined independently from party ties, as supporters of the military regime and its legacy. These elements tended to be more sympathetic to the UDI, but many of them also were leaders or militants of the RN. We call this element "Pinochetism," and we believe it impeded the development of an authentically democratic Right.

The main learning within the military leadership during this period from 1982 to 1988 came from its incorporation into the political dimension of government and from the necessity of respecting its own rules and institutions. Even though institutionalization diminished Pinochet's discretionary power, the fixed rules and timetables of the Constitution allowed the military to overcome the 1981-1982 socioeconomic crisis and a moment of weakness on the part of the regime without opening a damaging discussion on the future of the regime.

Learning during the Transition (1988-1990)

The learning process for the opposition fundamentally revolved around its desire to expunge the dictatorship, which involved modification of its previous vision of success both through insurrection or social mobilization and growth in ideological unity. In turn, this modification required acceptance of the institutional rules of the regime in order to change it and the adoption of a more instrumental view of the alliance to overcome trauma and distrust between members. However, political learning was not complete regarding the link between democratic crisis and the necessary conditions to reestablish a democratic regime. This link was to be the most important historical learning; it finally took place during the transition period itself and was reinforced during the first two democratic governments.

For analytical purposes, we define the transition period as beginning with the plebiscite of October 1988 and continuing through the inauguration of President Patricio Aylwin in March 1990, the first elected democratic government following the Pinochet regime. This period notably includes the presidential and parliamentary elections of December 1989. The most salient feature of this period was the decision by almost all the parties of the opposition to transform their coalition, Coalition of Parties for NO (Concertación de Partidos por el NO), which was formed to oppose Pinochet's military regime, into a governmental coalition for the first democratic period (Concertación de Partidos por la Democracia); in so doing, they negotiated a flexible implementation of the constitutional framework with the "soft" sector of the military regime National Renewal (Renovación Nacional — RN), prepared a Concertación governmental program, and selected common candidates to contest the first elections.

Three factors account for this crucial learning. First, success in defeating Pinochet in the plebiscite of 1988 suggested that the best possible scenario for elections was one similar to that of the plebiscite. Second, the institutional and electoral rules of the regime forced the opposition to present common candidates if it wanted to win elections. Third, a key lesson from international transition experiences was clear: Failure of the opposition to maintain its unity during the first period of reinstalled democracy posed a great risk of instability or authoritarian regression.

It was not only a question of learning from the examples of transition in other countries or from other historical experiences; these just formed the context for the broad learning about Chilean democracy and its breakdown in 1973. There were also the experiences of prior Chilean minority governments that attempted to make radical changes of the whole society without having majority social and political support, thus polarizing society. There was the further perception that this polarization was caused by the confrontation of the two big social political forces, the Center and the Left, which together now constituted the Concertación. So, emerging not only from the experience of fighting the dictatorship and the requirements for a successful transition, but also from the nature of the political crisis that ended the democracy, all lessons pointed to the necessity of a democratic, majoritarian government formed by the main axes of the opposition to the military regime. The learning cycle was thus closed with the link among past, present, and future.

In this period, designated as the transition, the sector of the Right (Renovación Nacional) hoping to project itself as the democratic Center-Right in the new regime (March 1990) appeared with a better defined profile. As mentioned earlier, the Concertación negotiated with this sector to change some aspects of the 1980 Constitution, but the existence of a hard-right wing, ostensibly committed to preserving the "legacy" of the dictatorship and the overarching presence of what we called "Pinochetism," impeded the democratic coherence of RN. Thus, RN was inclined to harden its position in order to compete with the "other" Right for the same electorate. Also during this period, the military established a new set of rules to consolidate some of the neoliberal reforms and authoritarian prerogatives it had imposed during the Pinochet government.

Learning in the Democratic Period (1990-1995)

All the lessons learned about Chilean democracy and the transition had to be applied by the governmental coalition formed by the Christian Democrats, the Socialist Party, the Party for Democracy, and other minor parties led by President Patricio Aylwin during his term beginning in March 1990. Let us recall the three main characteristics inherited from the transition by the new democratic government. First, the absence of an acute economic crisis spared the government from having to implement economic adjustment plans that could divide the coalition and erode social support. Second, the presence of authoritarian enclaves threatened completion of the transition; overcoming these authoritarian enclaves would require democratic consolidation through social democratization and moderniza- tion. Third, the significance of a majoritarian government in a presidential system, formed by what had been the formal opposition to dictatorship, was eroded somewhat by the limitations on the coalition's institutional power, due to the existence of authoritarian enclaves.

The learning process described above is demonstrated in characteristics of the new democratic government. The execution of a very gradual policy eliminated dramatic social and political transformations, and economic and institutional stability were recognized as the underlying constraints for governmental action. Furthermore, a policy of negotiation, also called "consensus politics,"[11] aimed for timely agreements with different sectors of the right-wing opposition but not for deep agreements on major issues. Other effects of learning were suggested by the predominance of governmental leadership and presidential authority over the coalition parties, in what is called a "supra-partisan government" or the "transversal party." This feature originated from an assessment of restrictions set forth by the institutional framework, particularly from the past experience of Chilean democ- racy, which was characterized by conflicts between the president and his party.

With the exception of macroeconomic policy, which is more of a program- matic question, the learning of the political class in government generally referred more to the style of politics than to the content of programs and policies. This learning was based on historical experience, which was marred this century by the confrontation between political forces and minoritarian governments that led society to democratic crisis and breakdown.

The limits and merits of learning by the Center and Left have been confirmed during the second democratic government of the Concertación, led by President Eduardo Frei. The coalition successfully survived all the divisive issues and debates that could have ruptured it, such as the composition of the government, the distribution of jobs, the priorities for social and political democratization versus economic modernization (which implies, among other things, privatization and productive re-conversions), and especially the human rights issue. This discipline illustrates the very substance of learning with regard to the content and identities of parties' projects: There is no viable democratic government without the Center-Left coalition, and this one has shown that it can solve its internal conflicts and differences through discussion and negotiation. However, qualifying this success, beyond the inadequate programmatic and ideological debate, the coalition still has not addressed the institutional question of how to maintain unity while permitting power alternation and internal competition for its leadership. (Note: This problem was solved in 1999 with the Concertación primary elections for presidential candidate the same year, which were won by the Socialist-PPD Ricardo Lagos over the PDC Andrés Zaldívar.)

Experiences during the democratic period also confirmed that participation in elections for municipal or national government favored the democratic pole of the Right over its more authoritarian segment. But this conclusion is unstable; demands for changes in the socioeconomic model, such as labor laws and tax reform, and the presence of authoritarian enclaves and the recurrent debate on how to overcome them, aggravated by judicial condemnation of crimes and rights violations incurred under the Pinochet regime, tend to reinforce the authoritarian and Pinochetist sector within the Right.

POLITICAL LEARNING: THE ACTORS' VIEWS

The Context and Types of Learning According to the Political Orientation of the Actors

From the actors' perspectives, the content of political learning has been varied. The learning that each person acknowledges for his or her own political sector, or for the other sectors, depends to a great extent on political alignment, on the cultural orientations relevant to that political group, and on the sector's role in the country's political history since 1970. In this section, we discuss manifest learning (the learning declared by political actors for their own organizations) and attributed learning (actors' views of learning by others).

The Content of Political Learning by the Right: Instrumental Governability. For the representative of RN who was interviewed for this study, the concept of political learning is related to the ideas of "efficiency, qualification, and knowledge." For others, as with one leader of UDI, learning means a reaffirmation and a triumphant view of their own convictions; in the opinion of another UDI leader, it was a revaluation of stability when contrasted with the uncertainty of the past; and, in the case of the entrepreneurs, an attitude of pragmatism and adaptation to circumstances. We can recognize these ideas in the following discussions on the subject.

The RN leader interviewed for this study[12] developed arguments linking political learning with concepts of efficiency, such as qualification, knowledge, performance, acceptance of ideas, and science. He observed that the parties of the Center and Center-Right have diminished in electoral support since 1988, and he identified the present situation not as an electoral crisis but as a crisis of leadership. He believes that even though parties are electorally significant in relation to the historical average, in the short and medium terms, they have no possibility of reaching political power and will, therefore, have to position themselves as the opposition. Furthermore, he stated:

> The right as a party is very new and therefore has all the characteristics of weakness, fragility, and inconsistency of any organization that is in development. In UDI you can see a corporative capacity substantially greater than that of RN, and obviously greater than that which UCC[13] could present. [The fact that RN is] a much more heterogeneous generation in terms of age explains that . . . and on another side, the particular mark of Jaime Guzmán[14] of the Catholic University, on one hand favoring an anti-political party discourse, but at the same time creating a group with cohesion and coherence, which in fact becomes a political party. And I would add an additional matrix: the tendency [of UDI] to incorporate the efficiency factor into its political work with great dedication; I think that the greater presence (in relation to RN) of economists, administrators, businessmen, industrialists, and civil engineers has a lot of influence in that, because they add an efficiency factor to the organization and procedures that in the case of RN is missing.[15]

This RN leader ironically qualifies UDI as a party of a "Leninist" cut with a greater corporative capacity, but he foresees that its growth has an electoral limit determined by its conservative cultural orientation. He believes the greatest weaknesses of RN are its lack of generational renewal (the unresolved Allamand/ Jarpa[16] struggle) and the inefficacy of its renewal processes (not in doctrinaire but in political aspects). According to this leader, RN needs to solve its leadership crisis because its bases are very heterogeneous, both socioeconomically and generationally.

The RN leader considers the Center and the Left to be sectors with great political efficiency. He recognizes that these parties have assumed a developed outlook because of the importance they assign to social sciences and the direct contact they have had with complex democratic regimes (during their members' exile). He also recognizes a factor of cohesion and identity resulting from the opposition's struggle against the military regime.

For this RN leader, the Center and the Left have developed a deep democratic culture that made the Concertación possible by incorporating the constitutional and sociological democratic culture of complex democracies. On another level, they also had practice as an opposition against a rigid military government that affected them directly, an experience absent on the Right. The Left opened itself to the global changes that took place at the end of the 1970s through the 1980s because of its practical experience with complex democracies during exile. This did not happen with the Christian Democrats, who generally remained in Chile during this period. He also credits the 1989 crisis of the Eastern bloc countries in this sort of renewal.

A UDI representative developed his arguments linking learning to the "triumph of the ideas of the Right and the crisis of the socialist paradigm."[17] He recognized an evolution in postulates, information, and styles, all of which have improved the Right's self esteem. What he calls the triumph of the ideas of the Right is centered on the present dominance of the economic concepts of the free market, the valuation of economic recourse, the idea of competition, and other notions associated with the social and economic philosophy that the military government "dared" to impose during the past regime.

According to this UDI representative, the big achievement of the military was trusting a "group of professionals who sustained a correct line of development." He asserted that this line is being followed today by the Concertación, which, he said, confirms that "we won the battle of ideas, though not of votes" and enables the Right to confront this period "with great internal strength." In his opinion, the parties of the Right have failed to obtain political power, but their political projects (the institutional and economic model of the military government) have not failed.

This UDI representative recognized the absence of an intellectual world within the Right as a traditional weakness that in the past permitted the hegemony and legitimacy of Center-Left ideas. This situation has changed, because the failure of Popular Unity (Unidad Popular — UP) and the social transformations under the military regime brought about positive learning in the sense that new forces and individuals are generating an intellectual alternative that gives the Right an important self-assurance for the future.

He put forward the need to increase public awareness that UDI is different from RN. In fact, in considering the efficacy of the Right's statements, he believes they have won support because, he said, "What appears to be intransigence is coherence; what seems to be harshness is firmness," reflecting the disposition of "Jaime Guzmán, who was an example." The UDI representative continued, as follows:

> The political experience in our sector during the past 20 or 30 years has been quite deep and has marked a very dynamic evolution — in the postulates themselves as well as in their formation, in their conceptualization, in their expression, in the style of political activity. If one compares what the right was before, it was marked by some sort of temptation to defense, an abandonment of political initiative. . . . The right has repositioned itself because the degree of progress one can see in different domains, today more clearly than yesterday, runs through certain ideas originated in yesterday's right, which today, a little more currently, is a center-right with a distinct positioning. A new economic and social philosophy has not been discovered, but certain instruments have been improved. But in the end, what has happened is that this [philosophy] has endured the growth, development, and expansion of different countries throughout the century, while the alternative positions, under the socialist umbrella, did not survive. When that is reevaluated, the self-esteem of the right sectors improves, as they realize that they don't have to be ashamed of believing in free economy, in the market, in the importance not only of human resources but also of economic resources, in the importance of competition, and in the importance of the market in the assignment of resources — things that seemed dubious before.[18]

For another representative of UDI, learning derives from the country's historical experience, specifically during the period before the military regime, which he defines as "traumatic."[19] The fundamental challenge was to overcome the uncertainties produced by alternating between governments of different political leanings. This situation condemned the country to underdevelopment because nobody knew what would happen under the next government. Today, instead, there is a stability that everyone appreciates and to which even immediate interests are subordinated.

According to this UDI representative, this change encompasses the whole of society and can be seen in the public opinion that "he who bangs on the table is lost." People appreciate the search for agreement, although it can impede the presentation of new ideas since to venture them, one must break the consensus in a climate where, he said, "People punish extremes." He continued speaking about learning:

> There is political learning: The leaders, people in the Parliament, act differently in Chile than they acted 20 years ago. That change is rooted in learning from the Chilean experience. There was a quite traumatic experience, when we were used to elections that were 'eagle or cross.' If one won, he would take it all, and those who lost were left with nothing. If Frei won, they took over the farms. If Jorge Alessandri won, they were returned. If Allende won, all the public administration was fired — let's have new ones. The system changed each time, and that made this a country of great uncertainty. Nowadays there is great concern for stability. Anyone who steps out of a certain frame is punished by public opinion. That is why, in my opinion, the Communist Party or certain extreme right ideas are out. This is the reason for this search for consensus.[20]

The Content of Political Learning by Leaders of the Concertación: Democratic Governability. For representatives of the Concertación, political learning is seen as a deeper process of reflection derived from the traumatic experience of democratic breakdown, which forced them to modify substantial beliefs regarding projects, doctrine, concepts, and political practices. An example is the very creation of a government alliance like the Concertación, which, significantly, is considered to be vital for future political success. In the opinion of the actors, this alliance was possible because of learning that for the DC meant abandoning its "own way" approach and for the Left meant abandoning its effort to force radical changes with minority governments.

The DC representative associates the idea of political learning with the changes occurring in the world during recent years. In the particular case of Chile, he relates it to situations experienced from 1970 onward: the Unidad Popular and the military regime, the shock of the coup, and international upheavals stemming from crises of thought. According to the DC representative,

> Basically, the idea of believing ourselves to be the owners of absolute truths, the conception of global and totalizing ideologies, from these sprang the factionalism, the excessive politicization, the lack of dialogue, of tolerance, of possibilities to generate structures or institutional mechanisms that will control the conflicts. The strongest change in the DC is to accept not only as a political issue, but also as a conceptual one, that we have to make coalitions. You have to reach agreements with the others. You must have dialogue with others.[21]

For the PS representative,[22] the main political learning can be found in the assessment of the inability of the Left and the DC, during the democratic period prior to the coup, to put forth a majoritarian political project. From this learning derives the existence and consolidation of the Concertación. The PS representative observed that all political parties, to varying extents, but more so for the Left, have undergone renewal processes and have struggled through deep identity and structural crises. Yet, there is another dimension of renovation that has not yet been realized. It refers to the "logic" or "lines" of thought, or the way of conceiving politics. The Socialist Party leader, a vanguardist, believes that voluntarist political style still exists among elites of the Left.

According to the same opinion, the Christian Democrats have suffered much less from an identity crisis and, therefore, have not experienced the same level of ideological renovation. They have relied more on their political strength and position in the party system than on ideological renewal; they have not suffered a major political defeat nor a worldwide ideological crisis, as was the case for the Left.

For this leader, the ideological or identity crisis is related to the structural dimension. New parties establish relations with old parties, and some of these tend to disappear. Further, a direct relationship between political elites and the electorate tends to bypass party structure, rendering it irrelevant. Finally, the parties' inability to control political elites or the processes of decentralization and regionalization gives way to the hegemony of de facto powers. So, the party system is breaking down and rebuilding at the same time.

Crises of identity and structure contribute to a serious crisis of representation, which, according to the Socialist Party leader, particularly affects the Left. The PS leader stated the following:

> I believe there has been an important collective renewal. I wouldn't dare to say that in the PS-PPD universe there are renewed and not-renewed people, whatever renewal means. . . . I believe that the most important political learning has been the drawing of lessons from the most negative aspects in both the governments of Allende and Frei. They had a common feature: the incapacity, for reasons I won't analyze now, to make a common and majoritarian project. The consequence was exaggerated political polarization, with all it brought along as a national phenomenon.[23]

The DC representative believes that the Right has not experienced any significant political learning. He sees only small changes in the minority liberal sectors of RN, which have, in his opinion, lost the battle of ideology. He said that the Right largely "feels victorious from a conceptual and even political point of view. They haven't acknowledged a crisis or shock situation that could make them change." Regarding the armed forces, he thinks that "they became conscious of a political power they didn't have before. This new situation is no threat for democratic stability but could impose a limitation on what popular will can do."[24]

In the eyes of the PS representative, the Right has "undergone a conservative renewal. For the first time in the last 30 years, it has a coherent body of ideas and an intellectual production" that can envision the means to "strengthen the thought of the Right," reinforcing its political cadres. He did make a distinction between the UDI and the RN. From his point of view, the UDI is a more structured party, with a future vision and a more defined political project. The RN appears as an assembly of interests, which makes it more difficult for the party to fulfill its role as a class representative.

The PS representative claimed that the armed forces are "in an interesting re-accommodation process, rediscovering their role as an institution. They've been more efficient than the Right in discovering their function and finding the means to achieve their goals. They are playing a self-assigned political role and at the same time recovering their professional identity."[25]

The Idea of Political Learning by the Alternative Left: A Critical Outlook on the Concertación.[26] For the Center-Left and Left sectors outside the Concertación, the concept of learning is associated with the development of a critical stance toward the current political class, which they think needs to go through a new learning phase in order to address the need for a political alternative with a more social and humanistic perspective, a utopian orientation missing from the present political landscape.

A representative of the alternative Left linked the idea of learning to the capacity for creating a new political alternative, radically different from the politics implemented by the dictatorship. From this point of view, the Concertación's political class has made no post-dictatorial learning. The interviewee believes that the Concertación was incapable of addressing the population's deeply felt desire for a nonauthoritarian situation and that "their politics were ruled by the parties and the political class, diluted in negotiation and administration." The alternative Left representative expressed these views:

> The option of supporting Manfred Max-Neef as a candidate was the intimate conviction of the country that there had been no political learning after the years of dictatorship. And deep inside, what the people wanted was something really new, the seed of the nonauthoritarian, the 'no-Pinochet' syndrome in its whole dimension. And the 'no-Pinochet' meant the participation of every one of us. Pinochet glorified exclusion, the marginalization of the Self, the expropriation of the Self and the subordination of that Self to the Other.

> The political class, including the most important political parties, began to exercise domination of political action, thus generating the feeling that what really had happened was a continuation of the authoritarian syndrome. This was assumed by the political class, excluding the new energy of building something up from the best we've got. We have the conviction that in general there is a delay in the perspectives and hopes for what the people thought would be the return of democracy and the role [they expected] of the political parties. [The parties] didn't pick up the people's themes: the themes of development; in the case of women, the new themes in a gender perspective; the theme of a return to nature; all the themes that had to do with the everyday, with the intimate feelings of the individual wanting to rebuild a constructive Self.[27]

The Idea of Political Learning in the View of Business and Workers: Triumph and Disenchantment. A business leader interviewed for this project linked the concept of learning fundamentally to the capacity for dialogue among the political leadership, the government authorities of the Concertación, and private enterprise. In global terms, his argument holds that there has been a change of mentality in politicians with regard to business and that the present situation has caused "an escalation of dialogue instead of an escalation of confrontation."[28]

This business leader maintained that the relationship between today's government headed by President Frei and entrepreneurs is much more fluid and inclusive than it was under the military government. In this sense, his reflection about learning is self-referent, meaning that the political leaders who have learned are those who interact more with private enterprise; he says nothing about learning within the business sector. According to this business leader,

There has been progress in the politicians' way of relating with the rest of the leadership. I believe that a big feature is the improvement of the quality of the dialogue between politicians. We have seen more interest from them in understanding what enterprise is, what the economic world is, as seen by businessmen. This is expressed in reduced antagonism and a serious interest in knowing our view of the problems. Now we have many more possibilities for checking our point of view in a technical way. There is an ability to comprehend the problems and less prejudice than they had before. What entrepreneurs did before was political pressure, and now it is persuasion.[29]

A union leader interviewed for this project had a rather skeptical position regarding the learning of the political class. He prefers to call it "accommodation" rather than learning. For him, the political conduct of the Concertación, having scores to settle, doesn't meet the expectations of the social sector.[30] This union leader linked real political learning to the living experiences of the working class as a collective and of individuals active in the social movement. He resents the Left's lack of identity (the loss of its dreams and quest for utopia) and the lack of its own project and said, "The Concertación, where PS and PPD are, is doing the same as the Right could have done." He considers the Concertación to be the product of special interests, sometimes personal, and thinks that politics has been restricted to a very small political class. Civil society has no participation at all. Referring to social mobilization, he believes democracy must allow broader spaces for participation without menacing stability. He claims that within the Concertación are sectors of the DC and also the PS and PPD, which do not assign any importance to the union movement; in his opinion, a society where only political parties count risks social explosions. The shaping of a Left project should encompass the creation of mechanisms for consultation and popular participation, something the present political leadership has not been willing to do.

Regarding the learning of the workers, the union leader believes that the union movement has demonstrated great responsibility for democratic stability:

> From unionism, we have demonstrated to this country that we are responsible. Nobody expected that the union leaders of the CUT could, 60 days after the installment of the government of the Concertación, go to make an agreement with the employers, who had been the worst knives [enemies] for us during the dictatorship; or that we were willing to reach agreements, even delaying our demands; or that we sent a message to look not for confrontation, but for consensus. This message played a fundamental role for the country, and this must be acknowledged. We did it because for us, a climate of social peace is much better than one of confrontation.[31]

Political Learning from the Perspective of the Military: The Armed Forces Have Not Learned What Democracy Is. The retired army general we interviewed took part in the first years of Pinochet's government, later moving away to a radically critical position, and was a member of the first democratic government. He directly associates the concept of political learning with the crisis of democracy. It is a learning that covers the whole of society and the political class, which directly conditioned a prudent transition. Among the main contents of learning he identified are a reassessment of the importance of economic development in the democratic process; the rejection of demagogy; and a collective, cultural revaluation of Chile's democratic tradition. The retired general asserted the following:

> The biggest political learning has been made by the Chilean people themselves,
> the mass of Chileans who have always been an actor with much greater balance
> than their own leaders. There is a clear conscience that we are moving from an
> authoritarian regime incompatible with the will and character of the Chileans to
> a system that does suit them: the democratic system.[32]

The retired general believes that the economic limitations of the 1960s, which prevented a movement toward social democracy, precipitated the crisis. Other factors were the political class's lack of knowledge about the military world and its internal tensions, accumulated over decades; the influence of the doctrine of national security within the armed forces; the demagogy of political parties; and the ignorance of the political class, which was attempting a transition to a social democracy without calculating its risks and concrete limitations. There was also the influence of interests on the Right that saw themselves in danger of extinction. All these factors are conditioning today's political behavior.

The general agreed that democracy cannot be maintained if all its elements are not submerged in the democratic culture, and said, "The Chilean Armed Forces are still not informed of what the country's democratic life is, and they continue to have a corporative view that is far from the perception the armed forces should have of the country's democratic life." He also believes that the issues revolving around the armed forces have been taboo, and he explained the distance between the civil and military worlds as follows, "Politicians do not dare to touch them, and that wouldn't be desirable for the armed forces because they would cease being the power factor they have assigned themselves." [33]

He finds that on the Right, some sectors clinging to their authoritarian vocation still persist and will always pay attention to what the military forces could do. These sectors have a lot to learn and are late, compared to others, because they did not have a chance to look beyond the military government.

Sources and Means of Learning

The actors recognize a diversity of sources and means of learning: living experiences, individual and collective reflection, travel, suffering, education, the discovery of alternatives, dialogue, academic activity, disenchantment, defeat, triumph. Processes of collective reflection and self-criticism are acknowledged in the Left and DC. The same is not true of the Right and the entrepreneurs, whose learning has been more "instrumental" or functional compared with that of the DC and the Left, which is more "substantive" in character.

Actors across the board credit the Chilean historical experience and international political change for their impact on learning. The interpretation of that historical experience, though, depends to a great extent on the political perspective of each actor. Different historical landmarks are judged as trauma or salvation, success or failure, and responsibility is assigned or acknowledged in a totally different way by actors from the Right, Center, or Left.

In any case, the absence of self-criticism in the Right is remarkable. They consistently tend to see the mistakes of their adversaries and to deny their own responsibility in, for example, the coup, the violation of human rights, or the use of violence. The Right values democracy but refuses to recognize the real content of authoritarian policies.

The Vision of the Right: The Historical Trauma of the Unidad Popular and Chile's Integration with the World. A UDI leader made the following comments:

> Aside from the trauma of the Unidad Popular, what encourages learning is the integration of Chileans with the world. I believe that Chile was to a great extent an island 20 years ago — in the economic, the social, everything. Today, Chile is integrated into the world for diverse reasons, and that also changes your perspective of making politics. In the case of our sector, a great number of people studied abroad on scholarships during the military government. In the case of the left, there are all those who were exiled. Those people came back with a different perspective and one very similar to ours, so to speak, not so much in political ideas as in having a similar set of instruments; people are more open, and they have more perceptions of new ideas, the 'Fernando Floreses,'[34] so to speak. That world has been vital in this learning.[35]

The Vision of the Concertación: Trauma of Military Coup, Crises of Thought, and Parties. From the vantage point of the DC leader, the main source of learning stems from the shock of the military coup. It is related to what he calls the crisis of thought on a world level, though he recognizes that this factor is more relevant for the Left than for the DC. He also recognizes processes of collective reflection and self-criticism, which he considers easier for his own party.

> Apart from what has happened in the world, which without doubt constituted a strong political learning, the experiences of Chile between 1970 and the end of the dictatorship have been the vital part, the strongest. [Those experiences] forced a personal reflection first and then a collective one that represents a change in almost everyone at the political leadership level. I believe that first is the shock of what we lived and in a second phase the parallel flow of the world crises around the crises of thought. . . . At the time of the military coup, I would say, we were so deeply involved in the historical moment that we saw it as something inevitable. We had a very strong reflection within the youth leadership. We demonstrated against the coup in front of the party's hall on September 10, 1973. At the moment of the coup, the situation was surprising — surprising to see so many happy people, to see so many friends trying to take resistance positions. It was a mixture of surprise and the feeling of inevitability. We were a generational segment of close friends, among whom political division was very humanized, with very collective views. From the point of view of the role of the DC in Chile, we have done a complete self-criticism. From the conceptual point of view of abandoning an integralist ideology, I would say our self-criticism is very honest. But there is a perception that the crisis that has occurred on a world level hasn't affected some theoretical DC bases so directly as to be essential, as might have been the case for the left. That is, for us, to have to accept the market as an important issue is not a denial of what we thought. Valuing democracy isn't a difficult issue, either. In that sense, it has been easier for the DC.[36]

For the Socialist Party leader, learning is linked to historical experience in a large sense, but he unfolded his argument by making more references to the present. For this leader, learning is associated with a crisis of political parties in general and of the Left in particular. The identity crisis is related to the radical change in ideologies all over the world, particularly affecting the Left, which has undergone an important process of renewing its organizations and projects ("collective" rather than individual renewal). He associates the renewal of content or ideology that started after the military coup with the critical evaluation of the Popular Unity government by Left elites. The Socialist Party leader said the following:

> I believe that many different phenomena are concentrated in the political parties. I would start from the fact that Chilean political society is the most factionalized in comparison to other Latin American countries. This means that here, politics is impossible to understand without the presence of political parties, from the mid-nineteenth century until now. Now, these political parties have cyclic structures. The point is that right now we find ourselves facing three phenomena that portend negatively for the political parties. One is a certain transformation in their structure. New parties are emerging and relating with the old ones, behaving in new ways among themselves. The second is the transition from a dictatorial regime to democracy, which is a second transit feeding back to the structural change in the parties, but different, of a different nature. And the third is the great ideological crisis of the political system altogether, above all of the progressive forces, which are the ones that historically have segmented in a more structured way.[37]

EFFECTS OF LEARNING ON POLITICAL CULTURE: IDENTITIES AND PROJECTS

Effects of Learning on Political Identities of the Actors

All the actors, without distinction as to political orientation, claim to value the democratic system and to accept the rules of democracy. It is in regard to institutional models that one can distinguish between political projects with more authoritarian or democratic features. There is also a diversity of identities and projects from one political actor to another. Among them, we can identify the following:

The Right: Issues of Self-criticism, Identity. Curiously, the Right's electoral failure (in the 1988 plebiscite and subsequent presidential elections) and internal criticism, far from blurring its identity, appear to be factors of cohesion and projection. The Right set optimistic goals for becoming a political alternative in the midterm; most optimistic are the leaders of UDI. Their "alternative" identity is reinforced by acknowledgment of their presence by the Left and the Center.

On the Right, both in parties and among entrepreneurs, one observes a discourse that is democratic but, nevertheless, contradictory in that these groups do not assume responsibility for the democratic breakdown. Moreover, many claim they would act again as in the past if they felt threatened. The question, then, is how deep a democratic learning has there been by the Right? It seems to be much weaker than in the Concertación and in the other Left sectors. For example, when asked about the degree of responsibility for the democratic breakdown they assign to the Right, the political leaders of the Right acknowledged none, assigning all the historical weight of those events to the Left and to Allende or even to the Frei government. This view was stated as follows by a leader of the Right:

I don't feel the right had great responsibility. In fact, they had been gradually disappearing from the political scene. The truth is that the right, the Conservative and Liberal parties, got nine seats in Parliament: six for the Liberal Party and three for the Conservative Party. And when they reconstituted their forces around the National Party, we are speaking of a party that, at its best, reached 20 percent of the voters. So it didn't have the strength . . . in politics to have influenced the facts. Their responsibility might have been in abandoning their positions, abandoning their convictions, leaving the politics of ideas for defensive positions, even on the socioeconomic front.[38]

This seems to be a prevalent vision in the entire right wing, but specially among those more closely linked to the military regime. At best, some on the Right recognize that the main blame for the 1973 crisis lies across the whole political spectrum that fed the country's extreme polarization. In this view, the Left parties are considered the most irresponsible, but one leader of the Right who belongs to the UDI said that he was student leader of the Right at the time of Unidad Popular and that he "was part of this group of people that behaved irresponsibly. . . thinking that the student strike should last until Allende's fall. . . . That is totally unusual. . . . Everybody is guilty, and no one cared about democracy."[39] From this perspective, the Right shares responsibility for the crisis, but in a reactive capacity, not as instigators of the breakdown.

The Right aligns unanimously behind the present institutional model, inherited from Pinochet's regime, and does not accept the argument that authoritarian enclaves or non-democratic institutions still exist. They consider the present model perfectly adequate for the transition and argue that it ensures stability because it forces agreements.

For one of the UDI representatives, authoritarian enclaves do not exist because, from his point of view, the armed forces have not done anything beyond their competence during the transition. He even finds that one should not speak of a dictatorial government, but of a strong government that used force for a "great transformation." This UDI representative went on to state the following opinions:

> The armed forces during the transition never questioned the institutional framework. Along the same line, some say that there are many authoritarian enclaves, that the organic law and the permanence of the commanders in chief should be changed. The truth is that one has to know that the armed forces as an institution, and its representatives, have never made one single intervention in the political, economic, social, or institutional debates we've had during these years (after the military regime). They haven't been for or against the tax laws, the pardon of terrorists, or anything at all. They have only raised their voices in themes that are concerned with their own institutions — and that is a very important issue, one I find very valuable. It is the proof that the armed forces are up to taking their place within the institutional framework . . . an issue the military themselves never thought would be like this 10 years ago. It is the great lesson that it wasn't a dictatorial government, but a strong government that used force only to generate a different socioeconomic situation that allows them today to stay on the sidelines.[40]

The RN leader interviewed, referring to the theme of constitutional reforms that the Right has not been willing to accept, expressed fear that changing the present institutional scheme would produce great instability:

> The big debate of the constitutional reforms is the military issue because, depending on how it is resolved, the problem of the institutional balance must be solved. The other key issue is regional and community autonomy. And another central theme is the electoral system. In my opinion, we must not change during this period. I would maintain it for some years yet. The binomial system is an educational element, and changing it today would be a disaster. It would feed a decomposition of the democratic system that would make the authoritarian temptation grow strongly.... The reinterpretation of the military government and the 1973 crisis — a phenomenon that will occur in some 10 years — together with the disappearance of General Pinochet (and his subsequent mythification) will clarify the pulverization effect that the proportional vote has in the party system.[41]

The Left and DC: Political Identity. Many of the statements by the Socialist Party representative warned about a process of disintegration or a crisis of identity for the party, due to the problems of representation (bridging the old and new elements), the difficulties of formulating a coherent ideological project, or the loss of an independent profile for the parties of the Left within the Concertación.[42]

Also problematic, in the eyes of the Christian Left (Izquierda Cristiana — IC) leader, is the need for sectors that belong to the Concertación to raise their voices, recovering their sense of social utopia, their diversity. They need to advocate different solutions to the problems of governmental administration.[43]

The only party that doesn't seem plagued by identity questions is the DC. This fuels the conviction of the other actors that the DC is less "renewed." This view is even shared by rightists, who recognize orthodox tendencies in the DC's actions and ideology. The DC representative himself agrees that DC did not have to "modify its doctrine," but rather had to update its procedures.[44] The PS representative believes this position is explained by strong electoral support and the notion that nobody has been able to dispute the Center (despite efforts by the RN and the PPD).[45]

The Future of Political Projects

All of the actors recognize having undergone some kind of learning. For the Right, it relates to the efficiency and qualifications of political actors and is, in this sense, associated with an instrumental conception of governability. For the Concertación, learning is more linked to substantive themes in its conception of democracy, which causes identity and representation crises in its Left components (PS and PPD).

The diverse contents the actors assign to their learning and to that of their adversaries, as well as the interpretations of recent historical experience, reveal that this learning has modified the Chilean political landscape. These changes are manifest in the behavior of the parties and social actors and also in the crystallization of a political system made tense, not only by inherited authoritarian enclaves, but also by the projections of the present coalitions and alignments among the Right, Center, and Left.

The Political Project of the Right. The arguments drawn by the leaders of the Right suggest that this political sector can emerge in the future with a better capacity to govern, as it will have regained faith in its political project. This renewed confidence results from the military intervention that ultimately achieved a socio-economic revolution and reestablished the importance and inevitability of marching toward a world organized around the traditional principles of the Right. From the opinions expressed by actors of the Right, one can conclude that their potential is still related to the institutions they inherited from the military regime. For this reason, the authoritarian temptation is less linked to the search for a new military intervention than to a political conception of a democracy that protects their institutional advantage and is bolstered by a rather authoritarian and conservative society that maintains, with "firmness and coherence, the values espoused by Jaime Guzmán."[46] Military intervention is regarded as an unlikely outcome, although the Right cannot discard it as a possibility in extreme situations. The problem here lies in the fact that presidential and parliamentary elections in December 1993 showed that the Right can no longer count on the surplus of votes from "Pinochetism" and cannot hope to govern without an alliance with another sector, namely, the DC; this could not happen without a breakdown of the Concertación. Will these structural political conditions reinforce more authoritarian politics from the Right?

The leaders of the Right agreed in pointing out that even if the Right has strengthened its identity with the "triumph of ideas," these parties are weak as a political alternative in the short term. "The parties have failed, but not the projects."[47] Nevertheless, the opinions of the interviewed leaders also reflect that the fate of the Right's project is threatened by internal differences and a lack of leadership. The RN leader, for example, repeatedly said that the great challenges of politics in Chile no longer derive from differences between economic or political models (in which he sees great agreement), but from a fundamental cultural conflict that may, in the midterm, result in new political alignments.

The RN leader highlighted the existence of a struggle within the Right (which also projects to the whole political spectrum) between the liberal non-Catholic and the conservative Catholic orientations. He foresees a resumption of the fight between liberals and conservatives from the last century. The RN leader speculated that this tension could give birth to a strategic coalition between the UDI and the DC in the midterm. He does not discard the theoretical possibility of a coalition between the RN and sectors of the PS-PPD that share the same line of reasoning (also thinking in the midterm).[48]

As can be seen in the opinions of the Right's leaders, their coalition is also subject to internal tensions. Both parties, the RN and the UDI, see the need for different profiles and both have hegemonic aspirations. The liberal-conservative tension seems important to this sector, dividing them more consistently than contingent political alignments.

The Political Project of the Center and Left. The arguments of the leaders of the Concertación centered upon having learned the "need for coalitions" to avoid minoritarian projects. Nevertheless, they also have certain doubts about how stable this political project and its future projection could be. The question that arises concerns the relationship between political actors and civil society: To what degree has the very meaning of politics changed?

As has been developed in other works,[49] transitions and the process of democratic consolidation tend to privilege the elite, professional sectors. Therefore, these sectors cannot acknowledge a deep cultural mutation of the relationship between the social and political. There is difficulty in incorporating the new issues and cleavages of society in the proposals of a very well-consolidated party system and even in maintaining a stable governmental coalition. This seems to suggest that, in the Chilean case, we are in the presence of an incomplete sociopolitical project and thus are facing the uncertainty of the Concertación beyond its role in coordinating the transition from the authoritarian regime to a democratic regime.[50] What is at stake is the future of its political project to deepen democracy in a situation where the Right has the power of veto.

According to the DC leader, the Concertación was born as an option for moving away from the dictatorship, and he was personally skeptical about the long-term viability of the coalition. He said it was Aylwin's government that facilitated understanding of the advantages of maintaining the alliance, the formation of teams, and so on. His evaluation does not deny the existence of tensions that could threaten the permanence of the Concertación. In his perspective, the real lessons are that "there are no irreversible processes in history" and that maintenance of the Concertación depends on loyalty to the government of the coalition. He accepts the legitimacy of internal competition but observes difficulties in the relationships between parties. He considers the coalition's relationship with the PPD more problematic than its relationship with the PS.[51]

The PS representative feels that, even if the PS and PPD have played an important role in the transition and have improved their presence, they live in a state of crisis, not fully knowing whom to represent, or how, or in what circumstances. For this reason, they are in search of their own identities and at the same time are riding the momentum of what they used to be.

These Leftist parties of the Concertación have undergone important collective renewal processes, both in the content and in the logic and style of political thought and action. The first phase represents a cultural rupture from what the Chilean Left was, resulting from the self-criticism following the Unidad Popular. As noted above, in the opinion of the Socialist Party leader, this phase of renewal has been totally completed. The second phase is an open process, dependent on how political society ultimately is configured. It will be contingent on alliances, on the Left's relationship with the DC, and on how this progressive world relates to a Right that is increasingly dogmatic.

According to the Socialist leader, the renewal of programmatic content in the DC is the slowest among the Concertación parties, and he maintained that they "rely on their political strength . . . and their privileged position in the political realm, dominating the center. At the same time, as a party, they are much more structured than the PS and PPD. They respond better to party logic."[52]

The Left's identity problem and the future of the Concertación open a space to the left of the Concertación that is different from the traditional Left; this sector presents itself as an alternative for what the governmental coalition is incapable of representing.[53] The people who supported the 1993 alternative Left presidential candidate have concluded that the Concertación does not have a new outlook on the processes that interest people. Therefore, they think it is crucial to construct an alternative that can offer what the Concertación cannot. Because it concentrated on the state's power and did not reflect the creativity of civil society, the Concertación was not capable of collectively building a country.

For the alternative Left leader, the main challenge of the alternative project is to build a political life and a party character that is permeable, open, and transparent. In his opinion, the current electoral support for the Concertación does not represent support for proposals, but rather for stability. According to the alternative Left leader, "The country isn't educated to vote for proposals and has to undergo a new [process of] learning, that there can be various answers to different themes, for example. We will progress if we have more national debates, if the country understands it is possible to give a different vote without menacing stability. Then room for other alternatives will open up."[54]

Independent of the electoral meaning of this political space for the non-Concertación Left, and with the possibility that the Right might attract DC to the Center-Right, the coalition represented by the Concertación will have to outline a long-term political project beyond the immediate post-authoritarian period.

CONSEQUENCES FOR DEMOCRACY

From a general perspective, we can affirm that the political class and, even more so, the whole of society have experienced political learning, fundamentally motivated by the historical experience of the last 30 years. In the Chilean case, one may ask about the implications of this learning for the very meaning of politics.

Tolerance or Accommodation of the Political Class?

A more instrumental learning allows the Right to analyze the present moment of democratic reinstallation with a pragmatic view. Those on the Right clearly perceive the advantages of the protected democratic institutional model created under the military regime. This model also places them in the position to veto any project to expand democracy, at least under the current power configuration.

For the Center and Left, learning is concerned with the deeper relationship between social transformation and political democracy. For political actors, the question is how to achieve transformations while maintaining and developing democratic institutions. This means not only recognizing the need for majoritarian governments, but also understanding that in the Chilean political system a majority can be attained only through the creation of broad alliances or coalitions with inclusive party projects.

In the actors' discourse, the margins of tolerance for alternative political outlooks have widened. Nevertheless, this tolerance is mitigated by a skepticism that makes the question of "how much change is recognized in the other" very relevant. In this atmosphere, the DC leader interviewed thinks the Right as a whole has learned little and that only a minority of Rightists has learned significantly:

> I have the perception that the sectors that have done some learning are the more liberal ranks in RN, and very few others. Their interpretation is that they feel victorious from the conceptual point of view and even, I would dare say, from the

political point of view. I believe they have not perceived a situation of crisis or shock that would make them come to a certain change. From that point of view, the liberal sectors have lost a fight. The right is much more instrumental [in its negotiations]. They played with the Pinochet possibility and they lost, but they were not shocked by the defeat. They feel empowered and influential, and in fact they are. I believe they know they are not a government alternative, but they feel a part of the system. I would say that the right shows itself tolerant in global terms but is tolerant toward attitudes it likes, attitudes that are sympathetic or functional, but we don't know the right's reaction to extreme anti-system attitudes or attitudes tending to change things.[55]

The discourse on the Right is no less skeptical. The UDI leader interviewed, referring to the Concertación, believes that a policy of dialogue and a search for consensus is not a natural choice for the coalition, but is an attitude forced by the current institutional rules limiting its members' capacity to act as hegemonic actors. The UDI leader elaborated on his views:

> There has been a learning about styles of making politics. There has also been learning in sectors of the Concertación about being a little more tolerant. There is more pragmatism, more respect for minorities. If one remembers the political discourse at the end of Frei's government [1970], it had a certain arrogance due to the vote obtained, or, in the language of the UP, the class struggle implied a contempt for the adversary. Abandoning that, the new political conception has brought a more convivial style. Now, I ask myself if this would have been so if the Concertación had all the power in the Parliament. I ask myself if their behavior would have been the same or if they wouldn't have flattened out the ground [run over their opponents].[56]

This mutual skepticism begs the question of the maturity reached by the Chilean democratic system. Do players actually allow and tolerate differences in projects, alternative policies, and real negotiation, or do they merely avoid conflicts?

Learning Defects and Overlearning

A so-called "policy of consensus" during the first period of democratic consolidation (1990-1994) has served more to sanction a modus vivendi than to produce basic agreements on fundamental issues that generate antagonistic positions.[57] In fact, until the arrival of better conditions, no political actor wants to touch an agenda of taboo matters: the status of armed forces; the role of the state, whose reform is vital; and political reforms that suit the type of democratic system desired, the delay of which is impeding the tasks of deepening democracy. Furthermore, these remain issues related not to political order, but to the strategy of development, socioeconomic issues, or cultural issues. Without a democratic debate on this agenda and the requisite game of majorities and minorities, there is risk of a breakdown in the apparent consensus of the political class as a whole and within each coalition.

Perhaps we are facing learning defects, such as *overlearning* and *traumatic* learning from the past, concerning both the crisis of democracy and the very polarized and ideological nature of politics. Such learning defects could thwart political actors from solving their conflicts in democratic ways; instead, they may hide conflicts and not engage in real political debate. This problem affects the political class as well as its relationship with the whole of society.

The question that arises from this situation is whether this distance or divorce is a consequence of the moderation policy implemented at the beginning of the democratic reinstallation, or whether, on the contrary, it is a profound mutation of the meaning of politics. If the latter, then we Chileans have passed to a model of democracy without social participation, or at least to one restricted to relevant actors such as the entrepreneurs and political elites. Social actors would be excluded in this new democratic configuration.

This problem is especially feared by the union leader interviewed. Important links have been created between entrepreneurs and the political class of both the government and the Right. They have "a technical agenda and a common language" that permit a new frame of conversation. In a simultaneous and inverse way, workers resent the rupture with what was part of the classical political culture: the overlapping of the political and the social and its traditional relationships. To the union leader, it seems that not even in their own political field is there room for the historical social actors: the unions and the workers' movement.[58]

Manifest and Latent Learning

What have the social and political actors really learned, independent of what they say they have learned? To put it in other terms, what kind of effective learning is not manifested in discourse, but is latent, for example, evident in people's actions?

If we look at the armed forces, we see that they have learned very little. Indeed, they demonstrate no self-criticism and frequently have said that there is nothing about their behavior to blame, so there is nothing to be forgiven by society. This discourse indicates the absence of manifest learning, but it hides a real and latent learning: the armed forces learned how to intervene successfully, at least for themselves, in politics. They learned how to govern society and how to treat civilians in a situation of crisis — that is, they learned authoritarian politics and have realized that the introduction of democratic mechanisms while they were still in power could be dangerous for them. What they failed to learn is how to behave in a democracy.

Beyond what has been said about discourse, the Right learned that in a situation of crisis, the armed forces are inclined to protect the Right's socioeconomic interest, but also will disarticulate and fragment its political parties. In a situation of crisis or polarization, this learning will not favor democracy. On the contrary, an institutional situation in which the socioeconomic interests of the Right are protected will reinforce the political framework. Finally, the Right learned that it was not possible to challenge the leadership of the Concertación without an internal division in the coalition.

Both Center and Left learned that their division contributed to the democratic crisis and that their alliance was a major factor in the recovery of democracy, generating a successful government without an alternative outside challenge. But the Christian Democrats learned that their party would most likely lead any possible alliance and that, as the leader, the party would subordinate the maintenance of the coalition to its own hegemony within it. In addition, the Christian Democrats learned that the institutional framework favored their leadership within the alliance, so they had little incentive to change. Along the same lines, the Left learned that even though the Concertación allowed it to participate in the government, it would be very difficult to overcome its subordinate position within the government. However, as more time passes and the risk of an authoritarian regression fades, the political incentives for maintaining the coalition could recede, even if the ethical incentives endure.

The business sector came away from the crisis convinced that it was the winner and that negotiations with other sectors, especially labor, were necessary only at the beginning of the democratic regime. Originally, in negotiations, the business sector sought to protect its achievements under the military regime, as agreements to change some aspects of labor laws have proved. With the passage of time, the business sector has been able to impose its views without further modifying the labor laws and without introducing redistributive dimensions to the economic model. Aggravating this progression, the workers' movement has learned that it can no longer rely, as in the past, on automatic support from the parties for its social demands; thus, it must depend more on its own weakened organizations.

The latent learning discussed above does not mean that manifest learning is not real. Both manifest and latent learning are effective; the concrete behavior of the actors is a combination of these complementary, but also contradictory, lessons.

Some Limits of Positive Learning

Chilean learning has centered on political style. Inadequate learning about the programmatic, content, and institutional dimensions, however, casts some uncertainty on the future. With respect to the programmatic dimension, trauma provoked by the 1973 democratic crisis, combined with the necessity of achieving more consensual and less ideological politics, may have distorted effects for political action. On the one hand, criticism of the previous ideology — almost a political fundamentalism — could render politics a mere instrumental exercise. The trauma of foundational and exclusionary projects may have been at the root of the decision by the Aylwin government, from the beginning, not to promote constitutional reform in order to overcome authoritarian enclaves. This implies that some opportunities are lost and cannot be regained. More seriously, the fear of politics as a means of really transforming society could eliminate, in the long run, the ethical dimension of politics and the search for the "good society" inherent in political activity. This could subsume politics in a kind of ideological minimalism, with consequences different from, but as serious as those of, the ideological maximalism of the past. All of this occurs in the context of "political realism," where everything is submitted to the calculus of costs and benefits; the debate about society and its destiny tends to disappear, and politics loses its appeal for people. It becomes an activity of professionals or of party and group elites.

On the other hand, the trauma of polarization and confrontation could lead to a distorted vision about consensus. In the classical vision of politics, consensus revolved around fundamental values and the rules of the game. It did not exclude conflict; instead, conflict was a way to produce consensus. Under the traumatic shadow of confrontation in the past, consensus on fundamental issues (socioeconomic model, political system, and human rights) is not sought, and current agreements hide the real conflicts of society. Conflict comes to be considered a pathology, and new contradictions arising from modernization, globalization, gender relations, state reform, and decentralization are not recognized by political institutions and organizations. This reinforces the distance between people and politics. The way human rights problems have been handled to avoid tension with the military is an example; this could lead to a general distrust of the judiciary and other institutions.

Perhaps one of the main weaknesses of the renewal of political thought in Chile is the lack of its expression in new institutions. Lessons about political behavior have been reduced to voluntarism by groups and individuals, without translation to norms and institutions. The most relevant example is illustrated by the military's status, in which military subordination to civilian political authority is not ensured by any norm or institution and has depended on Pinochet's assessment of the political situation. Additionally, political life lacks mechanisms that could reproduce, over time, the lessons of people and political elites. For example, the general perception that democratic stability requires governmental majorities and coalitions is not accompanied by modifications in the extreme presidential character of the political system. In the same way, the only important constitutional reform was the modification of the election procedures for municipal authorities, which merely reinforced the equilibrium of the central parties and said nothing about the meaning of democracy and social participation at the local level.

All of these considerations raise some questions about the durability of political lessons if the risk of authoritarian regression were to disappear and if changes in the electoral system were to favor the competition. Let us remember that the main change in the culture of the Chilean political class concerns the basic dimension of the model of collective action. We can say that we are dealing with the passing of a revolutionary, globalizing, and heroic model of political action, in favor of a more uncertain and ambivalent way of doing politics. Undoubtedly, this is a necessary step for a more rational society. But the limits mentioned above show that the high price to be paid could be political impotency and the inability of politics to address present and future social problems. Politics could become irrelevant.

Political Learning or Historical Trauma?

The final and deepest question that can summarize our conclusions and our interpretation of political learning is whether the behavior of the current political class — the Concertación, the Right, and even those actors critical of the Concertación — is a product of an unfinished transition or whether, on the contrary, it is the product of a new political and institutional (and socioeconomic) model based on an exclusive consensus of the political class. The latter implies that consensus was reached autonomously and outside societal debate or was based on society's giving up the project of deeper democracy and modernization that had been mandated by the "No" vote in October 1988, defeating Pinochet, and by the votes for the Concertación in 1989 and 1993.

From another point of view, one can ask, how much of this behavior is learning, and how much reflects fear of generating conditions of instability? If we look for a common factor among all the actors, we find a traumatic history for both sides. For some, it was the Unidad Popular trauma, the political polarization, and the menace to private property. For most, it was the trauma of democratic breakdown and the military regime's repression, violence, and exclusion. For some others, it was the trauma of the opacity of the transition and the death of the expectation of global change.

Is Chile building on democratic political learning or struggling to overcome the trauma of a history whose veil Chilean society refuses to lift? Time will have to answer the question. If political lessons have not been substantiated in institutional achievements (constitutional and political reform, real control of the military by a civilian government, profound changes in the justice system beyond the modernization of the judiciary, generation of new institutions that encourage participation and debate, modification of exaggerated presidentialism in order to foster coalition governments, institutionalization and public financing of political parties, decentralization, and promotion of democracy at local and regional levels), then the survival of the lessons learned will depend on caprice and on political will. Unfortunately, political will tends to weaken over time, as new political generations come to the fore without the benefit of learning from past traumas.

Notes

1. Preliminary versions of some parts of this and other sections were published in Garretón (1992) and, in a modified version, Garretón (1993).

2. The list of interviewees follows. All interviews were done between October 1993 and February 1994.

Francisco Javier Cuadra, ex-minister of Pinochet's government, linked at the time of his interview to Renovación Nacional (RN), which he quit in January 1995; since then, he has been an independent consultant close to Pinochet's sector.

Hernán Larraín, elected senator in 1993, vice president of UDI.

Joaquín Lavín, mayor of Las Condes, UDI leader and in 1999 elected candidate of the Right for presidential elections.

Gutemberg Martínez, deputy, president of Democracia Cristiana until 1994.

Osvaldo Puccio, member of the Programmatic Coordination of the Concertación, member of the Political Committee of the Socialist Party, ambassador of the Frei government in 1994.

Manuel Jaques, member of the Campaign Command for Manfred Max-Neef in the 1993 elections, member of the Dirección of Izquierda Cristiana.

Arturo Martínez, vice president of the Central Unitaria de los Trabajadores, member of the Socialist Party.

Pedro Lizana, president of the Sociedad de Fomento Fabril, the main association of large manufacturers, until 1996.

Horacio Toro, retired army general, ex-director of the Investigations Police under the Aylwin government.

3. In the text, we will state the full name of the political parties only once, using only the abbreviation from then on. The parties mentioned are the following: On the Right: Renovación Nacional/National Renewal (RN), Unión Demócrata Independiente/Independent Democratic Union (UDI), and Unión de Centro Centro/Union of Center Center (UCC). From the Center and Center-Left, united under the Concertación de Partidos por la Democracia/Concertation of Parties for Democracy (Concertación): Democracia Cristiana/Christian Democracy (DC), Partido Socialista/Socialist Party (PS), Partido Por la Democracia/Party for Democracy (PPD). From the Center and Center-Left outside the Concertación: Izquierda Cristiana/Christian Left (IC) and the Movement led by Manfred Max-Neef, presidential candidate in the elections of 1993.

Unidad Popular (UP) was the alliance supporting Salvador Allende from 1970-1973 (communists, socialists, and other minor groups in the Center and the Left), and the Concertación por el No was a broad coalition organized to vote against the 1988 referendum on a continuation of the Pinochet government for another eight years, which afterwards became the Concertación de Partidos por la Democracia.

4. On the concept of matrix and the processes of its dissolution and change in Chilean society, see Garretón and Espinosa (1992).

5. For example, abrogation of some articles excluding Left parties, reducing the presidential term, increasing the number of elected senators in order to reduce the importance of appointed senators, changes in the composition of the National Security Council, and so on.

6. That means theoretically that a list that obtains 35 percent of the votes nationally could get 50 percent of the seats of the elected Parliament. Remember that in the Senate there are nonelected Senators who were appointed by the military regime for eight-year terms.

7. The authoritarian enclaves are of three types: One refers to the institutional and constitutional framework, including Pinochet's appointed senators, electoral system, non-removability of commanders in chief of the armed forces, and the participation of the military in such high-level political authorities as National Council of Security and Constitutional Court. The second is ethic-symbolic and concerns the effects of human rights violations under military dictatorship. The third is constituted by actors reluctant to embrace democracy; in the Chilean case, these can be grouped under the label of "Pinochetism." On authoritarian enclaves, see Garretón (1990).

8. An analysis of the learning process of the Chilean political class during the military regime and in the first two years of democratic government, especially concerning the opposition to dictatorship and the democratic coalition in government, is found in Garretón (1989a and 1991). The story, main hypotheses, and trajectory of learning are developed in these works, and in this section we will present only a short synthesis because the main purpose of this chapter is to present the data collected through the interviews.

9. Specific examples include the experiences of the Russel and Helsinsky Tribunals, the actions in the United Nations Commission for Human Rights, the Journal *Chile-America* published in Rome, the publications of each political party, the amount available for scholarships for Chilean students and professionals and for research on the breakdown of democracy and military government, and the numerous seminars all over the world to discuss the causes of the failure of the Chilean road to socialism.

10. In this period, the most relevant attempt at grouping intellectuals and politicians of all the parties of the opposition, including Communists, under the public leadership of Christian Democracy was the Group of 24 or Group for Constitutional Studies. Its aim was to prepare a democratic constitution for the future, but it organized a series of other political and academic activities and was the place where distrust among opposition parties started to diminish.

11. See discussion about the so-called "democracy of consensus" in Garretón (1993a, 1995).

12. Whenever we quote this former representative of RN, we must bear in mind that he was one of the RN leaders at the time of the interview, but in 1995 he quit that party and has been closest to the UDI.

13. He refers to a third party of the Right, the UCC, a minoritarian party in the right-wing coalition led by 1989 candidate for the presidency Francisco Javier Errázuriz, which later changed its name to Progressive Center Union (Unión Centro Progresista — UCP).

14. Jaime Guzmán, the founder of UDI, took an active part in the military regime and is considered the main creator of the present institutional model. He was murdered by extremists in 1992.

15. Authors' interview with Francisco Javier Cuadra, former member of Renovación Nacional.

16. Andrés Allamand was a second-generation president of Renovación Nacional, following the first generation leader, Sergio Jarpa, who was founder of the National Party in the 1960s and minister of interior under Pinochet. After Allamand was defeated in the 1997 senatorial election, he went to the United States.

17. Authors' interview with Hernán Larraín, vice president of UDI.

18. Interview with Hernán Larraín.

19. Authors' interview with Joaquín Lavín, major of Las Condes.

20. Interview with Joaquín Lavín.

21. Authors' interview with Gutemberg Martínez, the president of Democracia Cristiana.

22. Authors' interview with Osvaldo Puccio, member of the Political Committee of the Socialist Party.

23. Interview with Osvaldo Puccio.

24. Interview with Gutemberg Martínez.

25. Interview with Osvaldo Puccio.

26. We consider here the views of a supporter (a member of a small group, Christian Left — IC) of Manfred Max-Neef, an economist linked to the philosophy of alternative modes of development, who, as a Leftist presidential candidate alternative to the Concertación in the 1993 elections, obtained 5.55 percent of the votes. In fact, this movement dissolved after the elections, and the IC party disbanded.

27. Authors' interview with Manuel Jacques, member of Izquierda Cristiana.

28. Authors' interview with Pedro Lizana, then president of the manufacturers association, Sociedad de Fomento Fabril.

29. Interview with Pedro Lizana.

30. Authors' interview with Arturo Martínez, vice president of the central labor federation, Central Unitaria de los Trabajadores.

31. Interview with Arturo Martínez.

32. Authors' interview with Horacio Toro.

33. Interview with Horacio Toro.

34. A former minister of the Allende government who became very successful in business management in the United States in the last decade.

35. Interview with Joaquín Lavín.

36. Interview with Gutemberg Martínez.

37. Interview with Osvaldo Puccio.

38. Interview with Hernán Larraín.

39. Interview with Joaquín Lavín.

40. Interview with Hernán Larraín.

41. Interview with Francisco Javier Cuadra.

42. Interview with Osvaldo Puccio.

43. Interview with Manuel Jaques.

44. Interview with Gutemberg Martínez.

45. Interview with Osvaldo Puccio.

46. Interview with Hernán Larraín.

47. Interview with Hernán Larraín.

48. Interview with Francisco Javier Cuadra.

49. See Garretón (1994).

50. See Garretón (1995).

51. Interview with Gutemberg Martínez.

52. Interview with Osvaldo Puccio.

53. That space was mainly occupied by the Max-Neef presidential candidacy in 1993, but there are other groups that have been trying to gather the non-Concertación Left since 1994. See the report in *APSI* (Chile) 495 (6-19 February 1995). However, the mere existence of a space does not ensure viable political actors.

54. Interview with Manuel Jaques.

55. Authors' interview with Gutemberg Martínez.

56. Interview with Hernán Larraín.

57. See Note 11.

58. Interview with Arturo Martínez.

References

Garretón, Manuel Antonio. 1989a. "La opposición política y el sistema partidario en el régimen militar chileno. Un proceso de aprendizaje para la transición." In *Muerte y Resurrección. Los Partídos políticos en el autoritarismo y las transiciones en el Cono Sur,* eds. M. Cavarozzi and M.A. Garretón. Santiago: FLACSO.

Garretón, Manuel Antonio. 1989b. "The Ideas of Socialist Renovation in Chile." *Rethinking Marxism* (Summer).

Garretón, Manuel Antonio. 1990. "The Feasibility of Democracy in Chile." *Canadian Journal of Latin American and Caribbean Studies* 15 (30).

Garretón, Manuel Antonio. 1991. "The Political Opposition and the Party System under the Military Regime." In *The Struggle for Democracy in Chile* 1982-1990, eds. Paul Drake and Ivan Jaksic. Lincoln, Neb.: University of Nebraska Press.

Garretón, Manuel Antonio. 1992. "El aprendizaje político en la redemocratización chilena." Presented at the Congress of Latin America Studies Association, September, in Los Angeles.

Garretón, Manuel Antonio. 1993a. "Aprendizaje y gobernabilidad en la redemocratización chilena." *Nueva Sociedad* (November-December).

Garretón, Manuel Antonio. 1993b. "La democratización política en Chile. Transición, Inauguración y Evolución." *Estudios Interdisciplinarios de America Latina y el Caribe* 4 (January-June).

Garretón, Manuel Antonio. 1994. *La faz sumergida del iceberg: Estudios sobre la transformación cultural.* Santiago: CESCO-LOM.

Garretón, Manuel Antonio. 1995. "Redemocratization in Chile." *Journal of Democracy* 6 (1) (January): 146-158.

Garretón, Manuel Antonio, and Malva Espinosa. 1992. "Reforma del Estado o cambio en la matriz socio-política?" *Perfiles Latinoamericanos* 1 (1) (December).

"Los nomades de la Izquierda." 1995. *APSI* (Chile) 495 (6-19 February).

CHAPTER FOUR

Uruguay: Democratic Learning and Its Limits

LUIS COSTA BONINO

INTRODUCTION

On March 1, 1995, a new government was installed in Uruguay, initiating President Julio María Sanguinetti's second term in office. An abrupt increase in political and social violence and the unprecedented tie among the three major parties in the November 1994 elections had cast a shadow of consternation over the new administration's stability and capacity to govern. The country had debated at length in the last few years the shortcomings of some of its constitutional "rules of the game." These rules, originally conceived in support of a rigid bipartisan system, were now obsolete in view of the realignments in the political party system. Formally speaking, the worst possible political scenario for Uruguay was the triple tie resulting from the 1994 elections because it signaled an ungovernable situation with a minority ruling party. Moreover, at the time, the traditional parties were fragmented political groupings that had never participated as a coherent whole in government coalitions.

Contrary to widespread predictions, however, the political catastrophe never materialized. Quite the opposite happened: After three years in office, the new administration found support in a solid government coalition that still remained firm. This coalition, which provided parliamentary support for initiatives by the executive, made it possible to enact fundamental legislation, such as social security reform and the reform of the national constitution, which adapted the rules of the game to the realigned political scenario.

What happened within Uruguay's political elite so that circumstances similar to those that had generated polarization, political violence, and a traumatic institutional breakdown were processed calmly this time around through bargaining and compromise, thus self-correcting the very parameters that endangered the country's democratic stability? The key to this "political miracle" was a change in the political elite's behavior through a process of learning.

POLITICAL LEARNING SCENARIO:
TWELVE YEARS OF DEMOCRACY IN PERSPECTIVE

Twelve years have elapsed since democracy was restored in Uruguay, allowing us to assess changes in behavior that will affect the future of the country's political democracy. Some of these changes have increased the legitimacy of the system, generated a greater ability to govern, created more fluid and productive interactions among the different actors, reduced ideological confrontations, and promoted further discussion and a new pragmatism. Other behaviors have produced friction and confrontations, polarized society, hampered the possibility of arriving at a consensus, and, as a result, threatened to reduce the legitimacy of the democratic political regime.

Some of the democratically oriented changes of behavior respond to assessments of past experiences that quite often have been traumatic. These assessments have not necessarily been explicit, but in the collective memories of society and of the political elite, there is a thread connecting certain past behaviors with the traumatic experience of military dictatorship. The majority recognize that violence, the ineptitude of politicians, the betrayal of democratic principles, the loss of public liberties, intolerance, and the irresponsible support of military adventurism were all factors that opened the door to the authoritarian regime. This recognition contributed to the changes in behavior observed in recent years, both in society at large and in the political class.

We call this process of reflection and evaluation political learning. We find that in Uruguay, learning from past experiences has resulted in behavioral changes that reinforce the democratic process. Positive learning from new situations has been harder to come by. In particular, some antidemocratic events and behaviors seem to prosper precisely because they go unrecognized and are not assessed in relation to other events of Uruguay's political life, especially events of the pre-dictatorship period.

In this study, we analyze in greater depth the content of political learning and its effects on the functioning of the democratic system. We also point out the limitations of such learning and analyze opposite types of behavior that directly or indirectly generate an antidemocratic inclination. This chapter first synthesizes the main elements that brought about the breakdown of democracy in Uruguay, then examines the content of the elite's political learning with regard to its discourse, its identity, the rules of the game, its relationships with others, and decisionmaking. Finally, this chapter analyzes certain events and behaviors that seem to run counter to the country's democratic learning — behaviors that although not antidemocratic in motivation, quite often tend to develop a logic that lessens the legitimacy of Uruguay's political democracy.

Context of the Breakdown

The breakdown of Uruguayan democracy, marked by the dissolution of Parliament on June 27, 1973, resulted from a complex set of factors, including political violence, guerrilla activity, gradual intervention of the armed forces in civil affairs, conflict between the branches of government, ineptitude or self-discreditation of the political class, and the resulting loss of prestige by political parties and by Parliament. All of this occurred amid an economic crisis perceived by society as serious, for which the democratic political regime seemingly had no solutions. Many of these same factors can be recognized in the breakdown of other democracies on the continent. During the 1960s and early 1970s, the beliefs and behaviors of the vast majority of Uruguay's political actors directly fed the processes leading to the breakdown of their country's democracy.

The macro or structural context that largely determined the breakdown of the Uruguayan democracy was a representational crisis that led to the collapse of the traditional bipartisan system. For more than a century, the political system in Uruguay was grounded on two solid pillars: the National or White Party (Blancos) and the Red Party (Colorados). These parties had been born in the first third of the nineteenth century, at practically the same time the country itself came into being, from large, communal (almost tribal) groups that followed *caudillos* with deep-seated roots in Uruguayan society. Each of the parties always had a liberal faction and a conservative faction. This peculiar arrangement rendered a history characterized by multiple pacts, sometimes between liberals of diverse parties, sometimes between conservatives. This was called, in Uruguayan terminology, "co-participation." Especially during the twentieth century, the governments of co-participation have afforded the Uruguayan political system a large measure of stability.

The Broad Front (Frente Amplio), a coalition consisting of the Socialist Party, the Communist Party, the Christian Democrat Party, left-wing organizations, and other factions that had split from both traditional parties, was founded in 1971. At its beginning, this heterogeneous bloc was united by a strong opposition to then-President Jorge Pacheco Areco. This broad alliance made it possible to double the number of votes that nontraditional political groups had been able to garner until that time, from 9 percent in 1966 to 18 percent in 1971, and this caused the strong bipartisan system to begin to crumble.

The representational crisis occurred for two reasons: as a result of the threat to the traditional values of co-participation and the harshly repressive regime of President Pacheco and as a result of the discontent spawned by an economic recession that the traditional parties seemed unable to correct.

A system that understood only bipartisan logic thus was unable to process some basic challenges, such as the lack of parliamentary support for the president. During Pacheco's term in office, between 1967 and 1971, this situation came to a head through confrontation. President Pacheco resorted to the so-called Emergency Security Measures, which translated into a state of martial law, allowing him to compensate for his lack of parliamentary support and to govern by decree. The fuel that fed the Emergency Security Measures, however, was the country's internal unrest, which legitimized his actions in the eyes of the public. Nurtured by those in the upper echelons of power, who used them as political tools, violence and repression escalated.

In 1972 and 1973, during Juan María Bordaberry's administration, the situation reached a critical stage because the bipartisan system had, in fact, disintegrated with the founding of the Frente Amplio. During this period, while dealing with the guerrillas, President Bordaberry treated Parliament as if it were also a subversive element. The deterioration of the political situation ended in the coup d'état of June 27, 1973.

During the 1970s, the military dictatorship incarcerated a large number of dissidents. Because of Uruguay's small population, this action resulted in one of the highest proportions of political prisoners in all the Americas. An even greater number of people went into exile. However, the military faced serious problems in legitimizing its permanence in power. In 1980, the military organized a plebiscite to justify its continued role but lost the vote. Between 1980 and 1984, the country slowly moved toward democracy, which was restored in March 1985 when President Sanguinetti took office.

In the subsequent 12 years of democracy, Presidents Sanguinetti and Lacalle took special care to avoid conflicts among the different branches of government and to negotiate parliamentary support. The challenge for democratic learning was to accept the end of the bipartisan system in Uruguay. Even recently, when various options for reform of the Constitution were being considered, many of the objectives discussed were rooted in a bipartisan system. The intent was for the president to have majority support in Parliament upon his election — a mathematically impossible situation in a system with three parties of equal electoral weight. This objective could be attained only through a radical revision of the proportional representation electoral system, which was politically unfeasible given its historical role in Uruguay.

Although this structural context can help to explain Uruguay's political processes, the analysis of concrete learning is more effective at the micro level. Thus, the following sections analyze the dimensions of political learning among individuals and groups.

POLITICAL DISCOURSE

In general terms, political discourse in Uruguay has become more democratic, in that proposals by political and social organizations are more pragmatic and are based less on ideological or mythological considerations than they were in the past. Politics is characterized by less dramatic, more feasible proposals that specify the means to carry out the proposed courses of action. This has resulted in less confrontation, polarization, and demagoguery within society and in a greater probability that political elites will solve the problems at hand. The downside is that as the number of contrasting ideas and proposals diminishes, interest in politics decreases and participation falls.

Uruguay's political discourse during the last decade basically has run along these lines. Curiously, many feel that the democratization of the political discourse has been more discernible in social organizations and unions than in political parties. Among the more apparent changes are the ways demands are expressed and the bargaining styles of unions. Most proposals come with a description of financing mechanisms for the benefits requested. This represents a major change in the practices of these organizations, which traditionally were ideologically driven, relegating the problem of securing the necessary resources for their demands to the business sector or to government officials.

Nevertheless, the democratization of political discourse also has been palpable in the parties. The two mainsprings for this evolution have been 1) the replacement of ideological components by more pragmatic postures and 2) the moderation of the more demagogic vectors of the traditional political style. The relative diminution of the ideological factor in political discourse has been much more evident in the left wing, for which the use of ideological schemes has lost effectiveness.

For traditional parties, a more "modern," technical style has become the modus operandi preferred over the old populist formulas. The crisis of the socialist models has helped traditional parties gain unexpected terrain in a realm that had been practically closed to them: the realm of ideas. For many years, the "parties of ideas" in Uruguay were primarily nontraditional parties. It is understandable, therefore, that traditional parties interpret their renaissance of political and economic liberalism as a convenient settling of intellectual accounts.

Ironically, this tendency can be seen as a switching of roles in the use of ideological weapons. For the left, the democratization of its own behavior and discourse has not been matched by traditional parties. According to Senator Reinaldo Gargano, secretary-general of the Socialist Party, traditional parties "have attempted to ride this alleged ideological victory to carry out an in-depth offensive and relentlessly impose their societal model on the country."[1]

The redistribution of roles also reached the flanks of the extreme left. Moderation and, in many cases, the "traditionalizing" of the classic left, composed of socialists and ex-communists, generated a compensatory action on the part of the more radical left, composed of ex-guerrilla groups. At least for now, this radical sector has abandoned explicit calls for armed confrontations and has focused on filling the ideological niche left vacant by the classic left. In this way, the country has witnessed a shifting toward and a concentration of political discourse and proposals in the center.

Beginning in the 1960s, the left, which later coalesced into the Frente Amplio, and the national labor unions shared a political platform. For more than 20 years, the identity of the left was characterized by a series of key proposals that included agrarian reform, nationalization of banking and foreign trade, rupture with the International Monetary Fund (IMF), and, more recently, refusal to pay the country's foreign debt. With time, these political ideas started to surface in the Frente Amplio's programs in a progressively more diluted way, until they virtually disappeared. In general, this process occurred in an implicit, almost undetectable way. However, the Frente Amplio's leadership became more explicit about its purposes after the decisive experience of gaining access to power in Montevideo in 1989, which resulted in a reasonable expectation of winning national elections in the medium term. Not only had agrarian reform fallen by the wayside, but left-wing activists also were compelled to accept the ideas that the foreign debt could and should be paid, and that privatization was no longer an abomination but an integral part of the Frente Amplio's municipal policies.

The failure of the world's socialist political models and the shift of points of reference internally left many activists with a conspicuous need for ideological structure and security. It is toward this segment of the political spectrum that the extreme left seems to be aiming its discourse. The Eastern Revolutionary Movement (Movimiento Revolucionario Oriental — MRO), whose most recent armed ventures dating back to the early 1990s were misinterpreted as street skirmishes and largely ignored, decided a few years ago to recycle its political stance by overhauling the political platform of the traditional left of the 1960s. Another minority sector, the more radical faction of the Frente Amplio, organized its discourse around the slogan, "To change the country, no change to the Frente."

The Tupamaro National Liberation Movement (Movimiento de Liberación Nacional Tupamaros — MLN-Tupamaro), legally recycled into political life through the Popular Participation Movement (Movimiento Participación Popular — MPP), has experienced considerable growth within the Frente Amplio under the ideological banner of coherence. Directly opposing Tabaré Vázquez and Montevideo Mayor Mariano Arana, Tupamaro leader Jorge Zabalza, from his seat in the Montevideo municipal council, brought about the defeat of the Frente Amplio's plans to privatize a municipal hotel. This action, which took place in September 1997, produced good electoral results for Zabalza in the internal consultation of the Frente Amplio at the end of that same month.

With the classic left (Socialist Party members, ex-Communist Party members) filling political niches that used to be occupied exclusively by traditional parties, with the old guerrilla groups now using the political repertoire of the classic left, and with the low profile of the extremist right, the Uruguayan political stage has been sheared off at the ends. The growing centrism of political discourse has contributed to democratic stability while diluting the debate over ideas. Although this trend reduces political conflict in the medium term, it does not necessarily protect the system from challenges to the rules of the game, as discussed below. Moreover, the democratization of political discourse is cyclical. During elections, the rules of the game change, demagoguery is accentuated, and ideological shrillness reappears. After elections, political styles go back to normal, and the tendency toward democratization of the political discourse is corroborated.

IDENTITY

The self-perception and identity of various political groups is a factor that determines the style of political life and the way changes are processed within a system. In Uruguay, the problem of identity surfaces in two main areas: in one, groups question themselves in relation to their specific characters and distinctive historical traits; in the other, groups seek their identities in relation to their roles within the system.

Without a doubt, the political left has been the sector exhibiting the greatest identity problems during this period. The collapse of traditional socialist regimes brought a profound ideological crisis to the Uruguayan left, with ramifications in the labor sector as well. Leftist groups found themselves in search of a niche in the political system. To redefine their positions and motivated by the prospect of gaining access to government, the parties that had grouped together in the Frente Amplio abandoned their past radical postures, somewhat blurring their profiles. The main cost for democratization of their behavior and for their full participation within the democratic system's rules of the game has been that they have become more like the traditional parties (excessively so, according to the radical sectors).

The identity crisis has not affected the left wing exclusively. Traditional parties also have a changing definition of their own identities, having shifted, for example, from social democratic to liberal messages. There are also generational differences. The question of identity is most accentuated among the young, who cannot recognize themselves in profiles shaped by history or by long track records. Many politicians of the second generation (including Juan Raúl Ferreira, Rafael Michelini, and Washington Abdala) coincide in characterizing the new generation of parliamentarians as agents of consensus. In the late 1980s, members of this new generation, for example, formed *cortes transversales* — interparty groups to discuss legislative initiatives.

The constitutional reform enacted in 1996 has also generated new identity problems for traditional parties, which were formed in communities defined by affective relations and traditional loyalties. In this sense, these political entities are more similar to clans, megafamilies, or tribes than to political parties defined as associative groups based on a common philosophy, ideology, or line of action. These party "tribes" preceded the Uruguayan state; each tribe comprised its own party system, including a liberal and a conservative wing; democratic and authoritarian tendencies; and identifiable leftist, centrist, and rightist factions. However, traditional loyalties predominated over ideologies and impeded the foundation of "pure" liberal or conservative parties. This process explains the chronic factionalization of Uruguayan traditional parties. Thus, the true "parties" are party factions or *sublemas*.

This peculiarity of multipartyism in a "bitribal" system generated its own adaptability in the introduction of the double simultaneous vote in 1918, which permitted voters to express their traditional and affective identities while choosing the candidate and ideology of their choice. The double simultaneous vote allows multiple party lists and presidential candidates to be represented by a single party, with total party votes calculated to determine the winning party. In presidential elections, for example, the party (or *lema*) winning the most total votes wins the presidency, and the person (and party faction, or *sublema*) winning the most votes within that party takes office. In this way, the double simultaneous vote combines a primary and a general election in one election. Similarly, legislative lists are presented by each party faction and are voted on by proportional representation.

The problem of governability became particularly critical after the breakdown of the traditional two-party system in Uruguay. This breakdown, which started in 1971 with the founding of the Frente Amplio, was consolidated in the 1980s. The system of presidential elections by simple majority, which guaranteed a majority in Parliament for the winning party, ceased to work when the number of parties increased. In addition, this problem was aggravated by the fact that the ideological distance separating the Frente Amplio from other parties was so great that its participation in government coalitions became untenable.

One of the learning experiences of the political elite during the past two decades has been that the existence of governments with a chronic lack of parliamentary support makes democracy infeasible over the medium or long run. The hardest task has been to arrive at concrete, systematic measures to solve this problem. The clearest consolidation of this learning was the December 1996 passage by plebiscite of a new Constitution that modifies the electoral system by mandating single candidacies per party and two rounds in presidential elections.

Along with its search for formulas to make the system more governable, the Uruguayan political elite has sought to regulate the action of political parties. There is a general feeling in the country that although they are located at the very axis of the political system, the parties still constitute its weakest link. During the last phase of the military regime, rules were put into place to regulate the internal functioning of political parties. Once democracy was restored, however, these rules were repealed because they were opposed by the military but not because of opposition to their content. The 1996 constitutional reforms returned to these ideas by requiring candidates to be chosen in party primaries based on the national voters list.

The new reality may even push voters with traditional party affiliations to define themselves according to "ideological families," to use an expression of President Sanguinetti cited in the press repeatedly during the constitutional reform discussions. The results of the 1999 elections will show whether ideological identity is truly stronger than communal roots.

RULES OF THE GAME

One of the most important lessons learned in Uruguay's democratic political life in recent years is, without a doubt, the general consensus about accepting the political rules of the game. In the 12 years of restored democracy in Uruguay, some extremely controversial issues, including the law of amnesty for the military involved in human rights violations, have been resolved. The amnesty law was challenged, and a referendum was held in 1989 by popular initiative with the intent of repealing it; instead, the law was ratified by the popular vote. Thus, despite the emotional overload of such issues, differences were resolved by resorting to constitutional procedures. The results were respected, and the issues were resolved.

Compliance with the rules of the game is not something that is verified solely ex post facto; it can be observed in daily activities and in political discourses. The change is particularly noticeable in groups with a history of challenging the rules — particularly the political left. This sector has rediscovered the instrumental advantages of democratic norms and has become a legitimizing force in the traditionally most brittle spot in the system.

Some argue that the new democratic thrust of the left is simply temporal, if not outright opportunistic, based on the downfall of dictatorships and the circumstantial rise of democratic forms. Although this may be true for some of the more staunchly authoritarian groups, it is not true for the majority of the left. The logic behind the left wing's compliance with the democratic rules is rational, based on its interests and political objectives. One of the two main elements of this logic was a radical change in the political scenario between the 1960s and the 1990s; in the

1960s scenario, the left could not win by means of the democratic rules, whereas in the 1990s, it could. Secondly, strictly in terms of learning, the experience of the military dictatorship proved to the left that there was too much to lose and too little to gain by obliterating the democratic rule of law.

In Senator Gargano's words, "We thought that formal democracy not only did not 'do it all,' but to a certain degree was the pretext used by the dominant classes to maintain their hegemony. . . . I believe the left has reconsidered the importance of the mechanisms of formal democracies, in the sense that the functioning of democratic institutions in and of itself is extremely important because these institutions are the only instruments available to the marginalized sectors of society for solving their problems, and they can in fact contribute to solving social conflicts."

During the 1960s, the left had not yet surpassed the 10-percent threshold of the total vote in any election. With such a scale of political impotence, this sector was reluctant to support rules perceived as preordaining defeat and exclusion. In other words, the left appeared to support the view that democracy was but a mere artifice enabling traditional parties to remain in power.

With the formation of the Frente Amplio in 1971, the left was able to break the 20-percent threshold of the vote, and in the 1994 elections it reached 30 percent. Initially, this increase was due to the breaking away of the liberal left wing of the traditional parties and its incorporation into the Frente Amplio during the polarized years of the early 1970s. Elections were becoming truly competitive and were perceived as the only route for the left's access to power. Obviously, it is easier to support rules with which it is possible to win than to support a game in which it is possible only to lose.

After being political outsiders during the 1960s and following the virtually complete political disarticulation that took place during the years of military dictatorship, the left underwent a process of rediscovering its identity and political capabilities with the return of democracy during the 1980s and 1990s. From distrust and merely ritual compliance with the old rules, the left has evolved in recent years toward a truly professional handling of constitutional provisions, fully using the possibilities these rules offer to exert influence and to gain access to power.

Use of the Referendum

Some new threats to the functioning of democracy in Uruguay, such as the proliferation of use of the referendum, occur partly because of the late discovery of democratic rules as tools for political action. This problem would seem to be comparatively minor as a threat to democratic stability, but use of the referendum as a central component of the left wing's repertoire for political action has changed the scenario, threatening the political regime in some sensitive areas.

Three basic problems have been generated in Uruguay by the use of the referendum: 1) the polarization of society, 2) the blocking of government work, and 3) the devaluation of Parliament. Two of the referenda held in recent years — one in 1989 that ratified the 1987 amnesty law passed by Parliament for military personnel accused of human rights violations during the authoritarian period and one in 1992 that partially vacated the 1991 privatization law — led to a marked polarization of society and to significant fissures within the political elite. In addition, the bargaining, agreements, coalitions, and all the political processes required for passing those laws in parliament were challenged and in one case were repealed, as a result of political moves by the groups that lost in the parliamentary arena. In a country such as Uruguay, in which the most vulnerable components of democratic legitimacy traditionally have been low political productivity and political gridlock, these difficulties seem particularly alarming.

Finally, the use of the referendum as a constant platform for political action threatens to depreciate the specific functions of Parliament by perpetuating the myth of direct democracy and the idea that it is better to legislate through the electorate than through representatives. This aspect of the issue is by no means unidirectional. Excessive use of the referendum does, in fact, take away from the political function of Parliament. It is also true, however, that the political space ceded by Parliament and the emergence of civil society also have been instrumental in generalizing this political tool that was conceived constitutionally as an exceptional course of action.

Important figures of the different parties concur in this appraisal of the situation. For Senator Walter Santoro of the National Party, society has "the possibility of achieving its goals without the need for Parliament" because power "is now distributed in a different way, with an important presence of social groups."[2] For Senator Luis Hierro López of the Colorado Party, it is clear that between 1985 and the present there has been "a restoration of community-based organizations, foundations, and NGOs," and it is also clear that Parliament "has not interfaced with civil society."[3] Along the same lines, Senator Danilo Astori of the Frente Amplio recognizes an estrangement of sorts between Parliament and "the way the people see the country and how they perceive the frustrations of the past. . . . There seems to be a growing disaffection. People live their lives thinking about certain things, and the Parliament goes about its business dealing with other things. The trend toward direct popular consultation, which has been increasing in the country and has become a problem, has a lot to do with that disaffection and finds in that disaffection an important mainspring."[4]

The political dynamic induced by systematic use of the referendum has shown itself at its worst around general election times. In the 1994 election year, several initiatives were held for referendum. One was an amendment modifying the electoral system; another abrogated newly legislated provisions regarding social security; and a third was a proposal by the Frente Amplio and labor unions to earmark a fixed percentage of 27 percent of the national budget for education. The latter two proposals were clearly inappropriate in the eyes of the majority of leaders of all the parties. And yet, prompted by the fear of losing electoral votes among social sectors supporting such measures, very few leaders formulated a clear and unequivocal posture with regard to these issues. The political debate became almost a festival of double discourse, with one position being defended in public while the opposite was defended in private.

The referenda defeated electoral reform, supported abrogation of the new social security laws, and rejected the education budget earmark. Within this context, the results of the referenda were incorrectly interpreted as "punishments" by the electorate of the (public) positions of political leaders.

Traditional parties were placed in a particularly uncomfortable position by this distortion in the political game. The Frente Amplio, with no national political responsibilities, was best able to play this game of irresponsible behavior and reaping of short-run benefits. As the main sponsor of these referenda, however, the Frente Amplio became more cautious about letting things go too far once the initial political benefits were won. This political sector now has ambitions to win national office and seems to realize that uncontrolled use of the referendum can threaten its own medium-term plans.

More recent caution in using this political tool was evident in the events that followed the passage of the law of Reform of the Social Security System at the beginning of President Sanguinetti's second administration in 1995. The reform was approved despite opposition by the Frente Amplio and the labor unions. However, the Frente Amplio's opposition was not uniform, and initiatives to repeal the law by means of a referendum were swiftly discouraged. Thus, after first learning how to use this democratic tool to its own advantage for political opposition, the Frente now is learning the implications of this same tool for the party actually in office.

The Antidemocratic Challengers

Certain pockets of authoritarianism, on both the left and the right, still exist. On the left, the most notorious of these are groups close to the ex-Tupamaro guerrillas; and on the right, some extremist military groups. What interests us most is to observe the reactions of the political class as a whole to the challenges posed by those groups, rather than to study the behavior of the groups themselves.

In the midst of the political unrest and polarization generated by the referendum on the Law of State Reform (privatization) held during President Luis Alberto Lacalle's administration, the more authoritarian groups abandoned their low profile and started harassing the perceived weakest link of the political system: the president. The objective apparently was to denigrate the image of the president; and for that purpose, both the Tupamaros and a well-known retired military commander resorted to a variety of insults.

From the Tupamaro perspective, the strategy was this: If the president did not react to the insults, the dignity of the position would be belittled. If he reacted as expected by sending them to jail, it would also be a victory from their perspective because there would be talk about political prisoners, and democratic legitimacy would be blemished.

None of this came to pass, because President Lacalle consigned the problem to the judiciary power. The political class also ignored the issue, and the insults by the Tupamaros and by the ex-military commander were dealt with by way of contempt charges that were prosecuted in court without much fanfare. Nobody went to jail, and these challenges by antidemocratic factions were largely ignored by the majority of the population.

Of greater concern was the behavior of certain political sectors regarding another problem related to military groups. In 1993, a shadowy affair cropped up, revealing ties between the military intelligence services of Uruguay and Chile. As this incident unfolded, the authority of the president as commander in chief of the armed forces seriously came into question. When President Lacalle tried to denounce the commander of the army (among others), one of the main opposition factions, led by former President Sanguinetti, refused to support the action. This attitude by the majority faction of the Colorado Party put President Lacalle in a very delicate situation, severely injuring the supremacy of civilian power and the efficacy and legitimacy of the democratic political regime.

For some political leaders, such as ex-legislator and Ambassador Juan Raúl Ferreira of the National Party, Sanguinetti's behavior was not a disloyal act to the democratic regime, but rather a political move to show that President Lacalle was an amateur in military issues. Nonetheless, according to Senator Rafael Michelini of the New Space (Nuevo Espacio) Party, with this attitude Sanguinetti was entering a "danger zone."[5]

Although Sanguinetti's behavior was surprising for its ambiguities, no less surprising was the solid and unanimous support the president received from the leftist rank and file during this crisis. Upon analyzing the logic behind this behavior, Socialist Senator Gargano clarified that this support was not directed to the person of the president but was intended to sustain a matter of principle. According to Gargano, Sanguinetti's attitude was patterned after a Colorado tradition — which Gargano considers unacceptable — of trying to enlist the army in the party and cash in later on loyalties. From the Frente Amplio's point of view, the principle of respect for the president by the military, regardless of party affiliation, should be vigilantly safeguarded since the problems a National Party president faces today may be the same problems a Frente Amplio president will face tomorrow.[6]

LEARNING VERSUS ELECTORAL REFLEXES

Street Violence and Resistance to the Extradition of Basque Terrorists

On August 24, 1994, there were three serious clashes between demonstrators and the police in the vicinity of a hospital where three Basque militants (Euzkadi Ta Azkatasuna — ETA) who were about to be extradited to Spain were detained. The demonstrators, mainly from radical left-wing groups tied to the Tupamaros, tried to impede the extradition of the Basque militants and were harshly repressed by the police.

Given the identity of the actors, this sudden burst of violence once again conjured up the dreaded specters of the past. Many felt that this episode heralded the reactivation of armed confrontations. The stern intervention of the police induced the left to draw parallels with the particularly repressive 1968-1971 administration of Jorge Pacheco Areco.

Paradoxically, however, the fear and grave concern following these incidents offered certain guarantees that the chain of events that led to the breakdown of democracy in 1973 would not reoccur. The general disapproval inspired by both the demonstrators' attitude and the excesses of the police reinforced the primary social learning of democracy, and condemnation of violence remained intact in Uruguay.

Nevertheless, it is important to analyze what other lessons supposedly already learned by the political elite were forgotten or obscured by other agendas, thus allowing these incidents to take place. Clearly, the key fact that legitimized the demonstrators' actions was the presence of Frente Amplio presidential candidate Tabaré Vázquez at the scene of the incidents. It may be hard to understand the presence of a well-respected, left-wing political personality at a demonstration against a court decision made in compliance with current international treaties with regard to three Spanish subjects charged with homicide and terrorism. The traditional antidemocratic elements of small, radical ultra-leftist groups received an unexpected legitimization from the "establishment" of the left through the appearance of its main leader.

Our explanation of this destabilizing political behavior is the following: This leader acted in that way because, as part of his coalition's strategy to win the national government, he had leaned too much toward the center, thus risking a rupture with the left. His presence at this demonstration responded to the interest of maintaining unity within the movement by making symbolic concessions at the weakest point of the coalition.

Without this intra-organizational interest by the Frente Amplio, no doubt things would have worked out quite differently. The bonds between the ETA and the Tupamaros fully justified solidarity among their militants, but the demonstrations themselves would not have gone beyond semi-clandestine levels were it not for the appearance of this well-known personality of the left. His very appearance escalated resistance to the court decision, generating an unprecedented and very dangerous situation. The Uruguayan National Labor Confederation (Plenario Intersindical de Trabajadores-Convención Nacional de Trabajadores — PIT-CNT) added its support, encouraged by Frente Amplio's endorsement.

Another factor stemming from the electoral campaign highlighted the distance between the official resolutions of the coalition and those of presidential candidate Tabaré Vázquez. Events developed as if there were a tacit policy of "reserved domain" in electoral issues, which authorized Vázquez to pursue his own strategies for securing votes. Vázquez, a trained medical doctor with little experience in the complex art of politics, unleashed a series of political events evidently without a clear idea of their sometimes dangerous possible consequences. The Frente Amplio's success in marginalizing extreme left groups and antidemocratic effects on the system was shattered by an electoral reflex lacking deliberation or political assessment.

This unexpected turn of events predetermined the response by the national government. After almost 10 years of democracy, the political spaces and the dynamics of the different sectors (including the ex-guerrilla factions) were fairly well defined. Their courses of action, which were reasonably predictable, were under control and in relative tranquillity. Suddenly, surprising even the left wing's main political actors, some of the most prominent political leaders of the Frente Amplio bestowed a powerful legitimacy upon the extreme left as a result of a combination of electoral strategy, naivete, and irresponsibility — and the Tupamaros took full advantage of it. At once the guerrilla leaders of old saw themselves spearheading a movement that dragged along with it a whole party representing one-third of the electorate plus the powerful labor confederation. All this took place amid violent acts, including Molotov cocktails, rock-throwing, and, in all likelihood, the use of firearms.

This violent mutation of the political rules of the game put the government and the armed forces in a state of extreme alert. When the time came, repressive forces pounded on the demonstrators with a degree of violence that upset the Uruguayan people. However, the government had limited options and definitely could not show weakness in defending a court decision when jolted by actions bordering on political subversion. One omission, one localized victory of the Tupamaro movement, and the government would have been in a position of blatant ineffectiveness, leaving a power vacuum that the military would not tolerate.

Structural Threat to the Rules: Ideologized Marginality

The above incidents, known as the Hospital Filtro events, inaugurated a new and dangerous mode of violence: ideologizing, activating, and mobilizing marginalized social sectors in the urban subproletariat around the violent premises of the ex-Tupamaro guerrillas. Electoral analysis has demonstrated that the Frente Amplio was starting to filter into the marginalized urban sectors. Traditionally, these segments of society had been the bastions of ex-Colorado President Pacheco. More recently, the radical faction of the Frente, centered around the MPP, has been recruiting from this populace as voters have shifted from the extreme right to the extreme left, both of which are characterized by authoritarianism, violence, and disaffection with the democratic rules of co-participation.

The MPP achieved this shift in allegiances through strategies that included moving some of its most prominent leaders (most notoriously, Tupamaro chief Jorge Zabalza) to the slums of Montevideo, into the precarious housing of illegal settlements surrounding the city. In addition to ideology, the MPP gave its socially marginalized militants a dignified identity. In Frente Amplio demonstrations, these sectors are quite visible as a class of tattered warriors driving horse-drawn carts and styled after the movie character Mad Max — a bizarre synthesis of revolutionary riders and nocturnal garbage rummagers.

Winning over the poorest urban sectors allowed the Frente Amplio to increase its electoral constituency to the point that it almost tied with the front-runners of the 1994 elections. But this created new concerns for its leadership. The radical wing, supported by marginalized social sectors, was ungovernable. On the very night of the 1994 elections, these groups generated such disorderliness in downtown Montevideo that they blocked all traffic, not just cars belonging to triumphant Colorado Party members.

The Frente Amplio's extreme left and the marginalized, ideologized, and mobilized social sectors are, without a doubt, the main challenges to the democratic rules of the game. Up to this point, these groups have been a source of problems for the Frente Amplio itself, which has had more difficulties with its own internal discord than with its political adversaries. However, these adversaries could turn into a risk factor for democratic stability at any moment, especially in a hypothetical future Frente Amplio government.

RELATIONSHIPS WITH OTHERS

The relationships among the members of the political elite have changed. The identity of each of the actors and the ideological models supporting their positions have varied, or, on the left, have suffered a serious crisis. The traditional styles of interaction, particularly confrontation, are no longer profitable in political terms. These changes have created new scenarios in which interactions between groups have become more frequent and less contentious. As a result, the universe of possible partners for certain political pursuits — in particular, for coalitions — has broadened. The reasons behind these changes are many, but they generally redefine the actors and endow them with political acceptability.

Discreditation

The two decades preceding the institutional breakdown were characterized by "cannibalistic" behavior on the part of the political class. By this we mean a type of behavior in which different political groups discredited other sectors of the political elite, principally in moral terms. Accusations primarily centered around corruption or political catering to a foreign power. This contributed to a widespread belief that the political class as a whole was immoral and corrupt. Even though actual corruption in Uruguay was quite low compared with other countries, society's perception of corruption was quite real. In 1972 and 1973, at the outset of its ascent to power, the military found its objective of delegitimating civil power already well advanced by the political elite itself.

After democracy was restored, the link between personal-attack tactics and the weakening of democracy did not go unnoticed by the majority of people, nor by members of the political class. Although old grudges lived on, the desire to avoid a repetition of the past moderated the behavior of politicians. Thus, the first administration of the restored democracy (1985-1989) was characterized by implicitly clean rules of the game that contained political conflict within certain boundaries. Senator Germán Araújo's unpublicized expulsion from Parliament for systematically generating conflict and personally attacking legislators evidenced the resolve of the political class as a whole not to tolerate major transgressions in interactions and debates among parties.

During the second democratic term (1990-1994), these tacit guidelines were not contested. Political leaders who deviated from the norms were sanctioned by political segregation from their peers. However, disqualification tactics have not played well in public opinion, which is why, in the words of Senator Rafael Michelini, the majority of the political class shares in the opinion that such tactics do not pay.[7]

The first half of President Sanguinetti's second administration, between 1995 and 1997, saw several charges of corruption and mismanagement of public affairs, mainly leveled against individuals of the Lacalle administration, but also against officials of the current administration, and, more recently, against individuals affiliated with the Frente Amplio municipal administration. These charges were processed by the judicial system, and two people were given prison sentences. The fear of a renewed dynamic of politically inspired accusations of corruption so far has not materialized, however, because 1) levels of corruption are significantly lower than in the rest of Latin America, 2) the offenses did not go unpunished, and 3) those leveling false accusations have been punished. This was the case with Frente Amplio representative Leonardo Nicolini, who was suspended from his functions for six months for presenting false evidence against certain government officials.

The relationships among political leaders clearly are closer and friendlier now than they were in the past. This is particularly noticeable with two of the main leaders of the coalition: President Sanguinetti and Alberto Volonté. Their political affinity, out of which a personal friendship has evolved, could be interpreted as a somewhat late discovery of the common ground uniting Blancos and Colorados in opposition to the Frente Amplio as a third political force. Volonté and Vázquez have been equally generous in their demonstrations of mutual regard. Perhaps this is due to recent learning of more civilized behaviors or because the new political dynamic of the second round in presidential contests calls for more respect toward adversaries since the votes to win the second round in all likelihood will come from their rank and file.

Alongside these and other assessments by the political class about the adverse effect of discreditation on the democratic process, the disappearance of certain ideological macro-references also helps explain the shift in behavior. The disqualifying style of the 1960s was patterned to a large extent after the world confrontation between superpowers. In the 1990s, no international context could legitimize the disqualification of a political adversary using the argument that the person was catering to a foreign power. Conversely, world changes have generated, at least among members of the left, great doubts about the left's tenets, contributing to a noticeable moderation of political postures.[8]

Broadening of the Universe of Possible Political Partners

The same factors that eliminated discreditation have been at work broadening the universe of possible political partners in the formation of coalitions. This tendency has also been reinforced by a belief shared by the vast majority of the Uruguayan political elite: Good performance is necessary to consolidate democracy, and performance and good governance are achieved by reaching parliamentary majorities. From this perspective, a central component of the Uruguayan political parties' strategies is to preserve an openness toward the others.

Until the 1990s, the universe of possible political partners for government coalitions did not go beyond the confines of the traditional parties. Perhaps the only exception was the small Unión Cívica — which, for many practical observers of Uruguayan politics, was no more than a group of Colorado Catholics frightened away by the slogan of anticlericalism in the pro-Batlle discourse. But groups that in some way sympathized with the ideological universe of the left were excluded in practice from all participation in government. This is why it was such an auspicious beginning when, during Lacalle's administration, a government position was offered to the moderate left Party for the Government of the People (Partido por el Gobierno del Pueblo — PGP). Although the PGP's participation in government never materialized, the offer symbolically pointed out an openness toward potential partners who previously had been excluded.[9]

In this regard, the party scenario during the 1994 electoral year was particularly eloquent. Hugo Batalla's PGP had formalized an electoral alliance with Julio María Sanguinetti of the Colorado Party, whereas the Frente Amplio had made an agreement with ex-mayor Rodolfo Nin Novoa of the National Party, creating the political grouping called Encuentro Progresista. These political movements set the pattern for a progressive weakening of interpartisan boundaries and for a change in the way others were perceived. This allowed for the possible universe of coalitions to broaden considerably.

This broadening of the eligibility of political groups to form government coalitions has been gradual and, according to some observers, preconditioned. Although the ideological threshold of acceptance of the different actors has expanded, distrust still persists, quite often passing from the political onto the social stage. In an interview conducted for the purposes of this research, Senator Reinaldo Gargano, a front-line leader of the Frente Amplio, was of the opinion that for some conservative sectors, the left was not eligible for government coalitions for social reasons; according to this point of view, politics is basically an occupation for the upper classes.[10]

DECISIONMAKING

An important long-term outcome of learning is a change in the decision-making styles of the presidents. From 1967 to 1997, Uruguay had five democratically elected presidents. Before 1967, the executive's responsibility was not unipersonal but was shared among a collegial presidency. From 1973 to 1984, the country endured a military dictatorship. The first president in this series, General Oscar Gestido, died nine months after taking office; so we will use as points of reference the two last presidents of the pre-authoritarian period, Jorge Pacheco Areco (1967-1972) and Juan María Bordaberry (1972-1973), and the two presidents of the post-dictatorship period, Julio María Sanguinetti (1985-1990 and 1995-2000) and Luis Alberto Lacalle (1990-1995).

One point of comparison in decision-making styles is the relationship between the legitimacy of mandates and the degree of use of constitutional emergency measures. The legitimacy of the last two presidents before the dictatorship, Pacheco and Bordaberry, was questioned on several accounts. President Pacheco assumed power not by direct popular vote but after the death of General Oscar Gestido, who had been elected president. Up to that moment, Vice President Pacheco had gone practically unnoticed, in part because of his lack of a relevant background and in part because of the scant attention paid to the office of vice president until then.

As president, however, Pacheco was able to overcome his initial lackluster image and become a central figure in Uruguayan politics and a true leader, albeit at the expense of an extreme polarization of society. The broad sectors opposing President Pacheco reluctantly acknowledged his legitimacy as president but loathed his brazenly authoritarian style. His years in office were characterized by a chronic lack of support in Parliament, for which he compensated by consistently resorting to emergency measures and governing by decree.

This problematic combination of limited legitimacy and abuse of power, which characterized the Pacheco administration, became critical during the presidency of Juan María Bordaberry. Charges of electoral fraud diminished the legitimacy of his mandate. In addition, the climate of internal unrest and lack of political support caused Bordaberry's government to drift into the coup d'état of June 1973.

During the years of the dictatorship, the learning of the political class, whether conscious or intuitive, caused post-military leaders to avoid using emergency measures and to provide political support to protect democratic legitimacy. When Sanguinetti was elected president after a difficult transition, the main opposition candidate, Wilson Ferreira Aldunate, still incarcerated, took special care to support Sanguinetti so that he would not lack political support or legitimacy in office. President Luis Alberto Lacalle, although no longer assailed by formal legitimacy problems, followed in the footsteps of his predecessor by taking special care to carry out his policies without major confrontations and without resorting to emergency measures.

Today, there seems to be a tacit rule of political cohabitation, according to which democratic legitimacy is not eroded and emergency measures are no longer included in the president's political tool kit. This new style adopted by the presidents of the restored democracy is grasped with all its nuances by the political class as a whole. For ex-Senator and National Party representative Juan Raúl Ferreira, the Uruguayan ambassador to Argentina, "Before the coup d'état, the President of the Republic was the leader of a political sector. . . . Now there is a sense of nation underlying the dignity of certain offices, which was previously nonexistent. . . ."[11]

The scope of action of the government's policies has clearly expanded in recent years. The presidents' styles are more open and acquiescent than in the 1960s and 1970s, and perhaps the only "reserved domain" of the president is control over economic policies. The economy is handled with a sort of technocratic pretension that seeks to remove itself as much as possible from sectarian pressures. Nevertheless, the decision-making style of the last decade is one of bargaining and consultation, much more than one of imposition.

This tendency has been even more apparent in President Sanguinetti's second administration (1995-1999). The singular circumstances that came out of the "triple tie" in the 1994 elections and the formation of the government coalition have generated a much more open and consultative style, to the point of forming a sort of "virtual government council" that harks back to times when the executive was collegiate in nature. This practice has obvious democratic advantages, because decisionmaking is done from the ground up on the basis of a great deal of consensus and legitimacy. It also has its disadvantages, because the search for agreement and consensus is basically processed outside the scope of Parliament. Adding referenda to this "virtual collegiate system" threatens the political role of Parliament in sensitive areas.

This new decision-making style has had some important achievements, such as passage of the 1995 Social Security Reform Law and the 1996 Constitutional Reform. In the latter, the above-described partnership agreements were decisive.

One of the major difficulties for reforming the constitution — be it the current one or others — is the perception by different parties of the electoral advantages or disadvantages of modifying the rules. In this case, the Colorado Party perceived its own interest, based on the current political situation, to lie in shifting from a system of accumulation of votes among multiple candidates for each party to a single-candidate-per-party system. President Sanguinetti himself had competed as a single candidate — in the absence of other Colorado candidates — and was not interested in giving the traditional adversary, the National Party, any advantages.

It is harder to understand why the National Party agreed to modify an electoral system that favored it, seeing that it had at least three good candidates who would have competed effectively. Perhaps it was because the dynamics of the coalition government supplanted party interests with the personal political interests of the participants of that restricted club. As the National Party leader with the greatest control over the structure and mechanisms of the party, Luis Alberto Lacalle was interested in adopting a primary system of internal elections such as the one proposed. His control over the structure gave him tremendous odds of winning his party's internal elections, which had been much less likely with the previous system. For Volonté, the leader of another faction of the party, reform did not offer any electoral advantages, but it was to his advantage to come to a political agreement with his powerful coalition partner, President Sanguinetti.

On the other hand, another proposal to introduce the ballotage (or second round) system was perceived by the left as an artifice to bar the Frente Amplio's entrance to the 1999 elections, so the majority of its supporters voted "No" in the December 8, 1996, plebiscite. Nevertheless, the reforms passed with the minimum votes necessary.

ATTITUDES OF SOCIETY

Societal attitudes toward a political regime will increase the chances of success of either a democratic or an autocratic ruler. Each country's political culture largely determines its long-term tendencies, and Uruguay seems to corroborate this thesis firmly. Public attitudes clearly are supportive of democratic institutions and may contribute as much to democratic consolidation as does elite learning.

A comparative survey implemented throughout Latin America about the attitude of the different societies toward democratic principles, rules, and institutions shows that Uruguayan society, in principle, is satisfied with the functioning of democracy, as expressed by a majority of 69 percent of its citizens.[12] More surprisingly, there is also a 59 percent majority that supports Parliament. These rosy data, however, are tainted with the distrust political parties engender in 64 percent of the population. The last result, which is positive, shows that 73 percent of the people interviewed trust the electoral rules of the game.

Table 1. Degree of Satisfaction with the Functioning of Democracy in the Country

	Uruguayans	Latin Americans
Very satisfied	11	12
Moderately satisfied	58	35
Little satisfied	21	32
Unsatisfied	9	20
Do not know	1	1

Table 2. Trust in the Functioning of Parliament

	Uruguayans	Latin Americans
Trust	51	28
Distrust	43	67
Do not know	6	5

Table 3. Trust in Political Parties

	Uruguayans	Latin Americans
Trust	25	17
Distrust	64	79
Do not know	11	4

Table 4. Trust in the Electoral System

	Uruguayans	Latin Americans
Trust	73	46
Distrust	24	51
Do not know	3	3

These data indicate that Uruguayan democracy overall remains firm on its principles and rules but that political parties are its Achilles' heel. The political elite is aware of this problem, and the number-one item on its political agenda is to draft a law for political parties that will render these structures more efficient.

CONCLUSION

S ome time ago, a humorist adapted a famous phrase for an article published in a Montevideo newspaper, "People who forget their past are doomed to make the same mistakes, and people who do not forget it are doomed to make new mistakes." This play on words candidly describes the Uruguayan current reality. It would be impossible to deny important learning experiences with regard to past events, both for the elite and for society at large, which point toward the strengthening of democracy. It would be equally nonsensical to pretend that antidemocratic pockets in society and in the political elite do not exist. The specific goal of this research is to focus on the set of mistakes that are not being repeated because the past has not been forgotten. But it is also interesting to describe the "new mistakes" committed by the elite in a democratic environment. These "new" antidemocratic behaviors illustrate the limits of democratic learning.

The "Triple Tie" and the Ability to Govern

The results of the 1994 elections immediately brought forth bleak predictions regarding the governability of the country. Separating the winning party, the Colorados, and the party that came in third, the Frente Amplio, were a mere 30,000 votes. The country's historical precedents were certainly worrisome. The disastrous effect of divided governments in the 1960s and 1970s was still fresh in the memories of Uruguayans over 40. The new reality of a tripartite system was even more difficult. Contrary to all predictions, the installation of President Sanguinetti's new administration encountered fewer obstacles than anticipated, and political stability does not seem threatened.

What new factors came into play in these political circumstances to moderate the tripartite results and the minority government? In my opinion, there are three decisive elements: 1) learning by the political elite, in the strict sense that it has tended to avoid the problems that stemmed from similar situations in the past; 2) individual learning by President Sanguinetti, which has generated a political authority in many regards the exact opposite of the type of legitimization and leadership exercised by ex-President Jorge Pacheco Areco almost three decades ago, which caused serious institutional problems; and 3) the Frente Amplio's political ambitions, which have created a perceived need to pass a vocational test of sorts in order to substantiate and legitimize its democratic principles and to allow it to be perceived as qualified to govern the country.

1. *Learning by the political elite.* The political elite's learning can be ascertained clearly in the care given by practically all sectors to defining their political relationship with the president. Generally speaking, there has been a broad support for issues that were crucial to the president's ability to govern. The parties or sectors that became aligned with the opposition made explicit their allegiance and

role as a loyal opposition. In this way, the negative predictions stemming from the election results worked as an alarm system that activated the democratic and self-preservation reflexes of the political actors. The fear that Parliament would lock horns with the executive or that the executive would resort to emergency measures and govern by decree (as in the past) to compensate for its lack of support in Parliament set off one of the crucial reflexes for the survival of a democracy: the idea that democracy must be taken care of, nurtured, and protected. Without a doubt, this impulse improved things even as the prognosis was looking somber and the ability to govern seemed threatened.

2. *Individual learning by President Sanguinetti.* The personal factor, President Sanguinetti's authority, is another fundamental, positive factor coming out of the post-electoral situation. A savvy politician, President Sanguinetti recognized that the style required by the circumstances was one of low profile, of building bridges to other parties, and of seeking a consensus in government. The president's level-headedness and open disposition yielded positive results. Based on agreements mainly with the National Party, he chose a cabinet with several ministers outside his party. This procedure assured him of parliamentary support for passing certain laws essential for the accomplishment of his government objectives.

Without question, the presidential style has had a positive effect on democratic stability. The relationship between use of constitutional powers and personal legitimacy, which had dire results in the Pacheco and Bordaberry administrations more than two decades ago, is currently at its most beneficial combination. This relationship is basically minimum authoritarianism and maximum authority, stemming from a low-profile, consensus-seeking style, supplemented by strong democratic legitimacy and a well-earned reputation for being a skilled manager of political transitions.

This summary portrayal of President Sanguinetti during his second administration is practically the complete opposite of the 1967-1973 Pacheco and Bordaberry administrations referred to elsewhere in this chapter. The relationship between authoritarianism and personal authority at that time reached record extremes.

3. *The Frente Amplio's political ambitions.* The ideological crisis of the left, the failure of "real socialism," and the absence of utopias and models have led the militants of old to realign themselves with different projects. There are at least two alternatives for the Uruguayan left today. The first is an option based not on ideology, but rather on open bargaining and pragmatism among various sectors mainly from the Frente Amplio, which has explicitly revalued democracy and is hoping to gain power in the upcoming 1999 elections. The second alternative reflects the need for an ideological identity and purpose, which has intensified the militancy of the more radical antidemocratic groups, for example, those most averse to negotiation with other groups, even within the Frente Amplio. At the same time, a great number of people from marginalized social sectors have joined the ranks of the more radical groups, which will probably have turbulent implications for the social and political peace of the country. A lumpen proletariat that traditionally had voted with the ultra-right swung to the other extreme of the political spectrum in the 1994 elections, and it did so without abandoning its authoritarian and violent reflexes.

Signals from the political left, then, are ambiguous. The strong electoral performance of the Asamblea Uruguay movement led by Senator Danilo Astori, which is clearly the most open and democratic faction of the Frente Amplio, sent out positive signals concerning democratization of the political debate. However, the fact that the Frente Amplio gave greater priority to militant legitimacy than to democratic legitimacy gradually eroded Astori's leadership, buttressing his internal adversary, Tabaré Vázquez, and the more radical sectors.

The radical sectors no longer have Vázquez's blessing. After he consolidated his leadership following a long tug-of-war with Astori, Vázquez began to distance himself from his old partners of convenience. During the last quarter of 1997, the extreme left destroyed plans for privatization put forth by the Montevideo mayoralty, generating a crisis that culminated with Tabaré Vázquez's resignation from the presidency of the Frente Amplio. As he expressed repeatedly to the press, he remains hopeful that he will be able to lay a new foundation for the Frente Amplio, which in political language means not to lose his strength and to wait to return with all the power.

This chapter has presented a series of actions and behaviors by Uruguay's political and social actors, which have resulted, we contend, from a process of learning from past experiences. This learning has been heterogeneous, both in its nature and in its impact on Uruguay's political system and democratic regime. Significant changes have occurred in the political discourse of different persuasions, which has become less demagogic and more pragmatic. There is a progressive and almost unanimous acceptance of the democratic rules of the game, and the relationships among actors have become less antagonistic. In addition, the universe of possible coalition partners has broadened, which should increase governability. Political styles and even the way decisions are made have adapted to a context of greater tolerance and consultation. After the country's political problems were analyzed by the political elite, a constitutional reform was passed. Finally, Uruguayan society is committed to the principles and institutions of a democracy.

This long list leads to optimism. Uruguay has moved forward, and the conscious linking of these new behaviors and past experiences enables us to conclude that, to a great extent, both the political elite and society at large have learned from past crises and mistakes. However, this confirmation does not end the discussion. It is true that there has been learning, but this learning does not unquestionably guarantee the consolidation of democracy or even the ability to govern. This learning only allows us to predict that if Uruguayan democracy falls into crisis again, it will not travel down the same road that led to its breakdown more than 20 years ago. This is the case because certain past actions have brought about learning, and current political behavior explicitly avoids repeating them. The antidemocratic potential of other actions, however, seems to go undetected simply because such behavior has no precedent and cannot be measured against any past experiences. The military dictatorship is still recent enough to ensure that certain deeds will not be repeated, but it is also sufficiently removed to decrease the perceived need to evaluate possible antidemocratic consequences of new behaviors.

In more precise terms, there is a definite consensus on formal curbing of antidemocratic behaviors, but there are no qualms about using the political assets of democracy in an antidemocratic manner. In the name of direct democracy, the role of Parliament is being eroded; and, in the name of economic democracy, the basis of political democracy is shifting. Democracy stands to win when past mistakes are avoided, but it stands to lose when antidemocratic behaviors are legitimized as vestiges of ancient Greek democracy.

Notes

1. Senator Reinaldo Gargano, interview with the author, November 30, 1993.

2. Senator Walter Santoro, interview with the author in Montevideo, Uruguay, February 26, 1996.

3. Senator Luis Hierro López, interview with the author, February 22, 1996.

4. Senator Danilo Astori, interview with the author, March 15, 1996.

5. Senator Rafael Michelini, interview with the author in Montevideo, Uruguay, February 14, 1996.

6. Senator Reinaldo Gargano, interview with the author in Montevideo, Uruguay, November 30, 1993.

7. Senator Rafael Michelini, interview with the author in Montevideo, Uruguay, February 14, 1996.

8. Communist Party representative Gonzalo Carámbula's testimony about this process has been particularly illuminating. Interview with the author, December 15, 1993.

9. The PGP leader, Senator Hugo Batalla, considers this novelty one of the most important learning instances for the political elite as a whole. He was interviewed by the author on December 3, 1993.

10. Senator Reinaldo Gargano, interview with the author in Montevideo, Uruguay, November 30, 1996.

11. Former Senator and National Party representative Juan Raúl Ferreira, who became the Uruguayan ambassador to Argentina in 1996.

12. This survey was carried out in October 1993 by the Uruguayan consulting firm DATOS and by a network of affiliated companies throughout Latin America.

CHAPTER FIVE

Venezuela: Old Successes, New Constraints on Learning

FRANCINE JÁCOME[1]

In contrast to most other Latin American countries, Venezuela for the past 40 years has had a democratic system that has obeyed the basic rules of liberal representative democracy and has avoided the "bureaucratic authoritarian" experience of other countries in the region. Beginning in 1983 with the devaluation of the currency, however, it became clear that Venezuela faced an impending crisis that was mainly economic in nature but with important political ramifications rooted in the earlier "oil boom" decade. The crisis erupted first in 1989 with the famous *Caracazo* rioting and again in February and November 1992 with two attempted military coups.

When considering these events and the history of the country over the past 50 years (1945-1995), the question we address is whether the political leaders' reactions to the economic and political crisis resulted from political learning. For this study, political learning is understood to be a process of acquiring knowledge that informs behavior and attitudes. We are particularly interested in democratic learning — learning that leads to individual or collective attitudes that contribute both to legitimacy and governability or to the ability to solve problems within a democratic context.

In the case of Venezuela, there have been different types of learning[2] during the past 50 years. We posit that "overlearning" and simple learning are salient features of the Venezuelan political elite. Although complex learning can be attributed to some individuals, it is not found to be a characteristic of the Venezuelan political elite as a group. Finally, a certain degree of divergent learning at both individual and group levels was evident between 1989 and 1995.

The predominant *overlearning* is evidenced by situations in which strategies and tactics that worked well before continue to be used when new circumstances arise, even when they are not the most appropriate solutions to these current problems. In other words, prior learning impedes or slows subsequent learning for new situations. This is related to Joseph Nye's (1987, 379) concept of negative learning (that is, strong beliefs block or distort new information that could otherwise alter them through learning), except that we are focusing on beliefs or perceptions resulting from prior learning experiences that subsequently block the processing of new information. *Simple learning* refers to changes in attitude that are primarily instrumental, in that they seek to further strategic interests of the actors or simply constitute adaptations to certain circumstances. Thus, simple learning produces changes in means, in contrast to the changes in priorities or underlying goals that result from complex learning. *Divergent learning* refers to different lessons that have been learned by various actors from the same experience.

This chapter argues that in Venezuela, overlearning has contributed to a political system that has become less legitimate, less representative, and less participatory, thus producing growing governability problems in the face of the current economic and political crisis. We posit that the absence of complex political learning among the political elite contributed to the crisis of the state-centric matrix (SCM) of economic, political, and social relations in Venezuela.[3]

HISTORICAL LEARNING (1945-1982)

Historically, democracy in Venezuela began in 1945 with a military coup organized with the participation of Democratic Action (Acción Democrática — AD) leaders. The Junta Revolucionaria de Gobierno, presided over by AD's leader, Rómulo Betancourt, came to power in October 1945 and remained in power until December 1947, when the first elections with universal, direct, and secret voting were held. Rómulo Gallegos, a famous Venezuelan novelist who belonged to AD, was elected president. Yet, in 1948, a military coup ended this first try at democracy, known as the *trienio*. This event proved to be a turning point for complex political learning for Venezuelan political leaders and a source of current overlearning.

The *trienio* period marked the setting in Venezuela for the development of both the economic and the political characteristics of the SCM. From an economic standpoint, the SCM's characteristics were "import substitution industrialization, closed or semi-closed economy, government-regulated market, and a pattern of 'moderate' inflation" (Cavarozzi 1991, 94). Likewise, the SCM was accompanied by a populist ideology that has been characterized as one that identifies nationalism with statism (Castillo 1990). Accordingly, the state becomes the main promoter of industrialization and development. These characteristics of the SCM were established during the *trienio* period and continued during the military dictatorship of 1948-1958 and under the liberal democratic system after 1958.

The most important political reforms set forth by this first AD government during the *trienio* were geared toward modifying the electoral system to allow for universal suffrage and the participation of other political organizations. Yet, the government acted with increasing sectarianism, furthering only AD's interests, and it increasingly alienated itself from economic, military, and political elites (Castillo 1990; Peeler 1985). AD, whose political discourse and actions were deeply oriented toward popular mobilization and action, was not able to win the economic elite's confidence, in large degree because this elite doubted that the government would favor its needs. The government's ties with the military deteriorated because the military felt that AD's party interests were being favored over national interests. The two other important political parties, the Social Christian Party – Committee of Independent Political Electoral Organization (Comité de Organización Política Electoral Independiente — COPEI) and the Democratic Republican Union (Unión Republicana Democrática — URD), were alienated by constant accusations of their supposed involvement in coup plans to overthrow the government.

Thus, AD managed to alienate itself from the different sectors that could have supported the government and allowed for the building of a democratic regime. When the military coup occurred in 1948, the vast majority of economic and political sectors favored the military, and AD's government did not receive the backing necessary to forestall the coup.

The next 10 years of military rule have been divided into three main stages (Castillo 1990): 1) a first stage in which there was institutional coherence around an economic and political program developed by the military; 2) a second stage that revolved around the personal dictatorship of General Marcos Pérez Jiménez; and 3) a third stage leading to his downfall as different groups, especially the economic and military elites, distanced themselves from the dictator because of widespread government corruption and political repression.

Carrying out an import-substitution industrialization strategy, the military government invested in infrastructure and social services and operated without a deficit because of the revenue from oil exports. Likewise, during this period, the expansion of production and export of oil and steel allowed for growing investments in industry and construction. Notwithstanding the economic prosperity, there was growing political discontent, especially after 1952 when it became clear that a personal dictatorship had set in under Pérez Jiménez. Both elite and popular discontent were channeled through the political parties. Thus, popular discontent was led locally by clandestine groups formed mainly by the AD, the Venezuelan Communist Party (Partido Comunista de Venezuela — PCV), and the URD.

Having learned from the *trienio* experience, the political elite-in-exile, led by AD's Rómulo Betancourt, sought alliances with the economic elite and sought the backing of the U.S. government. There was widespread consensus that the main objectives were to overthrow the military government and to develop a democratic system, both of which were more important than developing a given party's program, a lesson learned well by AD as a result of the *trienio* period. Even though two ideological tendencies — AD's social democratic populism and COPEI's Social Christian project — had emerged after the 1948 coup, there were no deep, conflicting social, political, or economic projects, and the main sources of tension were centered on who would hold power (Castillo 1990).

The diverse parties reached consensus, in large part, because they realized that the only way to overthrow the military regime and to develop democracy was going to be through cooperative action. The core groups formed the Unión Patriótica in 1957 in order to coordinate action to overthrow the government, and the exiled elite signed the New York Pact.

The military remained in power until 1958, when on January 23, a popular insurrection led by the Unión Patriótica overthrew the Pérez Jiménez government. A civil-military junta governed until December 1958, when AD's most important founder and leader, Rómulo Betancourt, won the elections. One of the salient features of complex political learning from the 1945-1948 experience with democracy was the signing of the Pact of Punto Fijo by leaders of AD, COPEI, URD, the military, the church, business, and labor. The Pact's main objective was to reach a consensus on the priority given to development and consolidation of the democratic system, above all other political values (Navarro 1995; Karl 1986). The Pact created a power-sharing arrangement that guaranteed all the signatory parties a share in the government, no matter who won, and with its ancillary "Declaration of Principles and Minimum Program of Government," it laid out a common economic and political program. The accord thus protected the vital interests of the major social actors in Venezuela and protected the new regime from partisan conflict by guaranteeing that each party had a stake in the survival of the system (McCoy and Smith 1995, 244).

Clearly, the 1948 coup and the 10-year military dictatorship had taught the political elite, especially AD's leadership, attitudes and practices necessary for developing democracy and for maintaining legitimacy and governability. The main lesson learned was the need to reach consensus on a general economic and political program. The political elite had learned that it could not govern alone and that a democratic political system could not be developed by one party. Instead, through a series of pacts and accords, political and social actors reached consensus on economic, political, and social policies that would reduce uncertainty and reduce the incentives for another military intervention. The resulting political system had "three main guidelines: state and party centralism, incorporation of the major special interest groups — business, labor, and trade associations — in government decisionmaking, and formulas for negotiation and consensus by means of pacts and economic subsidy policies" (Stambouli 1993, 32).

The framework for a corporatist system with a state-centric matrix was set, with "the goal of interest groups to maximize their integration into the government" (Peeler 1985, 104). A type of contradictory political behavior using participation and negotiation but also using authoritarian and arbitrary control took root in this system. On the one hand, a strong government settled economic and political disputes, creating a hyperpoliticized political system and society as a whole. On the other hand, electoral participation grew, but it did not lead to greater participation in the decision-making processes.

Venezuela's model of liberal democracy came to be characterized by honest elections and a pattern of alternation between parties in the executive and legislative branches. This provided a sense of stability and legitimacy based upon a pattern of elite accommodation. The rules of the game — elections and alternation — were respected, but the range of options was limited "by masking hegemony in pluralist, competitive, strongly centrist political processes" (Peeler 1985, 127).

In accordance with the political characteristics of the SCM and despite the consolidation of democracy, this model led to greater control over society and limited the participation of other actors within the political system, which then came to be dominated by the parties and the state. What developed was a "culture of agreements" based on the fact that the relatively stable economy allowed for consensus regarding distributive government policies. "Rather than implementation of a plan of action . . . governing consisted of the ability to heed and please groups, individuals, and clienteles" (Stambouli 1993, 37). The result was a restricted-authoritarian political system (Jácome 1989), or, as characterized by COPEI leader Eduardo Fernández in an interview for this project, "The model proposed in the Punto Fijo scheme was based on three pillars: centralism, statism, and partyism. It was a democracy not of the people, but of the parties."

Table 1. Percentage of Votes for AD and COPEI During National Elections (1958-1993)

	1958	1963	1968	1973	1978	1983	1988	1993
President	64.4	53.6	57.3	85.4	89.9	91.5	92.9	46*
Legislature	64.7	53.5	50	74.7	79.4	78.6	78.4	46*

Sources: Miriam Kornblith and David H. Levine, "Venezuela: The Life and Times of the Party System," in *Building Democratic Institutions: Party Systems in Latin America,* eds. Scott Mainwaring and Timothy R. Scully (Stanford: Stanford University Press, 1995); and Herbert R. Koeneke, "El sistema electoral en Caracas," paper presented at the III Encuentro Internacional Sociedad Civil y Reforma Electoral, in Caracas, Venezuela, November 22-23, 1996. *The asterisks indicate provisional figures.

Within the framework of the Punto Fijo Pact, a new Constitution was drawn up and approved in 1961, and the pattern of electoral power sharing between AD and COPEI began. Thus, AD's presidential candidate, Raul Leoni, won the 1963 elections; COPEI's Rafael Caldera won the 1968 elections; and AD's Carlos Andrés Pérez won the election in 1973. (See Table 1.) During the early 1960s, achievement of political stability was somewhat hindered by the development of a guerrilla movement led by the Communist party and the Revolutionary Left Movement (Movimiento de Izquierda Revolucionaria — MIR) and by military coup attempts. It is important to note that these coup attempts brought forth large public demonstrations that backed the government.

Apart from the formal Punto Fijo Pact, since 1969 an informal pact had been agreed upon: the "Institutional Pact," which allowed bipartisan election of the heads of the Senate and Deputies chambers, Supreme Court members, and other government officials. In accordance with the predominant role played by political parties, this allowed power sharing mainly between AD and COPEI, but smaller parties such as the Movement to Socialism (Movimiento Al Socialismo — MAS) also were taken into account by allotting them less important positions (Gómez Calcaño 1995). The political culture evolving in the first decades of democratic life thus was one in which the political elite monopolized decisionmaking and power while popular participation was limited to periodic elections. As political scientist and one-time director of *SIC* magazine Arturo Sosa stated in an interview for this project, this has led to "parties that have become terribly impoverished and have an extremely strong tendency to hold on to their privileges because a great many of the party leaders cannot compete outside the party."

In conclusion, the political leaders' first experience with democracy from 1945 to 1948 taught them that in order to develop and consolidate a democratic system, it was necessary to reach a certain consensus that would allow a stable political system. The Punto Fijo Pact was a result of this complex learning, and the elite consensus enabled the development of a democracy in the framework of stable economic and social conditions. Yet, as the next section of this chapter demonstrates, when political patterns became rigid and unresponsive and the economic system started deteriorating, Venezuela's elite struggled to respond to the new situation, failing to demonstrate new collective complex learning.

THE STRUGGLE OVER THE SCM:
PERCEPTIONS OF THE CRISIS (1982-1995)

Contemporary learning in the Venezuelan case is analyzed here within the framework of the unraveling of the SCM and the different economic adjustment policies and political reforms that were put forth, beginning in 1989, in order to face the perceived crisis. During the 1970s, the Punto Fijo Pact began to show signs of disintegrating when President Pérez made decisions without consulting or taking into account other actors' opinions, and the original signators of the Pact no longer had homogeneous interests. The economic characteristics of the SCM also persisted in Venezuela until the late 1970s and early 1980s. With income from the hike in oil prices in 1973-1974 and borrowing from abroad, the government in 1975 and 1976 nationalized important basic industries, including the iron ore and petroleum industries. The country achieved high growth and low inflation rates between the 1950s and the 1970s.

With petroleum prices declining in the late 1970s, the various governments attempted to further statist development by using foreign loans to continue with their projects. A second oil price hike in 1979 helped to postpone economic adjustment. With the Mexican government near default in 1982, however, foreign debt became a major economic problem, leading to a drastic drop in new loans by the international banking community. Venezuela suffered a fiscal and balance-of-payments crisis, which caused the government in 1983 to devalue the currency and set up a dual exchange control in 1983. Nevertheless, these were partial adjustment policies aimed at two basic goals: stabilizing the economy and launching a structural reform process (Márquez 1994). Fiscal and external balances improved, but, at the same time, there was growing economic recession with a significant increase in unemployment and poverty.

Aggravating the situation even further, in 1986 the price of oil fell again. The AD government postponed economic adjustment until after the 1988 elections. It drained international reserves, increased indebtedness, caused continued fiscal deficits, and drove inflation up (Márquez 1994).

Politically, even though the Punto Fijo Pact had become dysfunctional, its main tool of power sharing in order to maintain political stability continued through alternation of the two major parties in power. Therefore, COPEI once again came into power when Luis Herrera Campins won the 1978 elections, and, in the 1983 elections, AD's candidate, Jaime Lusinchi, was elected. The end of alternation between AD and COPEI in the executive branch of government, which had occurred since 1968, came when Carlos Andrés Pérez was reelected for a second term in the 1988 elections.

As of 1989, Venezuela started its process of shifting from a state-centered to a market-centered economy as a solution to its decade-long economic and political crisis. The economic adjustment plan proposed by the Pérez administration — The Great Turnaround (*el Gran Viraje*) — aimed to open up and put an end to government tutelage of the Venezuelan economy. Consequently, Venezuelans began to carry out reforms in three areas: structural adjustment of the economy, political reform and decentralization, and integration processes (de la Cruz 1992).

From the standpoint of the economy, the reforms were aimed at correcting an inefficient production apparatus, dependence on oil income, increased public spending, a monopolized economy, and the failure of the price control policies. This readjustment plan was designed to reach macroeconomic stabilization, fiscal balance, and commercial liberalization and to privatize public enterprises and develop social policies for the poor (Naim 1993). Yet, by the end of 1989, inflation had reached 84.5 percent, and poverty was at 53.7 percent.

Political reforms and decentralization also were addressed, and political elites were forced to accept certain reforms, as will be discussed further on. Because of the globalization trend in the international sphere, the Pérez government also developed a growing interest in integration processes. Ties with Colombia and Mexico were reinforced by developing the Group of Three (G-3) integration scheme, the country's participation in the Andean Pact was reinforced, and closer ties were sought with its Caribbean neighbors.

The first negative reaction to the readjustment policies announced in January 1989 was the popular uprising on the 27th of February, known thereafter as the *Caracazo* although it occurred not only in Caracas, but also in the majority of the country's other large main urban centers. Between 300 and 1,000 people were killed when the National Guard tried to quell the unrest.

In spite of this totally unexpected event, the government continued its adjustment process, which included devaluing the currency by 170 percent, raising interest rates from 13 percent to 40 percent, and renegotiating the public debt. A new tax system, including a value-added tax, was sent to Congress for approval, and by 1991 the economy was growing and showing signs of macroeconomic improvement, with inflation down to 31 percent (Naim 1993). Nevertheless, the social situation was declining steadily. More than half of the population lived below the poverty line, public services did not function, more than half of the working population was in the informal sector, and corruption was widespread. This situation led, in turn, to increasing public unrest, and on February 4, 1992, the first military coup attempt of that year took place; a second one occurred in November.

The government was subjected to mounting pressure, not only from its own party and other political parties but also from a vast majority of social actors, to abandon its readjustment policies. The government gave in to the growing pressure, postponing further adjustments and back-tracking on some policies. This was to be the beginning of the retrogression to the SCM.

Pérez's unpopular adjustment policies and the growing charges of corruption eventually led to his removal from office in 1993 after the Supreme Court decided that there was enough evidence to try him on charges of misallocation of public funds. A very weak interim government was chosen, led by the intellectual Ramón J. Velásquez, who achieved his main goal: Elections were held in December 1993, and Rafael Caldera was elected for his second term with 31 percent of the votes but with an abstention rate of 39.48 percent, the highest ever in democratic Venezuela's national elections. (See Table 2.)

Table 2. Abstention Levels During National Elections

Year	% Abstention
1958	6.58
1963	7.78
1968	3.30
1973	3.40
1978	12.40
1983	12.20
1988	18.10
1993	39.48

Source: *El Nacional*, Caracas, December 1993.

One of the grave mistakes made by the Pérez administration in its quest for instituting a new model was the emphasis on economic reforms, to the exclusion of political and social reforms. These economic reforms, aimed at opening the economy to the market, were attempted within traditional political institutions and political culture. How could a market-centered economic model function within the framework of a paternalistic, clientelist, and centralist society? The question implied the need for members of the political elite to change their attitudes and practices in order to develop a new economic, political, and social model that would substitute for the SCM. However, this did not occur.

Instead, economic, political, and social elites affected by the changes resisted government efforts to move away from the SCM and sought to have the state regain its role as guardian and redistributor. Furthermore, the negative consequences of the adjustment policies brought forth a tendency to hold the political parties and their leaders responsible. As in other countries of the region, this situation led to the emergence of "a new generation of 'caudillo,' presidents whose appeal was based on speeches and behavior with an antipolitical slant" (Cavarozzi 1993, 34) — these being fundamental characteristics of what Guillermo O'Donnell (1994) has called "delegative democracy."

Rafael Caldera, the founder and leader of COPEI, took full advantage of this situation when he campaigned in 1993. By appealing to antiparty sentiment and running for his second term as an independent, he built a messianic image of himself as the country's savior. Thus, in 1993, a new "caudillo" president was elected. Those who voted wanted the new president to solve the economic and political crisis. In response, the Caldera government moved to regain centralist control of the executive branch. An example of this occurred in January 1994, when an acute banking crisis erupted just as Caldera was to be inaugurated. The new government launched a "de facto government takeover" of the banking system, set price and exchange controls, banned any parallel foreign exchange market, and suspended a number of constitutional rights (Márquez 1994, 12).

Perceptions of the Crisis

Perceptions of the political crisis that erupted in 1989 expressed by the actors interviewed for this chapter in 1994 give important insights into their interpretations and consequent reactions. Several actors focused on the limits of the political system and culture created by the Pact of Punto Fijo. Teodoro Petkoff, the former guerrilla leader and minister of planning under the second Caldera administration, analyzed the role of authoritarian political culture in Venezuela in bringing about the crisis:

> The Venezuelan democracy, in my opinion, was born under clear authoritarian signs. The roots of the crisis go back to the inequalities among the three powers of government: Since 1958, we've had a democracy with a highly concentrated and centralized power in the dominant executive branch, with a weaker legislative branch and a judicial branch strongly influenced by the executive, political parties, and economic forces. In addition, the nature of the political party system in Venezuela is Leninist, with power concentrated in a *cúpula* (small controlling group) and very limited internal democracy. The Venezuelan state was also infected by these autocratic characteristics of the parties. The crisis, therefore, has to do with the contradictions between a system that proclaims the values of liberty, equality, and citizen participation, and the frankly restricted nature of decisionmaking.

With some parallels to Petkoff, the intellectual Rafael de la Cruz disassociated the political from the economic crisis and explained the problem of declining political legitimacy in terms of the emergence of new social groups not represented in the public decision-making process:

> The emergence of these new groups not included in the Pact of Punto Fijo began to redraw the lines between the state and society, which had been defined by the *concertación* (consultation) between AD and COPEI, the military high command, the church, and the private sector organized in FEDECAMARAS (Federation of Chambers of Commerce). New sectors with different ideas began to emerge in the private sector, regional groups, neighborhood organizations, professional organizations, and labor unions. This reflected a much more complex society with a greater awareness of its own possibilities and long-term projects. This group of people slowly began to untie itself from the tutelage of the state and the political parties and to produce a phenomenon of autonomy of grand sectors of the society. I believe this is the origin of the political crisis in Venezuela in the 1980s, in the face of which began to emerge proposals for the decentralization of the political system, reflected eventually in the creation of the COPRE (Presidential Commission on Reforming the State) in 1984.

Arturo Sosa, director of the magazine *SIC*, identified the rupture of the national consensus born in 1958 as an important source of the political crisis of the 1980s and 1990s:

> In 1958, there was a high level of consensus about the basic elements of the political system. Time passed, and this consensus lost its historic context as the participating actors' economic and political interests evolved. Simultaneously, a much slower transformation in the rhythm of the mass political culture occurred, in part as a result of the Pact itself and in part as a result of the contradictions produced by the Pact. For example, the Pact delimited the channels, levels, and

limits of participation. But now the society can no longer remain in this framework of limitation. There is a pressure, and there are types of participation that imply remaking the foundational pacts. . . . There is now a total incongruence between the social body and the bases of the political system, including the Constitution.

Other actors attribute the crisis to both economic and political frustrations. Former COPRE president Carlos Blanco argued that the crisis of the political system began at the end of the 1970s with the convergence of three fundamental factors: 1) deterioration of the economic possibilities provided by the rentier model, as a result of the decline in oil income and increase of external debt; 2) the growing incapacity of the political system to represent citizen demands, along with a democratic maturation leading to more demanding and more vigilant citizens; and 3) a serious social problem that became grave in the 1980s. Additionally, the increasing centralization of the political system and political parties impeded the capacity to adapt to changing circumstances.

Two political leaders of different ideologies attribute the political crisis of 1989 and beyond to frustrated expectations of the Venezuelan people. COPEI leader Eduardo Fernandez explained:

> In my opinion, the fundamental cause [of the political crisis of 1989] was the drastic fall in national income. In 10 years, Venezuela passed from a per capita income of about $5,000 to one of about $1,000. This would produce a critical situation in any country. Venezuela sold its oil at one moment at $40 per barrel, and by the mid-1990s, the average price had fallen to $11. This drastic fall in income produced consequences above all in the middle class, but also in the armed forces and the social indicators that form public opinion. . . . The political system, which was a pact of elites, ended up projecting an image of corruption, clientelism, and loss of capacity to interpret the reality of what was happening in Venezuela (and in good measure this corresponded with reality). Interestingly, the 1989 crisis follows a pattern of historic accidents in which there seems to be a traumatic crisis every 30 years, dating back to 1777.

Likewise, former Causa R (Radical Cause Party) leader Pablo Medina attributes the political crisis to both economic and political factors: "First, the political class elaborated a project for Venezuela in 1958 that created unmet expectations in political and economic terms. There is a collective dissatisfaction with the grand democratic project in Venezuela. Second, the coincidence of the 1973 oil price hikes and the consolidation of the biparty system by AD and COPEI that same year produced a corrupt political class."

POLITICAL LEARNING FROM THE CRISIS OF THE SCM?

Since 1958, Venezuelan political actors had worked toward a goal of democratic stability. However, this model evolved in such a way that stability was achieved at the expense of representativeness, participation, and legitimacy. Within the framework of the SCM, the Venezuelan political system had operated under three basic characteristics: 1) state and party control not only of the political system, but also of the economy and civil society; 2) government decisionmaking incorporating the different goals of diverse interest groups, with elections as the main means of political participation; and 3) underlying the political system, negotiation and consensus through pacts and subsidy policies.

After 1958, substantial civilian control over the military was established, but this process also deteriorated. As Alberto Müller Rojas, a former general who became a Causa R senator, stated in an interview for this project, the military, as in the case of the political parties, is not homogeneous. He pointed out that the military is deeply divided among three different groups. First is the group whose members have close ties with the traditional political parties, namely AD and COPEI, who act based on the need to defend the traditional two-party-dominated political system. Ironically, the deepening of the relationship between politicians and the military actually undermined civilian control. A second group, also with a political bent, revolves around the *bolivarianos* who staged the first coup attempt in 1992 and who see the need to change this traditional political system. The third group, the institutionalists, believe that the military should not intervene in politics.

The military rebels had learned from the overthrow of the Pérez Jiménez dictatorship the importance of the backing of a large social movement. In 1958, the population took to the streets supporting the ouster of the dictator. In a similar fashion, both coup attempts in 1992 seemed to depend on social backing, which they did not receive. In other words, the military leaders had learned that in order to change the government by force, it was necessary to count on social backing. Growing popular unrest during 1989 — seen clearly during the Caracazo — as well as the clear opposition to government and political elites seem to have prompted the coup leaders to think that they immediately would have popular support for their effort.

Events in 1989 and 1992 and the outcome of the 1993 presidential election do not seem to have prompted complex political learning by political leaders. On the contrary, the increasingly marked tendency toward a delegative culture would seem to point to overlearning and simple learning, which could, in the short and medium terms, lead to even greater governability problems than those Venezuela now faces. The crisis of the SCM meant a necessary change from one type of state to another. The centralist and paternalistic model run by party elites had to give way to an open, decentralized, pragmatic, and competitive model. This crisis and the need for economic and political change brought forth different reactions from the political elite. While political leaders repeated a lesson learned during the previous period by seeking to negotiate new pacts in order to stabilize the democratic system, they also recognized the need for reforms to decentralize the political system and to increase participation and representation, which would deepen the democratic system. A third issue arose because of the 1993 electoral results, in which the predominantly two-party system shifted to a multiparty one. Therefore, the SCM crisis led to conflicting solutions by the political leadership concerning these issues, as discussed below.

Seeking New Pacts

Exemplifying overlearning, the traditional political elite returned to the idea of pacts to address the new situation. Thus, as the SCM began to unravel, numerous proposals were made in the 1980s concerning the type of pact needed in order to face the growing economic and political crisis. These different proposals[4] were a repetition of the Punto Fijo Pact, in which the state and the traditional political parties remained as the main actors. Thus, the traditional political elite showed clear signs of persisting in its perceived role as the nucleus of economic and political decisionmaking through elite consensus and negotiation. Nevertheless, these proposed pacts failed to produce any meaningful results.

The two attempted coups in 1992 shocked the political system and led to renewed attempts to reach a national accord to preserve Venezuela's democratic system. President Pérez appointed an Advisory Council to the Presidency of the Republic and proposed a National Accord between AD and COPEI (Navarro 1995; Gómez Calcaño 1995; and Jácome 1994). The Advisory Council, composed of a number of prominent members from all sectors of society, advised Pérez on the different solutions needed to solve the crisis. Congress began to discuss amendments to the 1961 Constitution and to make reforms that would contribute to the stabilization of the political system. The National Accord turned out to be a short-lived agreement between AD and COPEI; however, COPEI backed the government by consenting to three of its members becoming ministers in Pérez's cabinet until he was ousted in 1993. Despite the difficulties, the shaken democratic system remained intact, and the interim government succeeded in conducting the 1993 national elections peacefully.

The 1993 election brought about a realignment from a two-party dominant system (AD-COPEI) to a multiparty system (AD, COPEI, Causa R, and MAS/Convergencia), as shown in Table 3. The traditional political elites, shaken by the Caracazo, two coup attempts, and the banking crisis, and with a minority government in power controlling no more than a quarter of the Congress, tried to adapt to a new political environment by returning to past practices.

As he had done in his first term in office, President Caldera turned to AD and, to a much lesser degree, to COPEI to form short-term legislative alliances that enabled each partner to survive politically. As political scientist and pollster José Antonio Gil Yépez stated in an interview for this project, "AD and COPEI will go on with their old traditional clientelist systems," and pacts and alliances will thus continue to be used as a tool to enable the traditional political parties to cope with the facts that their status (representing popular interests) and legitimacy have been seriously undermined.

Former Causa R leader Pablo Medina viewed the continued tacit pact-seeking between AD and COPEI in a similar vein: "Democratic Action and COPEI constructed this system of partnership based on mutual dependence. It is difficult for them. They must defend themselves to a society demanding political change. The two parties know that if one falls, the other falls; thus their mutual survival is at stake." One-time Causa R Senator Alberto Müller Rojas commented on the party's own learning experience regarding pacts: "We are not willing to participate in pacts among elites. We will participate in pacts that are structured around certain issues, but not in those that are organized on the basis of power sharing."

For AD, the alliance provided a much-needed image of a party willing to sacrifice its beliefs in order to guarantee political stability. At the same time, this special relationship with Caldera's government helped AD regain a certain "re-

Table 3. Seats in Congress by Party: 1993

Party	Chamber of Deputies		Senate	
	Number	%	Number	%
AD	56	27.9	18	34.6
COPEI	54	26.9	15	28.8
Causa R	40	19.9	10	19.2
MAS and Convergencia	51	25.4	9	17.3
Total	201	100.0	52	100.0

Source: Michael Coppedge, 1996, "Venezuela: The Rise and Fall of Partyarchy," in *Constructing Democratic Governance: South America in the 1990s,* eds. Jorge I. Dominguez and Abraham F. Lowenthal (Baltimore: The Johns Hopkins University Press).

spectability" by being associated with the government's anticorruption rhetoric. COPEI's role has been more ambiguous, displaying what could be termed as a "constructive opposition" position. Such alliances, then, are another good example of simple learning to adapt to a new environment.

President Caldera's actions also are a prime example of overlearning: He left his own party and led an antiparty campaign, yet depended on traditional party elites in order to govern. Rhetorically, he upheld deep criticism of AD and COPEI, but, in practice, he did not look toward emerging political and social actors for alliances, preferring the backing of the traditional parties. Caldera thus applied the lessons he learned more than 30 years before to a totally different set of present-day circumstances. Caldera tried to repeat the Punto Fijo Pact, of which he was a signatory, this time with the actors changed to AD and his newly founded party, Convergencia.

Political Project Dimension

This instrumental approach to pacts — to stay in power rather than construct a new national project to supersede the decline of the SCM — is closely related to the political project dimension of political learning. On the one hand, we have the parties or movements that say they have no ideology, as is the case with Causa R and Convergencia. Causa R's fundamental goal was the transformation of social relations by means of radical democracy, the production apparatus, and educational reform (Yépez 1993). Radical democracy, in turn, is seen as broadening decision-making levels and bringing democracy to society. There is no particular model that they strive to achieve; they feel that society must be built on the foundations of the current situation.

Likewise, Convergencia's plan was to bring together a number of sectors, members and nonmembers of COPEI, who decided to back Rafael Caldera's candidacy. Convergencia was established on the basis of antiparty sentiment and grew to back an independent candidate. This position is clearly reflected in Rafael Caldera's inaugural speech: "Between the two radical options, the populist and the neoliberal, I choose to commit myself to search for a *commitment to solidarity,* with a social accent" (in Rojas 1994). Nevertheless, a Christian Socialist tendency has arisen within Convergencia, which hopes to "rescue" true Christian Socialism (Jaimes 1994; Pérez 1994).

In both AD and COPEI, the various positions concerning political projects in the mid-1990s revolved around whether to keep the projects' definitions or reorient them to support modernization policies (Castillo 1994a). There have been two trends within AD: The so-called "reformers" had a neoliberal modernizing bent, while the so-called "orthodox" had a conservative bent that upheld the principles of Social Democracy (de León 1994; Castillo 1994a; Stambouli 1993). Until October 1994, this latter tendency was ratified as official party ideology. Inside COPEI, the difference was between those favoring a social market economy, for example, Eduardo Fernández and Oswaldo Alvarez Paz, and those who upheld Christian Socialism.

Although MAS was a party in which ideological discussion was considered important during the 1970s, this type of discussion was dropped, and party policies have come to be defined on a much more pragmatic basis. In an interview for this project, MAS member Víctor Rodríguez described the learning process within the party since the 1970s: "Within MAS, discussions, questioning, and criticism are an inherent part of the party. It is often said that the MAS is the child of differences of opinion." Nevertheless, Rodríguez said:

> Internal democracy has been misused, making it difficult to suggest definite policies because of the fact that multiple opinions have represented the party. . . . We have gone from one extreme to the other. At first, we were very oriented toward theoretical-ideological discussions. Yet, because of the changes that the country has undergone, now we are mainly concerned with providing solutions to very specific problems. This has led a certain group of us within the party to try to find a balance between theoretical-ideological discussions and those oriented toward specific and everyday problem solving.

Because of the economic and political crisis the country faced in the 1990s, one would expect the political project dimension to be important in discussing the economic and political goals and changes that are necessary. Nevertheless, although there has been some discussion of the changes needed in political projects, it has not been predominant. Internal party politics revolve more around power struggles between leader-oriented groups.

As for the discourse dimension of democratic learning, it is generally acknowledged that political parties are tending to be much more pragmatic and less ideological. This leads to the idea that there has been a movement "away from ideologization toward electoralism" (Combellas 1988, 67) within the Venezuelan political system. Community leader Angel Zambrano's statement in an interview for this project was, "Here, everybody is thinking about the next election of governors and mayors, the next presidential election. People are still thinking in terms of party clientelism." This view is shared by a large segment of Venezuela's population, which criticizes the attitude of the parties and thinks that they should be discussing and defining a national project that would go beyond demagogic discourse.

In this regard, some political leaders and other actors in civil society who were interviewed for this project look upon such pragmatism as an unfavorable feature of the political system. They stated that at present, political parties have no proposals; that there is no innovation in keeping up with the economic and political changes in the country; and that, as argued by Arturo Sosa, if the parties have nothing to propose, they are incapable of responding to the growing crisis. Having no project to propose, they improvise in the face of the economic, political, and social crisis, which does not benefit the country.

Likewise, José Antonio Gil Yépez stated in an interview for this research that there has been little learning evident among the parties to address the changes in the country: "The Causa R will not change; they will continue to oppose everything in order to capitalize on popular discontent, whereas AD and COPEI will continue with their traditional clientelism."

Political Reforms and Rules of the Game

With the depletion of the SCM, the situation in Venezuela since the late 1970s left no doubt that the fundamental issue to be faced was how to achieve the economic opening and political reforms needed without causing a state of "disorder" with the new, much smaller role that government would play after reforms were carried out. The problem, basically, was how to implement reforms without causing governability problems that could endanger the democratic system.

One alternative that recognized, at least to a certain point, the serious limitations of the workings of the political system and its institutions and responded to pressure brought forth by emerging political and social actors was the creation of the Presidential Commission on Reforming the State (COPRE) in 1984. This body, with very little input from other sectors of civil society, debated and then presented a number of proposals concerning necessary political reforms. Thus, apart from the various proposed pacts, political reform was also considered important for responding to the growing political and economic crisis. However, this alternative was set forth largely by a "technocratic" and more intellectual group, of whom some were politically independent and others had ties with the major political parties — AD, COPEI, and MAS.

One of the main goals of these changes was to eliminate the centralist model of political power and the inefficiencies of the state. In this regard, among the most important changes achieved in 1988 were direct election of state governors, creation of the office of mayor and direct election of the mayor, the changing of the electoral system from a solely election-by-slate system (proportional representation) to a mixed system that included direct election of some deputies (single-member districts), and various other steps toward decentralization.

With this framework in mind, COPRE presented to the political parties and executive branch the Pact for Reform, which was signed in December 1990. This pact's main objectives included the implementation of additional reforms that would renew the political system, enhance internal party democracy, depoliticize the judiciary system and electoral authorities, and restructure and further decentralize central government objectives (Navarro 1995). It is important to note that this pact was limited to political parties and the government. Though the pact formally stated that other social actors would be included in discussions on the different reforms, they were very rarely invited to discussion meetings, as was pointed out by Arturo Sosa during his interview.

Despite the important reforms achieved in 1988, the general opinion, especially among those interviewed who do not belong to political parties, was that the two major political parties — AD and COPEI — did not really support them or the additional reforms proposed in 1990 because they feared losing a portion of their power. Instead, they had finally agreed to the first set of reforms in 1988 in response to public pressure and to what at that time MAS leader Teodoro Petkoff called "demagogic competition" among party leaders in the heat of the 1988 electoral campaign:

> AD and COPEI were out of sync with the rhythm of social and economic transformations since the early 1980s . . . [transformations] such as the attempts to widen the frontiers of democracy with the direct election of governors and mayors. These reforms were made against the desires of AD and COPEI. They emerged not only from the growing pressure of public opinion, but also from the demagogic competition among some of the leaders of those parties. The direct election of governors emerged from the competition between Pérez and Fernández in the 1988 electoral campaign. Fernández, thinking that AD would never accept it, proposed the direct election of governors; when Pérez saw that he was going to be overrun by Fernández, he embraced the proposal and imposed it on his resistant party.

Likewise, Rafael de la Cruz, who directed COPRE's decentralization effort, explained, "The political leadership of this country does not believe in the reform of the state or decentralization; they are populists and clientelists. . . . Intellectuals promoted decentralization in the hope of generating political actors who would permit a progressive modification of the system." José Antonio Gil Yépez confirmed that the adoption of these reforms was not a result of conscious evaluation and learning by the parties about the need to deepen democracy, but rather a pragmatic adaptation to the political situation: "The most important reforms that the political system has undergone are due to civil society. Direct elections of governors and mayors and the *uninominalidad* (single-member district) system of congressional voting are a direct result of the pressure that the political elites received from civil society."

This interpretation is given credence by the fact that the main political parties failed to honor the Pact for Reform, which, together with representatives of the executive branch, they had signed on December 4, 1990. Instead, the parties in Congress stalled on additional reforms most directly affecting them, such as control mechanisms over their finances and the establishment of mechanisms that would guarantee internal party democracy.

With the 1990 Pact for Reform stalled in Congress, the discussion returned to constitutional reform. Then Senator Rafael Caldera presided over a special commission for revising the 1961 Constitution. After the February 1992 coup attempt, however, the commission began to discuss more far-reaching changes, and pressure began to build outside Congress to elect a new Constituent Assembly. The smaller parties and significant sectors of public opinion believed that the same politicians responsible for creating the political crisis would be incapable of reforming the Constitution. One of the issues discussed was the possibility of a referendum to recall elected officials, especially in light of the absence of clear impeachment proceedings in Venezuela. With public opinion divided, however, Congress decided to suspend discussions on constitutional reform in mid-1992.

Regarding future prospects for political reform, there was a widespread feeling among those interviewed, both political actors and persons belonging to civil society, that the reform process still faced serious obstacles, including party decision-making structures and central government control. First, as stated by Arturo Sosa, "The process lacked citizen participation due, to a large extent, to the lack of a participative political culture in the country." In this regard, one of the fundamental criticisms was aimed at the political parties themselves for having failed to move forward on internal democratization.

The decision-making structure within the two main political parties — AD and COPEI —traditionally has been in the form of a pyramid, with decisions being made from the top down. Through the various levels in these parties, the members or militants "delegate" their representation. For example, despite the fact that in recent years internal elections have been held to choose the presidential candidates, "debate in COPEI is democratic in form, but not very participative" (Combellas 1985, 76). Within MAS, the various internal groups have revolved predominantly around specific leaders, not around political projects. In AD, 20 or 30 members of the National Executive Committee (CEN) decide on the candidates for the various legislative bodies and the policies to be followed by the party (Coppedge 1995).

Former MAS leader Teodoro Petkoff and former COPRE President Carlos Blanco confirmed that decision-making power was still monopolized by a small elite, the *cogollo* (core). Petkoff analyzed the problems of internal democratization within the parties this way: "AD and COPEI have not been able to overcome these characteristics — the persistence of autocratic mechanisms at the top and the will to maintain an elitist relationship with the country, based on the Leninist notion of the party as the supreme conductor of life and other organizations as the transmission belt for the will of the party."

A second issue is the extent to which political and administrative decentralization gives real authority and fiscal power to local and state governments. As community leader Angel Enrique Zambrano remarked, "It is obvious that the central government talks a great deal about decentralization, but the facts show that it does not want to let go of authority or resources." Additional obstacles include the lack of full-fledged direct elections[5] and the ingrained presidentialist nature of a system based on the idea of a caudillo, a leader who prevents democracy from becoming more deeply rooted.

The resulting control of the traditional political parties perpetuated the model of "partyarchy" described by Michael Coppedge (1995). Causa R leaders, for example, felt that for their party the rules of the game were not honored, so the party was forced to turn to the courts for recognition of elections it won. At the time, Causa R leader Pablo Medina in an interview for this project contended that AD and COPEI kept a majority in Congress in 1993 by fraud and that these parties opposed the use of vote-counting machines to be able to continue committing fraud in elections.

At least insofar as discourse is concerned, the rules of the game have changed. Popular opinion in general and most civil society leaders interviewed hold that the parties are no longer the sole or even the most appropriate channel for communication between government and the rest of society, although this mediating relationship has always been considered an essential part of the ability to govern. The discrediting of the traditional political parties was demonstrated in an August 1993 poll in which two-thirds of respondents viewed AD unfavorably. On the other hand, only 30 percent viewed Causa R negatively (USIA 1993). Continued low ratings of the party system along with contradictory beliefs about its desirability for democratic functioning are shown in 1997 polls presented in Tables 4 and 5.

When the decision-making process within the parties is evaluated, however, the question arises whether this democratic discourse on honoring the rules of the system is not merely rhetoric. As Teodoro Petkoff so rightly asked, how are the leading political parties going to accept participation by the citizenry at large if they have not been able to achieve internal democracy?

Both MAS and Causa R (Yépez 1993) have claimed that decisionmaking within their parties was based on debates and discussion with an effort made to achieve a consensus. In contrast to Causa R, MAS has held internal elections when consensus was not possible; MAS has claimed that it was the first political party to use this system to elect both its leaders and its candidates for legislative bodies. The acceptance of different internal tendencies within MAS has been acknowledged by the party, and the various orientations have been assured proportional representation in the party's decision-making process. These groups, however, have tended to revolve more around individuals than around programmatic proposals (Ellner 1993-1994).

In Causa R, which is defined as an "organization of organizations," each individual organization or movement has chosen its own leaders and has developed its own local policy. This structure has been contrasted with that of a Leninist-type organization in which decisions are made on the basis of democratic centralism. Alberto Müller Rojas commented on what the Causa R had learned from AD, COPEI, and MAS regarding internal organization: "We fear any form of bureaucracy. Therefore, within our movement there is no organizational structure with positions such as an organizational secretariat or a disciplinary tribunal. The only figure we have is that of secretary-general, and that is due to the fact that the political party law requires this." Pablo Medina confirmed this conscious reflection within the party: "From the beginning, we decided to create a political organization unlike the rest . . . without vertical structures and democratic centralism. . . . We arrive at accords through debate. This has generated an internal culture in which we don't perceive that we have lost a debate, but rather that we have gained a discussion. Sometimes, of course, this causes difficulties because we don't always agree at the end of a debate; in that case, political experience indicates where is the truth and where is the possibility."

Outsiders, however, have a different view of Causa R. According to Guillermo Yépez, "In structure, Causa R has a level of tight, closed cadres, with stringent requirements for entry, zealously guarded, and a number of broad organizations, teams in which militants and friends take part." (1993, 76). Despite the openness, Yépez says that there is a small group, the political team, considered to be the "core"

Table 4. Youth Opinion on Political Parties

Political Parties	
They inspire little or no confidence.	82%
They create more problems than the solutions they offer.	80%
They are indispensable for democracy.	64%
They serve no purpose.	61%

Source: *Primicia* magazine, Caracas, December 16, 1997.

Table 5. Institutions Necessary for Democracy

Mass media	41%
Armed forces	40%
Universities	38%
Catholic Church	29%
Judicial system	28%
Congress	27%
Neighborhood movements	27%
Political parties	19%
Mayors and State Governors	17%
Private enterprise	11%
Police	10%
Labor unions	8%

Source: Fundación Pensamiento y Acción, 1997, *Cultura democrática en Venezuela: Informe analítico de los resultados de una encuesta de opinión pública* (Caracas, January).

(1993). Although MAS and Causa R criticize the other parties for their centralism and for allowing a small group to hold all the power, other sectors accuse MAS and Causa R of exactly the same thing.

Within Convergencia, there is no policy aimed at the creation of a political organization; even the suggestion by some party leaders that it was necessary to create a Leninist-type organization was rejected. Basically, the organization is a parliamentary group organized around one person, Rafael Caldera. In this regard, there is a contradiction between stating that Caldera "is obviously our leader" and that "the party has a horizontal structure" (Ramón Ramirez López, cited in Jaimes 1994).

Despite the fact that primaries were held for the 1993 presidential elections, the resistance to internal party democratization within the traditional parties is illustrated by an August 1994 incident. A group of AD leaders, led by former party presidential candidate Claudio Fermín, argued the need to hold already planned internal elections; Fermín said, "Without elections, there would be no way of incorporating one's own criteria in major decisions and in day-to-day actions, since decisions and lines would be reserved to a small group and every day the shaping of collective directions will move further away" (Fermín, cited in Chirinos 1994a). The response was to call a meeting of the National Directors Council (CDN), which decided to replace executive committee members who backed Fermín and to postpone the internal elections (Chirinos 1994b).

The two main parties continue to use a decision-making process that is limited to a small elitist group, while other parties, although denying it, seem to have accepted this same pattern within their own internal party structures. In this regard, Angel Enrique Zambrano stated in an interview that his neighborhood association movement learned from AD and COPEI what they do not want in terms of decisionmaking: centralism and elitism. The parties, in contrast, had learned how central party control ensured governability in the first decades of the new democracy.

This reluctance to reevaluate internal structures has impeded the ability of the parties to respond adequately to the serious problems facing the country. COPEI leader Eduardo Fernández commented on the capacity of Venezuelan political leaders to learn how to respond to political and economic crises: "There has been very little analysis, and, in a certain way, events have given way to spasmodic answers. The answers to the crisis have not tackled the real situation. . . . The analysis of the crisis is taking place in very prestigious academic centers. Yet, up until now, these centers do not have the capacity to influence the decision-making process, nor do the political leaders look toward these centers in order to receive advice." With regard to COPEI in particular, Fernández said he believed that COPEI "must promote a great dialogue with the country; it must open up and listen to what the country has to say. The party must promote an open mind. It cannot continue to look only within itself; it cannot continue being sectarian."

Political scientist and magazine editor Arturo Sosa confirmed this view of political learning by the parties: "The case of the political parties is an important one for analysis. They were the proponents of the Pact [of Punto Fijo], yet they have been incapable of maintaining their consistency regarding ideological and political creations. . . . Therefore, instead of initiating new political projects, political parties have become the administrators of an outdated project."

Neighborhood leader Angel Enrique Zambrano felt that learning was completely absent within the parties: "The political parties have not understood what is happening and, much less [has] the state [understood]. We are presently in totally different circumstances, yet there has been no process of adaptation. They [parties and the state] believe they can continue to administer [the country] in the same traditional manner, applying the same outdated policies. . . . This proves that they have not understood that there are changes underway. Also, they have not comprehended that the image of politics is deteriorating very rapidly." Likewise, intellectual Rafael de la Cruz sees a "political elite that comes from the old model we have been combating with decentralization, that has not been capable of facing the nation and explaining what the country needs. . . . This old political elite has not learned and will not learn."

In conclusion, both economic and political reforms became stalled. Political leaders seemed not to have learned how to respond to the changing social structure and growing demands for crisis management. Instead, they demonstrated simple or instrumental learning in adopting the political reforms of 1988 and 1989 in response to public pressure during an electoral campaign, and then they retrenched when faced with renewed pressure during the political crisis of 1992. The parties' blindness to their declining legitimacy, however, led to a dramatic fall in popular support and to the apparent shift to a multiparty system in the 1993 elections.

Two-party Versus Multiparty System

Although this may be a short-lived phenomenon, the Venezuelan political system did undergo two important changes as a result of the electoral reforms and the 1993 election results. First and foremost, the country elected as president a leader who departed the party he had founded and ran as an independent, even though he was still clearly among the traditional political elite. The second change was the election of a multiparty legislature (see Tables 1 and 3), which raised questions of governability without a governing majority coalition. Former COPRE President Carlos Blanco, when interviewed, stated that the multiparty Congress would not lead to problems of governability per se; however, such problems might arise as a result of what he considered would be "a lack of programmatic willingness on the part of the country's political and institutional forces to reach fundamental understandings. . . . There are certain groups that have not understood that the best way of staying in power in these circumstances is by sharing power." In this sense, he criticized the highly centralized decision-making process both within political parties and in the government, and he lamented that the political elites had not yet learned that this style was no longer functional in the current system.

Therefore, the ability to govern within this new multiparty legislature would depend on the policies followed by the various political, economic, and social groups in this multiparty context. As for the workings of Congress, there were two basic schools of thought among those interviewed in 1994: one, that, given its current composition, Congress was dysfunctional. Those holding this opinion said that, taking into account the number of seats held by each of the various groups in Congress, decisions requiring a two-thirds majority could not be made. This point of view, exemplified by former Causa R leader Pablo Medina, was in accordance with the idea that the existing Congress should have been closed and a Constituent Assembly elected. The other viewpoint, shared by other political leaders such as COPEI's Eduardo Fernández, MAS's former leader Teodoro Petkoff, and Convergencia's Ramón Ramírez López, was that it would be necessary to find formulas that would both allow Congress to work and make it possible for the relationship between the legislature and the executive branch to maintain stability within the political system.

This latter proposal, which gained the most support, again led to the subject of pacts. The various social and political groups feared that, once again, the situation would be one of short-term negotiation aimed at gaining or holding onto shares of power. In this regard, the majority of interviewees not belonging to the political parties felt that AD and, to a much lesser degree, COPEI negotiated with the Caldera government in order to provide it with the political backing it needed in return for their shares of power. Thus, they perceived the traditional parties as continuing to exclude the new political and social forces, even in a multiparty system. Party interests led COPEI and AD to argue instead that democratic stability depended upon an elite alliance between them and the workings of a two-party system. This manifestation of overlearning may turn out to be a shortsighted view, as independents again were rising to the top of the polls as the 1998 elections approached.

ANALYSIS OF THE VENEZUELAN LEARNING PROCESS: A CASE OF OVERLEARNING

As Jennifer L. McCoy indicates in Chapter One of this volume, interaction, self-reflection, and a change of membership are the three main methods of complex political learning. In the Venezuelan case, however, we have found little evidence of these methods. There is scarce evidence that interaction between the political party leaders and other social actors has led to any change in the behavior of this political elite. Neither does anything point toward interaction with outside actors that has influenced members of the local political elite to change their attitudes in reaction to the crisis.

As for reflection, only Eduardo Fernández and Teodoro Petkoff stated that they had given critical thought to the mistakes of their own parties and other party organizations. Their criticisms focused mainly on the enduring presence within the parties of an elitist leadership that stands in the way of rank-and-file participation, centralism in government, and an authoritarian decision-making style at both party and government levels. Nevertheless, they agreed with other actors in civil society that, in general terms, political leaders in the country have failed to reflect on the crisis that the political and economic systems face. Thus, reflection leading to complex learning has occurred primarily at the individual level.

Furthermore, there have been no major changes in membership or leadership within the political parties, which might have prompted some reflection and a change in traditional attitudes and views. As a matter of fact, one of the main criticisms from the general public is that the main parties are still led essentially by their founding members. There has, therefore, been little generational change; to the extent that it does occur, the younger leaders who have been brought up through the party tend to perceive party politics in the same manner as their elders.

The traditional political parties in Venezuela are accustomed to being the sole representatives of social interests. They have no desire to change this, and they do not accept the idea of sharing power with emerging social and political actors such as, for example, non-governmental organizations (NGOs) and the emerging parties. For this reason, it seems highly likely that the political system will not be the subject of significant change through actions taken by political leaders.

Within the framework of the economic and political modifications Venezuelan society is now undergoing with the end of the SCM and following examination of the various parameters set for assessing democratic learning among political leaders, our conclusions are not optimistic. There is no question that the changes taking place in Venezuela call for a variation in the goals, values, and assumptions of the political elite — all the more so because their overlearning has been found to be an underlying cause of the crisis. Moreover, the maintenance of democracy in the near future may very well depend on a process of complex learning.

Despite all this and aside from some specific exceptions mentioned above, there is little indication that any changes aimed at making the democratic political system more legitimate have been made. In this regard, one of the fundamental problems is that the political system revolves around the subject of stability. The result is that political leaders tend to reject proposals for needed political and economic modifications, instead arguing the need for stability. Their assumptions about this need, stemming from a static view of Venezuelan reality, affect not only the legitimacy of the political system but governability as well.

If democratic learning is understood to be a process for learning practices and attitudes that make it possible to solve problems within a democratic context (see McCoy, Chapter One in this volume), or if it is defined more specifically as an individual or collective change in attitudes that leads to increased legitimacy of the democratic system (see Costa, Chapter Four in this volume), then we must conclude that there is an absence of recent democratic learning in the Venezuelan case. In the first place, despite reaffirmation of tactics and actions that proved effective in the past, these are not leading toward solution of the present political crisis, nor are they leading to increasing legitimacy. Instead, they tend to do the opposite, exacerbating the crisis of legitimacy.

Political leaders did learn from the 1945-1948 experience, and this learning also was reflected within the political parties. However, when changes were necessary both at a political and economic level, they did not come about. Since 1980, the political elites have tried to solve new problems by old means. They have done the opposite of learning: Instead of preventing the crisis, they have, to a large degree, exacerbated it. Their refusal to acknowledge that both domestic and international spheres have been subjected to important modifications and that there is, therefore, a need for new economic and political models has led the country to its most serious crisis in 40 years.

The existence of internal divisions within the parties does not mean that there is discussion regarding either different positions as to how the crisis should be handled or different economic and political models. Instead, discussion within and among parties tends to be oriented around power struggles involving different factions and individuals. Although there has been some discussion in the 1990s revolving around positions labeled "neoliberal" and "populist," these are fundamentally name tags that certain groups use either to defend or attack each other. There is little substance to this discussion. Positions within parties still are predominantly defined by leader-centered groups. Even though a group may be called "orthodox" or "renovating," as is the case in AD, the general public perceives that the groups revolve around leaders and have little to do with theoretical or political project differences. Table 5 shows the results of an opinion poll in which the institutions deemed necessary for democracy were rated. As we have seen before, political institutions such as Congress and political parties did not rate very highly.

Therefore, we conclude that the Venezuelan case includes instances of individual complex learning by some political leaders, evidenced by the fact that they have proposed and, at times, tried to implement new economic and political models. These individuals' learning processes have resulted from reflection and the acquisition of new knowledge from past and foreign experiences. The problem is that these learning experiences have been predominantly individual or very small group experiences. Yet, the problem could also be that these leaders have not learned the means of reaching their goals. As an example, Carlos Andrés Pérez and his governmental team tried to implement economic reforms, but the decision-making process was very authoritarian; they did not first build a consensus around a new economic and political model. Therefore, although there were new goals, which could show democratic learning, the means chosen included the traditional imposition of decisions upon the majority. Moreover, Pérez and his team did not even employ the traditional mechanism of elite consensus.

In contrast, emerging social groups did exhibit learning processes. As discussed above, newer political parties and neighborhood groups assessed the consequences of the centralized decision-making structure of the parties and decided not to replicate them. Intellectuals promoted decentralization as an exit from the political crisis. Rafael de la Cruz argued that the change in the electoral rules of the game opened the door to learning on the part of both the voters and the directly elected politicians: "The people sensed that these new political structures would open space for participation in political decision-making to those sectors that had been isolated from the mechanism of elite *concertación*. . . . Now there are mayors and governors, persons who have been elected in a more direct form, that are beginning to realize what can effectively happen in the country, and who, through a process of renovating party leadership, could eventually have a larger participation than the old elites now have."

In conclusion, the main obstacles to complex political learning among political elites have been an authoritarian and delegative political culture, which will be discussed below, but also overlearning from past historical experiences. Unfortunately, it would seem that in this case a deeper national trauma will be necessary in order for political parties and their leaders to modify their goals, attitudes, and values. The foreseeable traumas could be hyperinflation and/or pressures brought on by increasing social discontent and movements that could arise because of this. Another social outbreak such as the Caracazo is a permanent worry for both the political and economic elite as well as for the general population.

CONCLUSIONS:
DEMOCRACY AND GOVERNABILITY

On the matter of what the most important topics for democracy are, we found that the majority of the political leaders interviewed upheld that maintaining democracy and coping with governability problems posed by the current crisis were a priority. This, fundamentally, is the position of the leaders of the traditional parties. Within the new multiparty system, however, we found that two parties stressed the need to make democracy more deeply rooted: Causa R and MAS. Both parties criticize what has been called "limited" democracy, and they believe that it is necessary to establish channels that will allow the general population to take greater part in decisionmaking and to make their various stands known.

In addition, the other actors interviewed also recognized the need to maintain democracy and overcome governability problems. However, the majority focused on the need to deepen democracy or to find formulas that are more truly democratic. In other words, they want to move forward from the current rhetoric about democracy and actually put it into practice.

Beginning in 1958, Venezuela's intention was to build a representative democracy; nevertheless, Venezuelan democracy evolved into an increasingly clientelist and centralized democracy. Overlearning by political leaders and simple learning have become ingrained and have caused a deterioration in the model of democracy. Venezuela seems to be sliding back to a delegative democracy from what could have been the consolidation of a truly representative democracy. Table 6 shows that neither participation nor elections are now highly regarded as to what best defines democracy. Table 7 shows a high degree of dissatisfaction with Venezuelan democracy.

Table 6. Words That Best Define the Desired Democracy

Justice	48%
Employment	40%
Liberty	28%
Equality	27%
Accountability	21%
Authority	20%
Productivity	18%
Well-being	18%
Respect	18%
Peace	16%
Participation	13%
Necessary Provisions	13%
Salaries	10%
Elections	6%
Consensus	2%

Source: Fundación Pensamiento y Acción, 1997, *Cultura democrática en Venezuela: Informe analítico de los resultados de una encuesta de opinión pública* (Caracas, January).

Table 7. Levels of Satisfaction with Venezuelan Democracy

Levels of Satisfaction	%
Very satisfied	4
Somewhat satisfied	20
Somewhat unsatisfied	45
Very unsatisfied	30

Source: Fundación Pensamiento y Acción, 1997, *Cultura democrática en Venezuela: Informe analítico de los resultados de una encuesta de opinión pública* (Caracas, January).

The absence of complex political learning in Venezuela has led to governability problems, which have threatened the democratic system, as seen above. This research suggests that these governability problems are to a large degree a result of the breakdown of the SCM and of a deeply rooted delegative political culture. Compounding these problems are two fundamental characteristics of the Venezuelan political system. The first is that clientelist projects prevail over the designing of a national project that could determine the policies to be followed. The second is the deeply rooted nature of elitism and authoritarianism, which is the end product of delegation, in opposition to the representativeness and legitimacy that could be a result of a participative political culture.

In Venezuela, the first step toward overcoming the governability and legitimacy crises is the rethinking of the national project, beginning with the indispensable debate as to the type of democracy to be fostered, given that a large majority of the population is unsatisfied with the post-1958 democratic system. As long as the delegative-authoritarian political culture remains in place, this cannot occur. Therefore, in order to begin developing a participative political culture, it is essential to foster complex democratic learning, not only by political leaders but by civil society as well.

We suggest that this complex political learning could be guided by the discussion and analysis of six main points: First, discuss and put into practice mid- and long-term national plans that respond to the changes that the economic and political systems are undergoing because of the breakdown of the SCM. Second, carry out an internal democratization process within the political parties. Third, for the traditional parties, carry out a dialogue and consultation with emerging political and social actors. Fourth, discuss the need for changing political institutions, policies, rules of the game, and decision-making schemes. Fifth, implement and consolidate political accountability mechanisms, which are very precarious in the Venezuelan case. Sixth, overcome the Venezuelan tendency to define governability in terms of stability, and modify the corresponding role this definition assigns to the political parties.

Notes

1. The author gratefully acknowledges the research assistance of Andrea Domínguez. All interviews with Venezuelan leaders for this chapter took place during the first semester of 1994. Those interviewed are listed in the Interviews section.

2. This brief discussion on the different types of political learning is based on Jennifer L. McCoy's first chapter in this volume and on discussions held in 1995 in Bellagio, Italy, with the other project team members — Marcelo Cavarozzi, Luis Costa Bonino, and Manuel Antonio Garretón. I gratefully acknowledge their important contributions to this chapter.

3. Marcelo Cavarozzi (1991, 1993) analyzes the transition from an SCM, which had predominated since the 1930s, toward a new matrix with characteristics that have not yet been well defined for Latin America.

4. These were the Tesis de la Concertación Nacional (Thesis of National Dialogue) by Rómulo Betancourt in 1981; Tesis de la Concertación Nacional y un Acuerdo Nacional (Thesis of National Dialogue and a National Accord) by COPEI in 1982; and the Pacto Social (Social Pact) by Jaime Lusinchi in 1984.

5. The 1993 elections introduced single-member districts for the first time in Venezuela, though they were used in only half of the elections of congressional deputies. The other half continued to use election by proportional representation in closed party lists.

References

Arroyo Talavera, Eduardo. 1988. *Elecciones y negociaciones: Los límites de la democracia en Venezuela.* Caracas: Fondo Editorial CONICIT/Pomai.

Blanco, Carlos. 1994. Interview.

Carvallo, Gastón. 1991. "Una visión de coyuntura del sistema político venezolano." *Cuadernos del CENDES* 17/18 (April-December): 269-292.

Castillo, Alcides J. 1994a. "Fermín y López harán una 'retirada estratégica' después del CDN." *El Diario de Caracas*, August 25.

Castillo, Alcides J. 1994b. "Alfaro sacó por 'conspiradores' a cinco miembros del CEN." *El Diario de Caracas*, August 26.

Castillo, Ocarina. 1990. *Los años del buldozer: Ideología y política 1948-1958.* Caracas: Fondo Editorial Tropykos/Asociación de Profesores U.C.V./CENDES.

Cavarozzi, Marcelo. 1991. "Más allá de las transiciones a la democracia en América Latina." *Revista de Estudios Políticos* 74 (October-December): 85-111.

Cavarozzi, Marcelo. 1993. "Transformaciones de la política en la América Latina contemporánea." *Análisis Político* 19 (May-August): 25-38.

Chirinos, Exequalidades Q. 1994a. "Fermín propone amnistía en el CDN para alcanzar un entendimiento en AD." *El Universal*, August 14.

Chirinos, Exequalidades Q. 1994b. "Fuera del CEN los poderes perecistas y aplazadas elecciones internas de AD." *El Universal,* August 26.

Colomine, Luisana. 1993. "AD de rodillas: Otro round que gana Caldera al sector político." *Economía Hoy*, August 1.

Combellas, Ricardo. 1985. *COPEI: Ideología y liderazgo.* Caracas: Editorial Ariel.

Combellas, Ricardo. 1988. *La democratización de la democracia.* Caracas: IFEDEC.

Coppedge, Michael. 1995. "Partidocracia and Reform in Comparative Perspective." In *Venezuelan Democracy under Stress*, eds. Jennifer McCoy, Andrés Serbin, William C. Smith, and Andrés Stambouli. Coral Gables, Fla.: North-South Center at the University of Miami.

Coppedge, Michael. 1996. "Venezuela: The Rise and Fall of Partyarchy." In *Constructing Democratic Governance: South America in the 1990s*, eds. Jorge I. Domínguez and Abraham F. Lowenthal. Baltimore: The Johns Hopkins University Press.

de la Cruz, Rafael. 1992. "La estrategia de la descentralización en Venezuela." In *Descentralización-Gobernabilidad-Democracia,* ed. Rafael de la Cruz. Caracas: COPRE/PNUD/Editorial Nueva Sociedad.

de la Cruz, Rafael. 1994. Interview.

de León, Ignacio. 1994. "Acción Democrática?" *Economía Hoy*, August 31.

Ellner, Steve. 1993-1994. "Deepening of Democracy in a Crisis Setting: Political Reforms and the Electoral Process in Venezuela." *Journal of Interamerican Studies and Work Affairs* 35 (4): 1-42.

El Nacional. 1993 Caracas (December).

Fernández, Eduardo. 1994. Interview.

Fundación Pensamiento y Acción. 1997. "Cultura democrática en Venezuela: Informe analítico de los resultados de una encuesta de opinión pública." Caracas (January).

Gil Yépez, José Antonio. 1994. Interview.

Gómez Calcaño, Luis. 1995. "Crisis de legitimidad e inestabilidad política en Venezuela." *Revista Venezolana de Economía y Ciencias Sociales* (April-September): 2-3.

Gómez, Iraima R. 1994. "Las actuales medidas reinvindican mi programa de gobierno." *El Diario de Caracas*, August 28.

Guevara, Pedro. 1989. *Concertación y conflicto*. Caracas: Universidad Central de Venezuela, Facultad de Ciencias Jurídicas y Políticas, Escuela de Estudios Políticos y Administrativos.

Hernández, Clodovaldo. 1994. "Congreso podría darle largas a la suspensión de garantías." *El Universal*, August 2.

Hillman, Richard S. 1994. *Democracy for the Privileged: Crisis and Transition in Venezuela*. Boulder, Colo.: Lynne Rienner Publishers.

Jácome, Francine. 1989. "Los rasgos autoritarios de la democracia venezolana." *Revista Occidental* 6: 39-57.

Jácome, Francine. 1994. "La crisis del sistema político venezolano." *Homines* 17 (July 1993-June 1994): 291-307.

Jaimes, Humberto. 1994. "Convergencia: ¿Más de lo mismo?" *El Universal*, August 5.

Koeneke, Herbert. 1996. "El sistema electoral en Caracas." Paper presented at the III Encuentro Internacional Sociedad Civil y Reforma Electoral in Caracas, Venezuela, November 22-23.

Kornblith, Miriam, and David Levine. 1995. "Venezuela: The Life and Times of the Party System." In *Building Democratic Institutions: Party Systems in Latin America*, eds. Scott Mainwaring and Timothy R. Scully. Stanford, Calif.: Stanford University Press.

Márquez, Gustavo. 1994. "Sísifo en el trópico." Paper presented at the Seminar "Comparación de los sistemas políticos y económicos de Colombia y Venezuela," Santa Fe de Bogotá (July).

Marta Sosa, Joaquín. 1993. "Partidos democráticos de nuevo tipo y necesidad de nuevos partidos." In *Venezuela, del siglo XX al siglo XXI: Un proyecto para construirla*, ed. Carlos Blanco. Caracas: COPRE/PNUD/Editorial Nueva Sociedad.

McCoy, Jennifer, and William C. Smith. 1995. "From Deconsolidation to Reequilibration? Prospects for Democratic Renewal in Venezuela." In *Venezuelan Democracy under Stress*, eds. Jennifer McCoy, William C. Smith, Andrés Serbin, Andrés Stambouli. Coral Gables, Fla.: North-South Center at the University of Miami.

Medina, Pablo. 1994. Interview.

Molina Vega, José, and Carmen Pérez Baralt. 1994. "Venezuela: ¿Un nuevo sistema de partidos? Las elecciones de 1993." *Cuestiones Políticas* (13): 63-89.

Müller Rojas, Alberto. 1994. Interview.

Naim, Moisés. 1993. *Paper Tigers and Minotaurs*. Washington D.C.: The Carnegie Endowment for International Peace.

Navarro, Juan Carlos. 1995. "In Search of the Lost Pact: Consensus Lots in the 1980s and 1990s." In *Venezuelan Democracy under Stress*, eds. Jennifer McCoy, Andrés Serbin, William C. Smith, and Andrés Stambouli. Coral Gables, Fla.: North-South Center at the University of Miami.

Nye, Joseph S. 1987. "Nuclear Learning and the United States: Soviet Security Regimes." *International Organization* 41 (Summer).

O'Donnell, Guillermo. 1992. "Interview by Jorge Heine." *LASA Forum*, Vol. XXIII, No. 2, Summer 1992: 7-9.

O'Donnell, Guillermo. 1993. "Estado, democracia, y ciudadanía." *Nueva Sociedad* (128): 62-87.

O'Donnell, Guillermo. 1994. "Delegative Democracy." *Journal of Democracy* (January): 55-69.

Peeler, John A. 1985. *Latin American Democracies: Colombia, Costa Rica, Venezuela.* Chapel Hill, N.C.: The University of North Carolina Press.

Pérez, Nidia. 1994. "En Convergencia la palabra es plata y el silencio oro." *El Diario de Caracas*, June 5.

Petkoff, Teodoro. 1994. Interview.

Primicia. 1997. Caracas. December 16.

Ramírez López, Ramón. 1994. Interview.

Rodríguez, Víctor. 1994. Interview.

Rojas, José M. 1994. "Ni populismo ni neoliberalismo: 'Compromiso de solidaridad'" *El Diario de Caracas*, February 3.

Romero, Carlos. 1994. Interview.

Salazar, Gregorio. 1994. "Los venezolanos votamos pero no elegimos." *Economía Hoy-V Aniversario*, May 30.

Sonntag, Heinz R. 1992. "La democracia en Venezuela: Una visión prospectiva." In *La democracia en América Latina: Actualidad y perspectivas,* eds. Pablo González Casanova and Marcos Roitman Rosenmann. Madrid: Editorial Complutense.

Sosa, Arturo. 1994. Interview.

Stambouli, Andrés. 1980. *Crisis política: Venezuela 1945-1958.* Caracas: Editorial Ateneo de Caracas.

Stambouli, Andrés. 1993. "Déficits democráticos y gobernabilidad del sistema político venezolano." In *Venezuela, del siglo XX al siglo XXI: Un proyecto para construirla,* ed. Carlos Blanco. Caracas: COPRE/PNUD/Editorial Nueva Sociedad.

USIA. 1993. "Democracy Stumbles in Venezuela." Washington, D.C.: United States Information Agency. December 10.

Villasmil, Alejandra. 1996. "No hay voluntad." *Economía Hoy*, June 21.

Yépez, Guillermo S. 1993. *La Causa R: Origen y poder.* Caracas: Fondo Editorial Tropykos.

Zambrano, Angel Enrique. 1994. Interview.

Interviews

The following interviews were held during the fall of 1994.

Blanco, Carlos. Former President of the Presidential Commission for State Reform (Comisión Presidencial para la Reforma del Estado — COPRE) and later Minister of State and President of this Commission. He is currently the Director of the weekly magazine *Primicia*.

de la Cruz, Rafael. Expert on decentralization and political reforms in Venezuela. Former Director of the Decentralization Area of COPRE. He is a professor and researcher at IESA and was a member of the team that drew up Irene Sáez's Presidential Program.

Fernández, Eduardo. Former presidential candidate and former Secretary-General of COPEI. He is the President of the Fundación Pensamiento y Acción and was one of COPEI's pre-candidates for the 1998 elections.

Gil Yépez, José Antonio. Political scientist and Director of a leading public opinion polling firm.

Medina, Pablo. Former Secretary-General of Causa R until its division in 1997 and member of Congress representing Causa R (1993-1998). He is one of the main leaders of the newly created Patria Para Todos (PPT).

Müller Rojas, Alberto. Former Governor of what is now the state of Amazonas and former General of Venezuela's Armed Forces. He was a Senator (1993-1998) first for Causa R and later for Patria Para Todos (PPT).

Petkoff, Teodoro. Former guerrilla leader, MAS presidential candidate, and member of Congress. He was the Minister of CORDIPLAN (Planning Ministry) and one of the most important economic spokesmen of Rafael Caldera's second government. He resigned from MAS in 1998.

Ramírez Lopéz, Ramón. Member of Congress representing Convergencia (1993-1998). Member of the Comisión de Asuntos Regionales (Commission on Regional Policies) of Congress.

Rodríguez, Víctor. Member of MAS. During Rafael Caldera's government, he worked in FUNDACOMUN (Foundation for Community Development).

Romero, Carlos. Acting Director of the Ph.D. Program in Political Science of the Universidad Central de Venezuela. He teaches courses in political science both at the pre- and post-graduate levels at the same university.

Sosa, Arturo. One-time Director of the magazine *SIC*, he has a Ph.D. in political science. As a Jesuit, he is considered one of the important and outspoken leaders of the Catholic Church, though his views often do not reflect the official views of the church. He actively promotes community-based work.

Zambrano, Angel Enrique. Community leader. Founder of the Citizen Decision Movement (Decisión Ciudadana). He was elected as one of the first independent mayors of the Baruta Municipality of Caracas in the 1992 elections.

CHAPTER SIX

Comparative Lessons

JENNIFER L. MCCOY

We have defined learning as a process of reflection on experience and new information that affects attitudes and behavior. It leads to a cognitive change involving changes in beliefs and perceptions about how the world works. These altered beliefs can lead an actor to change goals and priorities in complex learning or simply to change tactics to better reach his/her goals in a process of simple learning.

Our primary interest has been to try to discern how and under what conditions political actors and groups learn democratic behavior, whether because they value the democratic norms and rules for their own sake (normative valuation of democracy) or because they value them as the best means at the moment to further their own private interests (instrumental valuation of democracy). This distinction, of course, will have consequences for the survival and nature of the democracy. We also asked what is the manifestation of learning in actual behaviors: How have the new perceptions or attitudes been translated into actions, and what are the consequences for democratic survival and governability? Finally, we wanted to know how and whether learning is transmitted to new groups and new generations or whether there are real limits to learning.

In this chapter, the experiences of our four country cases — Argentina, Chile, Uruguay, and Venezuela — are compared to identify the conditions under which democratic learning has occurred. The limits of learning and the consequences for democratic governance are examined. The chapter concludes with suggestions for future research emerging from this initial study.

LEARNING FROM TRAUMA: DEMOCRATIC BREAKDOWNS AND REVIVAL

Each of the four countries experienced an extreme crisis in the breakdown of democracy and learned from the crisis. Trauma as a source of learning tended to result in the reevaluation of both goals and means on the part of the opposition in each country: The broad principles of democracy and human rights were given higher priority than they had received prior to the breakdowns, and the survival of the democratic regime became paramount, at least in the short term. In Venezuela and Chile, in particular, the trauma of democratic failure led to power-sharing and consensus-seeking strategies by political oppositions to the military regimes. Uruguayans returned to their prior institutions and rules and then adapted those rules to the changing electorate. Argentines responded to the crises of human rights abuses and hyperinflation but faced a different challenge: to end a cyclical pattern of democratic/authoritarian regimes.

Chile

In Chile, the preeminent learning from the democratic collapse and subsequent attempts to restore it were on the part of the major opposition parties to the dictatorship, who learned from experience that in the Chilean tripartite ideological system (center, left, and right), no single political force alone can form a majority government capable of incorporating demands for social change. Instead, alliances and coalitions are required to ensure governability and democratic survival. Corollary lessons included, first, the need to join forces to oust the dictatorship by using both the institutional framework of the military regime itself and social mobilization, while discarding insurrection. Second, leading members of the opposition learned that they could in fact join forces, both to oust the military and subsequently to govern, if their alliance were based on negotiated strategies and specific policies, rather than on an attempt to compromise on ideological or programmatic terms that had divided them in the past.

The successful alliance to win the 1988 plebiscite with the "No" vote was repeated with the formation of the Concertación, a coalition of Christian Democrats, Socialists, and the Party for Democracy (Partido por la Democracia — PPD), for the 1989 elections. Unlike many other alliances born in opposition to an adversary, the Chilean parties sustained the coalition beyond the defeat of their opponents in the 1989 elections, presenting a unified slate for the 1994 elections as well. The coalition partners had learned well from the pre-1973 failed attempts to govern alone and from the 1988 and 1989 successes of unity.

Nevertheless, the traumatic source of the learning brought its own limitations with negative implications for the future functioning of the democratic system. Two points in particular raise questions about the nature and durability of the fundamental lessons learned by the Concertación. First, a type of *overlearning*[1] occurred in which the opposition became so afraid that divisions would return the country to the instability and the trauma of the past that the search for consensus became the overriding goal. Consensus-seeking, however, has a downside for democratic functioning in that dissent and debate about alternative policies, programs, and visions for society are suppressed, thus limiting the government's capacity to find the best solutions to pressing national problems. Furthermore, the opposition's reluctance to confront conflict prevented it from successfully negotiating a change in the rules to eliminate the authoritarian enclaves before the transition. Consequently, the first post-military government under Patricio Aylwin could not muster the legislative supermajority necessary to change the Constitution, subordinate the military, and institutionalize and guarantee the means of governability in the future.

One of the consequences of this overlearning was the anxiety produced in Chile with the detention of General Augusto Pinochet in October 1998 in London, in response to an extradition request by a Spanish judge to try Pinochet in Spain for human rights abuses during his regime. The arrest reopened the wounds and unmasked the carefully constructed consensus that had sought to avoid a return to conflict. The action of an external actor could finally force Chilean society to, in Manuel Antonio Garretón's words in Chapter Three of this volume, "lift the veil" of a traumatic history that it had thus far refused to do. The Christian Democratic government, along with the opposition right and the Socialist Party leader and presidential precandidate, all argued on the basis of national sovereignty that Pinochet should be returned to Chile for trial. They argued that this was an issue for Chileans to resolve, not a foreign government, even though it was clear that there was very little chance that the General would actually face a trial in Chile. Parts of the Socialist Party and human rights activists, in contrast, argued that sovereign immunity should not protect crimes committed by a head of government while in office. They further argued that Chile itself was not in a position to address the human rights abuses because of the amnesty the military had granted itself before departing office for crimes committed between 1973 and 1979 and because of the authoritarian enclaves described in the chapter on Chile in this volume. Seven months later, the issue was still pending in the English courts, and Chileans had not reforged the consensus that had been cracked open by the actions of a single Spanish judge.

The second threat to the lessons learned by the Concertación concerned the inability of the Concertación members to establish institutional means for majoritarian rule. This meant that governability after 1989 depended on the political will of the members of the Concertación to form alliances. Right up to the primary scheduled for May 31, 1999, to determine the next Concertación presidential candidate, it was not clear whether the Christian Democrats would accept a victory by a Socialist candidate who was leading in the polls nor whether Socialists would accept another Christian Democratic candidate after supporting Christian Democrats in two previous elections. In the end, the Socialist candidate, Ricardo Lagos, won resoundingly, and the Christian Democrats accepted his candidacy for the 1999 presidential elections. Nevertheless, the coalition members have not formally incorporated any new rules to encourage the same type of cooperative behavior after the first decade of post-military government, when different actors or different generations, lacking the same collective memory and interpretation of history, may have gained power. In brief, political behavior changed as a result of learning, but these lessons have not yet been translated into new rules or institutions that could guarantee their survival in the long term. Only when the institutions are built will we be able to answer the question raised by Garretón, whether the coalition-building and conflict-avoidance behavior is truly a result of learning rather than a product of the fears of a traumatized society that they could regenerate instability.

Venezuela

In Venezuela, the failure of the first democratic experience — the Trienio of 1945-1948 — and the experience of the Marcos Pérez Jiménez dictatorship in the following decade produced clear learning by the major political parties, especially Democratic Action (Acción Democrática — AD), during their second chance at ruling. As Francine Jácome describes in Chapter Five of this volume, the Pact of Punto Fijo, including its corollary political and economic agreements, was a deliberate attempt by its signatories to avoid the unilateral rule that they believed was the downfall of the AD government during the Trienio. Consequently, not only did the leaders of AD, Social Christian Party – Committee of Independent Political Electoral Organization (Comité de Organización Política Electoral Independiente — COPEI), and Democratic Republican Union (Unión Democrática Republicana — URD) agree to share power regardless of who won the 1958 elections, but they and associated social actors also began to practice a form of pact-making, alliances, and tacit cooperation that would endure for the next 30 years.

As in Chile, the overriding goal of democratic survival and stability was achieved, in part due to the pact-making strategy of political and social leaders. However, this lesson from the trauma of democratic collapse and authoritarian rule also had clear tendencies of overlearning and a "competency trap."[2] The repeated use of pacts as a successful strategy eventually impeded the learning of new means of dealing with new types of problems and crises. Political elites became comfortable with their handle on power, and political office became the means to share the spoils of an oil economy. The strategy was unsustainable, however, as the perception that the two major parties that alternated power throughout Venezuela's democratic history were becoming increasingly centralized, corrupt, and out of touch with the needs of the general population led to their eventual demise.

When the economic, institutional, and political crises erupted from 1989 through 1992, the first reaction of Venezuela's political elite was to turn to the "tried and true" pact strategy in an attempt to resolve the crises and return the political system to normal. As Jácome describes, however, several such attempts failed, with the consequences being not the collapse of the regime but the destitution of one president, the political realignment of the electorate, and a severe crisis of legitimacy and governability reflected in the political elite's inability to resolve social and economic problems.

The dramatic collapse of the party system in the 1998 elections provided a severe lesson for the traditional parties. In an election in which neither AD nor COPEI ran its own candidate, Venezuelans voted among a failed coup leader, an independent former governor, and a former beauty queen who became an independent mayor. The overwhelming victory of Lt. Colonel Hugo Chávez Frías from a platform calling for a cleansing of the political system, a new constitution, and economic redress for the average Venezuelan demonstrated the electorate's deep desire for change and its rejection of the traditional parties. The makeup of the new Congress also illustrated a political realignment, with Chávez' coalition controlling 34 percent of the deputies, followed by AD, COPEI, and a new party, Venezuela Project (Proyecto Venezuela), led by the second-place presidential candidate, Henrique Salas Romer.

A revolt within AD the week before the December 6, 1998, presidential election illustrated both the rigidity of the party and its potential for reform. As Jácome describes in Chapter Five, AD had consistently resisted internal democratization. One of the proponents of internal elections, Claudio Fermín, had been rebuffed by the AD leadership and ran an independent presidential campaign in 1998. AD chose its lackluster Secretary-General, Luis Alfaro Ucero, as its presidential candidate for the 1998 elections. With Alfaro Ucero never topping 6 percent in the polls in the months and weeks leading up to the elections, the newly elected governors in the November 8 regional elections demanded that he drop out of the race and that AD support Henrique Salas Romer, an independent candidate. Alfaro, heretofore master of the AD political machine, refused to resign, and the party had to oust him, leading to an electoral crisis — who would become the party's candidate less than a week before the election? In the end, the National Electoral Council ruled that the party, rather than the candidate, retained the position on the ballot, and AD threw its support to Salas Romer.

The resistance to internal change limited AD's capacity to respond to the growing complexity of the Venezuelan society and demands from the populace, as predicted by Jácome in her chapter. Nevertheless, the growing strength and independence of governors representing the traditional political parties indicated a new source of reform and potential resurgence of AD and COPEI.

Uruguay

In Uruguay, the trauma of the dictatorship from 1973 to 1985 carried clear lessons for both political and social actors. The perception of most of those actors was that it was the behavior of politicians and their adversaries that caused the breakdown, rather than the political institutions or rules (González 1992; McCoy and Costa Bonino 1992). Therefore, with the return of democratic rule in 1985, the previous Constitution was restored, and there was no immediate attempt to change the preexisting rules of the game.

In Chapter Four, Luis Costa Bonino argues that the lessons of the previous breakdown produced a clear change in strategic behavior in three important respects. First, the social and political violence and disruption that preceded the coup were no longer accepted as legitimate means or methods to challenge government policies. Second, the extreme personal attacks and discrediting of political opponents that characterized the pre-coup period were no longer evident. Third, the first three post-dictatorial presidents were careful not to repeat the unilateral decision-making style of the pre-coup presidents; instead, they strove to work diligently with the Congress. Legislators, too, showed a renewed interest in accepting their responsibility as a co-equal branch of government, in contrast with their self-abnegation of power and responsibility preceding the coup.

Perhaps the most significant illustration of the positive effects of political learning occurred after the 1994 elections. With a virtual triple tie and a mere 30,000 votes separating the winning party from the third-place party, the circumstances were reminiscent of the crumbling of the bipartisan system prior to the democratic breakdown in the early 1970s. Furthermore, because of Uruguay's unique double simultaneous vote system, a president could not even count on the support of the multiple formal factions within his own party. Pessimists predicted that Uruguay would again become ungovernable in 1995. Instead, newly elected President Julio María Sanguinetti forged a solid government coalition that was able to carry out such fundamental reforms as a change in the social security system and revision of the national Constitution to change Uruguay's peculiar electoral system.

Costa Bonino argues that three factors explain the positive learning on the part of Uruguayan political actors regarding governability in Chapter Four of this volume. First, the political elite consciously tried to avoid a recurrence of the pre-coup institutional instability in a similar tripartite context after the 1971 elections, when the executive resorted to exceptional measures and rule by decree and the Parliament harassed the president. The dire predictions of ungovernability following the 1994 elections reawakened an essential reflex for the survival of democracy: the idea that democracy is not achieved and assured once and for all but instead must be constantly nurtured and protected.

The second factor was President Sanguinetti's own learning from historical experience, in which he perceived that the best governing style for the political moment of 1995 was low profile, building bridges to other parties and seeking consensus through negotiations. This style combined with his personal prestige produced, in Costa's words, "a minimum of authoritarianism and a maximum of authority." The third factor was the perceived necessity on the part of a majority faction of the Broad Front (Frente Amplio) to abandon ideological dogma and to play the democratic game with the aim of legitimating its own ambitions of winning power in the 1999 elections.

Nevertheless, these lessons from traumatic experience have their own limits. As Costa Bonino points out, political violence has not been extinguished and may even be resurging a decade or more after the democratic transition. More explicit rejection of violence, especially on the part of political leaders on the Left, would help to mitigate this potentially dangerous phenomenon. In addition, the Uruguayan case demonstrates the potentially temporal nature of traumatic learning. As the vulnerability of the democratic regime was perceived to decrease, political leaders returned to a demagogic electoralism during political campaigns, which threatened to undermine the credibility of representative institutions by raising expectations to unrealistic levels. Nevertheless, this behavior, rather than indicate a memory loss of past lessons, may instead reflect a certain calculated risk on the part of political actors as they seek electoral advantage during the campaign, common to any democratic system. After the election, they have tended to recover a degree of responsibility toward democratic governance and stability once a new government is installed and faces the tasks of governing.

Argentina

Argentina's is unlike the other three democratic breakdowns in that it represents cycles of hybrid regimes, rather than a single major military interruption. In Argentina, democratic political learning stems from the assessment of a history of democratic/authoritarian cycles since the 1940s. Marcelo Cavarozzi demonstrates, in Chapter Two of this volume, that the Radical Party changed its goals and strategies in response to a deliberate evaluation of the political cycles of 1955 through 1973. The party first manifested a new disposition to accept pacts with its traditional political enemy — the Peronists — and to promote a party system that would legitimate both parties in 1969. A continued change in orientation to accept the full consequences of the possibility of party alternation in power occurred in the 1970s, culminating in 1983 when the Radical Party presidential candidate Raúl Alfonsín sought and achieved a victory over his adversaries.

Peronists were slower to learn lessons that would contribute to democratic governance. They arrived at the 1983 transitional elections still reluctant to accept institutional rules and the peaceful resolution of internal conflicts. However, a process of learning stimulated by evaluation of recent experience and international contacts beginning in 1982 became evident with the formation of the Renovación (Renewal) faction within the party. This faction was instrumental in the party's denunciation of the barracks uprisings in 1987, electoral victories in the 1987 mid-term elections, and the 1989 presidential election. Peronist Party members' learning from their divided past, however, may not be deeply entrenched. By 1999, President Carlos Saúl Menem had not only changed the rules that allowed for his reelection to a second term in 1995 but was also trying to run for a third term, a decision that divided his party. The Radicals, in contrast, had recognized the need to expand the universe of coalition partners and joined in a coalition with the Left for the 1997 mid-term elections and the 1999 presidential elections.

The Argentine case shows traumatic learning based on the human rights abuses of the last military period as well as the economic trauma of hyperinflation. The major lesson learned by the Argentine society was the need to reconstruct public authority, weakened by cycles of ineffective civilian and military governments. One of the aspects of that learning was how to submit the military to civilian rule, evidenced most clearly by Radical leaders who made bold innovations by putting the military on trial in civil courts. Even the military eventually learned to appreciate the institutional and legitimacy costs to the armed forces, leading to a military put-down of insurrections within its ranks against democratic rules, and, after 1989, to self-criticism and acknowledgment of the disappearances and other abuses of the "dirty war" of the 1970s. In contrast to the other cases, then, Argentines appear to have undergone a dramatic learning process with regard to civil-military relations. The political class learned the risk of military intervention, and the military learned the costs of political involvement.

In Uruguay, a deep learning process was not as necessary because the military involvement was more a historical accident than a regular pattern of behavior. Both the military itself and political and social actors perceived the Uruguayan military intervention to be a failure, symptomized by its defeat in the 1980 constitutional plebiscite.

Chile's military learned how *not* to be controlled; that is, it learned to retain its prerogatives under democratic rule, while the political class still needs to learn how to remove the authoritarian enclaves and deal with a military institution different from the pre-1973 years.

Venezuela presents another case of a competency trap with regard to civilian control of the military. The successful measures enacted to control the military after 1958 — civilian oversight over promotions, improved budgets, rapid rotations of high-ranking officers, divided services — eventually undermined civilian control, as members of the military bred their own resentments about partisan interference in military affairs, rivalries among the services, and pay inequities. In particular, dissension between mid-ranking and high-ranking officials over these issues fed into the attempted coups of 1992 and the eventual electoral victory of a paratrooper in December 1998.

The second trauma experienced by Argentines was high inflation from 1975 to 1991, with bouts of hyperinflation. Cavarozzi argues that the Argentine state had been able to avoid high inflation for decades, as economic actors depended on the state to protect them against deterioration of the value of money in the face of irresponsible fixing of prices and salaries by unions and businesses. However, the state could never generate a consensus that would have permitted it to reach full monetary stability. When new mechanisms of indexation and dollarization of savings began in the 1970s, the state lost its capacity to control inflation, and the costs of devaluation became explicit, leading to high inflation.

Learning from the trauma of hyperinflation in Argentina took place in stages. Large capitalists evaluated the economic policymaking of the 1976-1983 military regime and concluded that its arbitrary and isolated policy-making style impeded their own access to decisionmaking and the regime's ability to rectify failed policies. These business leaders also linked the discretionary decisionmaking of authoritarian rulers with politicized state intervention, so that when the crisis of 1982 forced a process of depoliticizing the economy, these leaders were ready to support the democratic transition. Indeed, the actions of large capitalists as a group were decisive in the process of democratic consolidation in the 1980s.

In contrast, President Raúl Alfonsín and the Radical Party were slow to learn from the economic trauma. Cavarozzi argues that they became political and psychological captives of the state-centric matrix, failing to perceive that the new context made statist policies and populist reflexes counterproductive. Their beliefs were shaped by their experiences and cognitive association of the military regime with a failed economy and neoliberal policies. Consequently, Radical Party leaders associated economic recuperation not only with democracy, but also with a return to Keynesian income policies of the 1946 to 1975 period.

Peronists learned from the Radicals' economic failure as it became clear that the state-centered matrix had entered an irreversible crisis. Their learning was manifested in two ways: during the Radical period of government, the Peronists attacked the government but defended the democratic system, reflecting a reevaluation of democratic rules of game. As a result, the crisis of hyperinflation did not lead to institutional rupture, as it might have in the past. By the 1989 elections, the extreme uncertainty created by hyperinflation made severe adjustment programs more acceptable to the populace and lowered demands for higher income levels and public services. This change in attitudes opened the door for Menem to redefine Peronism, restructure the economy within a democratic framework, and revamp the matrix of state-society relations.

INSTRUMENTAL LEARNING

One of the most difficult problems of learning theory is to distinguish empirically between valuative or ideational learning and instrumental learning. In valuative learning, actors adopt new beliefs, ideas, or values in response to new experiences and information. In instrumental learning, actors learn to adapt their tactics to new circumstances to reach their goals and serve their interests more effectively. For example, is a change in government policy from protectionist to open market trade policies 1) the result of new ideas learned by a strong leader, or 2) a rational adaptation of a government to changing international economic circumstances, or 3) a bureaucratic power game wherein the winning bureaucracy chose the liberal trade policy as the best means to enhance its own power and prestige? The third explanation is an example of instrumental learning, as described by James Moltz (1993) to explain how Soviet bureaucratic leaders borrowed those economic ideas from abroad that would advance their own strategic political position within the bureaucratic game in the Soviet Union. Amy Searight (1998) makes a similar argument to explain the Ministry of International Trade and Industry's (MITI) change toward liberal trade policy in Japan.

Nevertheless, both the rational pursuit of interests and the revision of goals or values are legitimate forms of learning. Changing tactics to better reach one's prior goals can be a product of learning from new information or new experiences if the new input has changed one's perceptions about how the world works. This would be simple or instrumental learning and has been called simply "adaptation." The adoption of democratic rules by authoritarian actors (whether military, economic elites, or vanguard parties) to further their own interests may be instrumental and temporal; yet, this constitutes a form of learning.

Changing goals or priorities because of new values or ideas, however, is complex learning. The promotion of democracy because one values human rights, freedom, or the ability to choose leaders and hold them accountable is an example of valuative or normative learning. This decision may be based on a very negative experience with alternative forms of rule that lead a group or individual to revalue or reprioritize democracy, as we saw in the cases in this book.

As George Breslauer points out, a purely interest-based theory of politics is hard pressed to explain *change*. This theory is much better at explaining and predicting continuity. A learning theory, however, allows for the possibility of interest redefinition; it ". . . incorporates a political dimension by requiring a collective and institutional redefinition of interests and assumptions" (Breslauer 1991, 848). Instrumental learning, then, reflects the interaction of interest-based politics and learning.

In our cases, we have several examples of instrumental learning that contribute to the democratic process. The Uruguayan Left's use of the referendum is an excellent example of instrumental learning. The leaders of the Frente Amplio learned from their initial success in the 1971 elections, their growing electoral strength in the post-dictatorial period, and the election of Tabaré Vázquez to Montevideo mayor in 1989 that they could, in contrast to the 1960s, play the electoral game with the possibility of winning. Therefore, they moved from distrust of democratic rules of the game to respect for them in the 1980s and 1990s.

Leaders of the Frente Amplio also learned to use a constitutional tool — the referendum — to great effect to achieve policy goals they did not possess the legislative strength to attain. In the first and most dramatic instance, the Left proposed a referendum in 1989 to repeal the amnesty approved by the legislature for human rights abuses during the military period. After an intense, polarizing debate, the repeal was narrowly defeated, and the amnesty stood.

In subsequent attempts, the Left was more successful in achieving its policy aims through the use of the referendum. A 1992 referendum promoted by the Frente Amplio and the labor unions repealed a privatization law approved by the legislature, and a 1994 referendum both repealed a constitutional reform project approved unanimously in the legislature and abrogated social security reform.

Luis Costa Bonino argues, however, that this instrumental learning of the use of referendum as a tool for political action may actually have negative consequences for democracy. The overuse of the tool runs the risk of degrading the representative function of the Parliament, since majority votes within the parliament can be overturned by a popular referendum. Although its proponents rationalize the instrumental use of the referendum with the concept of direct democracy, Costa argues that an indiscriminate use of this tool risks devaluing representative institutions.

Instrumental learning is also evident on the part of the military and the Right in Chile. In particular, the military learned to govern and to deal with political actors using its institutionally guaranteed prerogatives and leverage. The Right learned to use its political veto capacity and influence to maintain its political and economic programmatic goals, especially those tied to the legacy of the military regime. Learning on the part of these two actors, however, appears to be instrumental, based on their acquiescence to democratic rules as long as their own interests are served or as long as the benefits outweigh the costs.

Venezuela's move toward political decentralization beginning in 1984 was a product of instrumental learning on the part of traditional party elites. Pushed by voters and grass-roots mobilizations from below, particularly the flourishing neighborhood associations, party elites reluctantly accepted a series of political reforms — direct election of governors and mayors in 1989, *uninominal* (single member district) elections in 1993, and even some party primaries to choose presidential candidates in 1988 and 1993.

Even though the reforms threatened to undermine the hierarchical, centralized control of the powerful party *cogollos* (bosses), party leaders also recognized the discrediting of political parties by voters and feared a voter backlash. Nevertheless, loath to give up control, party elites resisted further political reforms and sought to compensate for their loss of power in other ways.

CONSEQUENCES FOR DEMOCRACY

Chile

The manifest learning by political actors in Chile is mostly about style and democratic methods. A learning deficit with regard to the programmatic content and institutional dimensions of democracy raises uncertainties for the future. For example, the trauma of polarization and confrontation led to a distorted view of consensus, eliminating debate over fundamental visions of society. Even more serious, the fear of politics as a means for transforming society could eliminate the ethical dimension of politics in the long term, leading to an ideological minimalism in which decisions are submitted to a calculus of costs and benefits, debate about the destiny of society disappears, and politics loses its appeal for the population.

The lack of institutionalization of the lessons learned is another limitation of democratic learning in Chile: the subordination of the military has not been ensured by any norm or institution; the lesson of majorities and coalitions has not been accompanied by new rules or incentives to sustain it in the future; and decentralization has been stunted by the failure to increase social and political participation at the local level.

The consequences of these limitations to learning may be a denigration of politics, similar to the case in Argentina, where the political process is incapable of coping with present and future social problems and thus risks becoming irrelevant. Garretón argues that it is still unclear whether the current behavior of the political class is a product of an unfinished transition or a new political, institutional, and socioeconomic model based on a narrow political consensus arrived at without a societal debate. Venezuela may be a point of reference for Chile as well. In Venezuela, a politics of power-sharing and consensus to preserve democracy eventually transformed itself into a means for the parties to divide the spoils of the oil wealth. This strategy was unsustainable, as the events of 1998 and 1999 demonstrated, and may serve as a lesson for other countries in the region.

Venezuela

We said earlier the main question for Venezuela was whether political actors would increase their learning curve fast enough to prevent a collapse of the democratic system. Could the political parties learn to recover their representative function in a party-dominated system where parties no longer effectively represented social demands nor served as the channel of communication between government and society? Could existing political elites manage a transformation of state-society relations within the existing political rules, and would they continue to learn from new challenges and experiences long after an initial trauma (such as the military regime of 1948-1958)?

The evidence suggests that new learning was retarded by overlearning in the past, particularly regarding the reliance on pact-making as a political tool. The successful pacted transition in 1958 eventually led to its own demise as political actors failed to adapt to changing social and demographic dynamics.

If trauma generates learning, the problems Venezuelans experienced from 1989 to 1995 appeared not to have constituted a sufficiently deep trauma to spur a fundamental reevaluation of goals and strategies. Instead, an incomplete learning process occurred on the part of traditional political elites, spurred by the necessity of adapting to a new set of social and economic conditions, a reorientation of popular attitudes, and new political and social actors emerging on the scene. The results were improvised policy responses to crises rather than well-defined, programmatic learning.

Neither did generational change within the traditional Venezuelan political parties produce substantial complex learning. Instead, the first generation of party leaders continued to hold power in many instances. Even where younger leaders began to emerge, they displayed many of the same attitudes regarding political practices as their elders. The result of this absence of complex learning was finally the populace's rejection of the traditional parties in the 1998 national election.

Uruguay

Uruguayan political actors do not appear to have forgotten the lessons learned from the trauma of democratic breakdown. Even a new generation, without direct experience of democratic breakdown, has learned a greater pragmatism and tolerance of opposition groups from the decline of ideology in the 1980s and 1990s, as well as from the vicarious experience of their elders. The lessons are evidenced in the greater acceptance of new political groups as potential coalition partners, the pragmatic orientation of the large majority of political actors, and the willingness of all but the extreme left to play by the democratic rules of the game. When the electoral rules were revised to accommodate the changing electorate and growing tripartism, positive learning for democratic governability took place.

Nevertheless, though Uruguayans learned well how not to repeat past crises and mistakes, some new types of behavior could possibly have more negative, unforeseen consequences for democracy. For example, the use of the referendum as a form of a more direct democracy may actually weaken representative institutions and threaten governance in the longer run.

Argentina

Major political actors strengthened their commitment to democratic rules of the game after a period of regime cycles in the post-World War II era and the failure of the last military regime. Both civilian and military leaders learned the costs of military involvement and achieved a dramatic change in civil-military relations that augurs well for democratic governance.

On the other hand, the economic failures of the military regime and Alfonsín administration and the trauma of hyperinflation led to a generalized disillusionment with political authorities and a collective retraction from politics. Marcelo Cavarozzi, in Chapter Two of this volume, argues that fear of returning to extreme instability induced the society to accept a drastic contraction of the spheres of state action and regulation. At the same time, decreased expectations about politics — what and how much can be resolved through political processes — led to less popular participation, greater disaffection, and less accountability of authorities.

Although the greater room for maneuver of government officials allowed for a successful economic stabilization program from 1991 to 1994, the devaluing of politics raises questions for democratic governance in the longer term in Argentina. The delegation of authority to the president has weakened representative institutions and the possibility of resolving distributive conflicts through them. A historical fear of monetary instability and the government's focus on this issue, through the successful currency board regime that fixed the value of the peso, contributed to a diminishing state capacity to process the social consequences of economic reform. The Argentine population's patience appeared to be wearing thin in the face of high unemployment and stagnant growth in the mid- and late 1990s, which led to renewed demands that the government do more than just protect the value of the currency.

In sum, positive learning about the need for economic reform and a new matrix of state-society relations in Argentina produced political stability in the medium term; however, in the long term, this process and the societal and political changes it caused may have negative consequences for democracy because of the very devaluing of democratic institutions.

CONCLUSIONS

Under what conditions does democratic learning occur, and what are its limits? Our cases suggest that political groups learned from failures and successes, from trauma and a gradual accumulation of knowledge from trial and error or study, and from direct and vicarious experiences. However, the successes were more likely to produce an overuse of a strategy (a type of competency trap); trauma was likely to produce overlearning and incomplete learning; and direct experience was more important than vicarious experience.

Learning theory posits that formative events and crisis situations are likely to produce learning because they are strong enough to shake up prior beliefs, assumptions, orientations, or routines. The four cases support this hypothesis, but they also suggest significant limits to learning that carry their own risks for future democratic governance. The failure of political elites to manage governability and economic challenges led to the traumatic experiences of military dictatorship and/ or high inflation among the four countries studied in this volume. These traumatic experiences, in turn, stimulated a process of complex learning through individual and collective reflection on the causes of failure and through trial and error experimentation with solutions to the problems.

In all four cases, the breakdown of democracy led to a reorientation of goals/ values and of strategies, as normative democrats revalued democracy and instrumental democrats acquiesced to democratic rules. These changes in orientation led to changes in behavior as well. Political actors changed electoral strategies to deal with problems of governability in increasingly multiparty systems. They rejected and punished antidemocratic behavior, whether from military ranks or radical social elements.

Nevertheless, traumatic learning has its own limits. *Our cases suggest that traumatic experience as a source of learning tends to result in overlearning, in that political actors learn to solve one problem at the expense of other problems.* Motivated primarily by a fear of returning to the uncertainty and instability of the past, political actors applied the lessons of "the last war" so strongly that they impeded the learning process for new problems and situations. Chileans sought to avoid conflict through seeking political consensus at the cost of stifling debate over national problems. Argentines delegated authority to conquer hyperinflation at the expense of representative institutions. Venezuelans relied on pact-making to guarantee the early survival of the regime, while failing to enlarge the circle of participants and modify tactics as the society evolved and new challenges arose.

In contrast, the absence of trauma may impede learning as well. Both the relative economic equilibrium in Argentina before 1975, when inflation was tolerated and negotiated by groups, and the political stability in Venezuela before

1989 tended to blind political and social actors to the warning signals of underlying tensions, impeding their perception of emerging problems. Only when the system became dysfunctional and the trauma of high inflation and political violence broke out in Argentina did political actors conclude that the costs of the hybrid political formula were intolerable, leading them eventually to discard the authoritarian component and accept a severe economic adjustment program. In Venezuela, the shock of the 1989 riots (*Caracazo*), two attempted military coups, and a serious banking failure failed to produce a fundamental reevaluation among the political elites of political and economic goals and strategies to resolve the problems, while the population moved ahead of the politicians and eventually rejected the political elites.

Learning from trauma poses a paradox, then. A traumatic experience can produce fundamental learning about the perceived cause of the trauma but may impede learning about new kinds of problems and situations. In the absence of trauma, political actors tend toward the status quo in their attitudes and behaviors with regard to democratic processes. By ignoring nascent tensions and problems until very late, political actors contribute to the development of new traumas. Learning can, of course, occur in a noncrisis context, as illustrated by the Uruguayan success of dealing with the post-coup governability challenge. However, the obvious question raised is, under what conditions will political actors learn to read the warning signs and avert crises before it is too late?

A second hypothesis from learning theory is that failure tends to produce more learning than does success. The explanation for this is that failure motivates reflection and evaluation, while success tends to allow complacency and a competency trap. *Our cases suggest that success can reinforce orientations and behavior resulting from past learning, but it also risks reinforcement of complacency and competency traps.* The Venezuelan political elite's early success with pact-making led its members to an overreliance on this one political tool, ignoring new actors and weakening representative institutions. When legitimacy and governability problems erupted in 1989 and later, those same actors tried to apply the old pact-making tools to new situations with little success.

Likewise, the change in attitudes and behavior with regard to coalition-building in Uruguay and Chile reflects learning through trial and error and building on success. *Nevertheless, the very effectiveness of the learning process in Chile, in particular, raises the risk that the lessons will not be institutionalized through changes in the rules.* In other words, even though current political actors have changed their behavior to address the governability problems of a multiparty system, for example, or to submit the military to civilian rule, their success depends on the political will of actors who have had direct experience and memories of the trauma or on those who have only an instrumental commitment to democracy. In Uruguay, on the other hand, constitutional reform in 1996 reflected an attempt to institutionalize the lessons learned and modify the electoral rules to better accommodate the changing electorate.

The benefits of learning may often be tenuous and temporary. Depending on political will rather than institutionalizing new rules and norms is not a secure means of ensuring the survival of lessons beyond the current actors, especially given the likelihood of generational change or a subsequent redefinition of interests by instrumental actors. The Venezuelan case, nearly four decades after a democratic transition, does not provide clear answers to the generational dilemma, since to a large degree the traditional political parties continued to be dominated by the generation of 1958 or their lieutenants. Thus, direct experience with the Pact of Punto Fijo continued to characterize the traditional political leadership of Venezuela, even while a new generation of leaders in new political groups and social movements was emerging to challenge the attitudes and assumptions of the traditional leaders. A key test for future learning will be whether the new political parties, especially the Fifth Republican Movement (Movimiento Quinta República — MVR) and Proyecto Venezuela, learn from the mistakes of the traditional parties, and whether the lessons learned translate into more democratic behavior of and within the parties.

Finally, what is the process of learning in political groups? We found that a conscious process of reflection or evaluation of the causes of failures was more common among groups of the Left. This can be attributed to several factors: a) a historical tendency of self-criticism within the Left; b) a global process of declining ideology and the failure of socialist projects, producing identity crises among Leftist groups; and c) a position of political weakness.

The change in attitudes of the Right toward democratic rules, illustrated by Argentine capitalists and Chilean Rightist parties, reflects a redefinition of interests (itself a learning process), based on the widespread adoption of their economic programs. The lack of collective self-reflection on the role of these groups in contributing to past crises is striking.

FUTURE RESEARCH

The preliminary conclusions from our comparative case study suggest avenues for future research to explore further the nature of political learning and democratization. First, the role of political culture may help to explain variations in the content and application of democratic learning. The autocratic tendencies still evident in the Venezuelan and Argentine political cultures contrast with the negotiating style of the Chilean and Uruguayan political cultures. Political culture and historical inertia together may shed more light on the durability of learning or explain when learning does not occur.

For example, in the autocratic cultures, deep trauma is apparently required for a change in political attitudes, constituting what we have defined as democratic learning. In Argentina, after a history of alternating military and semi-democratic regimes, the deep trauma of the "dirty war" finally resulted in a dramatic change in civil-military relations. Similarly, the trauma of hyperinflation produced different learning curves among the actors but eventually resulted in a widespread recognition of the need for a change in state-society relations. The Venezuelan trauma since 1989 produced tactical changes (simple learning) among political elites yet was insufficient to stimulate a similar complex learning across the traditional political groups. The conditions may finally be met for such learning due to the shock of voters' rejection of the traditional parties in the 1998 elections. However, an underlying autocratic culture in Venezuela may impede democratic learning, leading instead to a similar pattern of centralized, exclusionary control by and within the new political parties, perhaps even moving toward a greater militarization of the political arena.

In contrast, noncrisis political learning appears to be more likely in the negotiating political cultures. Learning from trial and error and the cumulation of knowledge from past successes has characterized the attempts of both Uruguayan and Chilean political elites to deal innovatively with the multiparty systems they both now face.

Second, specifying "trauma" more precisely is an important task for future research. Can we predict a priori what levels or nature of trauma will produce learning and what will be the limits to learning in these circumstances? Our cases suggest that historical experience and political culture will influence the effects of different types of trauma in different settings.

Third, how is elite political learning translated into mass learning? Although this study did not address mass learning, theories of elite hegemony, cultural change, and socialization will be of use in moving to this next stage. Likewise, another question is under what conditions does mass learning lead elite learning, as the Venezuelan case seems to suggest.

Fourth, can we disaggregate the adoption of norms versus institutions as a result of a learning process? In other words, do different learning processes and timelines produce new norms and new institutions? And how is learning passed on from one generation to the next?

Finally, can we specify more precisely the different types of learning identified in our cases: overlearning, incomplete learning, negative learning, and even unlearning or forgetting lessons of the past? Understanding the conditions that produce these different types of learning will require more comparative case studies in different settings, including new democracies, reemerging democracies, and established democracies undergoing strains or crises.

Notes

1. We define overlearning as learning that impedes or slows subsequent learning for new situations.

2. See note 10 in Chapter One of this volume.

References

Breslauer, George, and Philip Tetlock, eds. 1991. *Learning in U.S. and Soviet Foreign Policy*. Boulder, Colo: Westview Press.

González, Luis Eduardo. 1992. *Political Structures and Democracy in Uruguay*. Notre Dame: University of Notre Dame Press.

McCoy, Jennifer, and Luis Costa Bonino. 1992. "Political Learning in Reemerging Democracies: Framework for Analysis and Illustrations from Uruguay." Presented at the Congress of Latin American Studies Association, September. Los Angeles, California.

Moltz, James Clay. 1993. "Divergent Learning and the Failed Politics of Soviet Economic Reform." *World Politics* 45 (January).

Searight, Amy. 1998. "MITI and Multilateralism: GATT and the Evolution of Japanese Trade Policy." Ph.D. Dissertation. Stanford University.

Contributors

Jennifer L. McCoy is Associate Professor of Political Science at Georgia State University and Director of the Carter Center's Latin American and Caribbean Program. She is a co-editor of and contributor to *Venezuelan Democracy Under Stress* (North-South Center, 1995).

Marcelo Cavarozzi is Chair of the Department of Politics and Government, Universidad Nacional de San Martín, Buenos Aires, Argentina, and author of *El Capitalismo Político Tardío y su Crisis en América Latina* (Buenos Aires: Homo Sapiens Ediciones, 1996).

Manuel Antonio Garretón is Professor of Sociology at the Universidad de Chile, Santiago, and the author of *Hacia una nueva era política: estudio sobre las democratizaciones* (México: Fondo de Cultura Económica, 1995; translation and revised version in English forthcoming from University of North Carolina Press).

Malva Espinosa is a Researcher in the Department of Labor in Santiago, Chile, and holds a master's degree in sociology from the Facultad Latinoamericana de Ciencias Sociales, Quito, Ecuador. She has published two working papers with the Department of Labor: "Tendencias sindicales: Análisis de una década," Working Paper No. 2, 1997; and "La encuesta laboral 1998," 1999.

Luis Costa Bonino is a Political Scientist and Campaign Consultant from Montevideo, Uruguay. He is the author of *La Crisis del Sistema Político Uruguayo, Partidos Políticos y Democracia hasta 1973* (Montevideo: Fundación de Cultura Universitaria, 1995).

Francine Jácome is the Director of the Instituto Venezolano de Estudios Sociales y Políticos and Professor at the School of International Studies of the Universidad Central de Venezuela. She is the editor of and contributor to *Sociedad civil e integración regional en el Gran Caribe* (Cries/Invesp/Nueva Sociedad, 1998).

Index

A

Abdala, Washington 79
"accommodation" 53
Acuerdo Nacional para la Democracia Plena. *See National Accord for Complete Democracy*
AD (Democratic Action — Acción Democrática) 100-101, 103-104, 107-116, 118-119, 122, 133-135
Adler, Emanuel 3
Alessandri, Jorge 50
Alfonsín, Raúl 22-25, 27-31, 136, 138, 142
Alianza. *See Alliance*
Allamand, Andrés 48
Allende, Salvador 42, 50-51, 56-57
Alliance (Alianza) 29
Alvarez, Carlos "Chacho" 26
amnesty law 80-81
    of 1987 81
Andean Pact 105
Anderson, Richard 3
Angeloz, Eduardo 26, 28
Arana, Mariano 78
Araújo, Germán 87
Argentina 1, 6-7, 15-20, 23, 25-29, 32, 90, 131, 136, 138, 141-145
armed forces 18-20, 22-24, 32, 74, 84, 86, 137
Astori, Danilo 82, 95
attributed learning 37, 47. *See also learning*
Austral Plan 22, 24-25, 27-28
authoritarian

enclaves 1, 7, 41, 46-47, 57-58, 64, 132-133, 137
regimes 1, 15, 20, 24, 30-31, 43, 54, 60, 74, 132
rule 134
autocratic regimes 6, 20
Aylwin, Patricio 38, 45-46, 60, 64, 132

B

Balbín, Ricardo 18-19
banking crisis 106, 110
Basque 84
Basque Fatherland and Freedom. *See ETA*
Batalla, Hugo 89
Beagle plebiscite 28
Bermeo, Nancy 4
Betancourt, Rómulo 100-101
binomial 40
    system 58
bipartisan system 73, 75-76, 135
bitribal system 79
Blancos. *See White Party*
bolivarianos 109
Bordaberry, Juan María 75-76, 89-90, 94
Born, Jorge 26, 31
Brazilian miracle 31
breakdowns 1, 4, 15, 131, 136
Breslauer, George 3, 139
Broad Front (Frente Amplio) 75, 77-79, 81-89, 91, 93-95, 136, 139, 140
"bureaucratic authoritarian" 99
business sector 17, 19, 21, 52, 64, 77

C

Cafiero, Antonio 31-32
Caldera, Rafael 8, 103, 105-107, 110-
    111, 114, 117, 119
Campins, Luis Herrera 104
cannibalistic 87
capitalists 6, 18, 21-22, 31, 138, 145
Caracazo 8, 99, 105, 109-110, 122,
    144
Carapintada 31
Carciofi, Ricardo 17
Casella, Juan Manuel 25
caudillo 75, 106, 115
Causa R (Radical Cause Party) 108-
    111, 113, 115-117, 119, 122
Cavallo, Domingo 26-27
Cavarozzi, Marcelo 6-7, 15, 136, 138,
    142
Center 41, 45-48, 54, 56, 58, 61, 63.
    See also Christian Democrats
    -Left 38, 40, 47, 49, 52,
    -Right 44-45, 47, 61
Chávez Frías, Hugo 8, 134
Chicago School 43
Chile 1, 7, 83, 131-134, 137, 140-141,
    143-144
Christian Democracy. *See DC*
Christian Democrat Party 75
Christian Democrats 41-42, 44, 46,
    48, 51, 63-64, 132-133
Christian Socialism 112
civil society 7, 16, 21, 39, 53, 59-61,
    82, 108, 112-115, 120, 124
co-participation 75, 86
Coalition of Parties for
    Democracy. *See CPD*
cognitive
    process 3
    psychology 5
cogollo (core) 115
cogollos (bosses) 140
collective
    learning 3, 42. *See also learning*
    reciprocity 16

Colorado Party/Colorados (Red Party)
    75, 82, 84, 86, 88-89, 91, 93
Comité de Organización Política
    Electoral Independiente. *See*
    COPEI
Committee of Independent Political
    Electoral Organization. *See COPEI*
Communist Party 44, 50, 75, 78, 101,
    103
communists 41
competency trap 5, 134, 137, 143-144
complex learning 2, 5, 99-100, 103,
    120-122, 131, 139, 141-143,
    145. *See also learning*
Concepción, Alfredo 24
Concertación 37-41, 45-46, 48-50,
    52-53, 55-56, 58-62, 64-65, 132-
    133
concertación 107, 122
Concertación de Partidos por la
    Democracia. *See CPD*
conflict 18, 46, 50, 63, 65, 132-133,
    143
    -avoidance 133
    cultural 59
    distributive 16, 142
    government 74, 76
    internal 31, 47, 136
    open 40
    partisan 102
    political 20, 78, 87
    politics 16
    social 81
Congress 105, 110, 114-115, 119,
    134-135
consensus politics 46
conservatives 18, 59, 75
    faction 75
consolidation of democracy 21, 95,
    102. *See also democracy*
Constituent Assembly 114, 119
Constitution 7, 29, 39, 40-45, 73, 76,
    80, 91, 103, 108, 110, 114, 132,
    134-135

Constitutional Reform 29, 40, 58, 67-68, 95, 114-115, 140
1996 79-80, 90, 144
elections 29
contemporary learning 104. *See also learning*
Convergencia 110-112, 117, 119
COPEI (Social Christian Party – Committee of Independent Political Electoral Organization — Comité de Organización Política Electoral Independiente) 100-104, 106-116, 118-119, 134-135
Coppedge, Michael 115
COPRE (Presidential Commission on Reforming the State) 107-108, 113-115, 119
corporatist 102
corruption 87, 101, 105, 108
cortes transversales 79
Costa Bonino, Luis 8, 73, 135-136, 140
CPD (Coalition of Parties for Democracy — Concertación de Partidos por la Democracia) 37, 45. *See also Concertación*
crisis 5, 17, 22-25, 51, 54-55, 63, 84, 87, 95, 99, 104, 107-108, 113, 120-122, 138, 143
banking 106, 110
bipartisan system 75
business sector 64
democracy 38, 53, 62
breakdown of 131
democratic 4, 45-46, 63-64
Eastern Bloc 48
economic 5, 7, 23, 32, 46, 75, 107
electoral 47, 135
global 44
hyperinflation 138
identity 51, 58, 79
ideological 51, 78, 94
leadership 48
management 119
of 1973 58
of 1982 31, 138
of legitimacy 121, 134
of political parties 55
of representation 51
of the SCM 22, 108-109
of the state 23
perceptions of 104, 107
political 45, 99-100, 104, 106-108, 110, 112, 114, 119, 121-122
and economic 120
spectrum 57
systems 56
Radical Party 29
representational 75
social 113
socialist model 77
socioeconomic 44
cúpula 107
currency board 142

D

DC (Christian Democracy — Democracia Cristiana) 37, 50-51, 53-55, 58-61
de la Rúa, Fernando 29
decentralization 51, 65-66, 104-105, 107, 113-115, 118, 122, 140-141
declining ideology 145
delegative
democracy 106, 123
political culture 122, 124
Democracia Cristiana. *See DC*
democracy
consolidation of 21, 95
deeper 65
direct 82, 96, 140, 142
internal party 113-114
democratic
breakdown 1, 4, 7, 41-42, 50, 56, 66, 131, 135-136, 142
consolidation 4, 16, 31, 38, 46, 60, 62, 91, 138
crisis 1, 4, 45-46, 63-64
game, rules of the 4-5
governability 4. *See also governability*

democratic, continued
learning 3, 5-7, 32, 56, 73-74, 76, 93,
99, 112, 120-122, 124, 131, 141, 143,
145-146
process 29
political culture, participatory 9
Democratic Action. *See AD*
Democratic Republican Union. *See*
URD
democratization 4-5, 19, 30, 39, 46,
76-79, 95, 115, 124, 134, 145
internal party 117
theories 1
dictatorship 6-8, 15, 20-23, 30, 39,
41-46, 52-53, 55, 60, 74, 76, 80-81,
89-90, 95, 100-102, 109, 132-133,
135, 143
differential learning 41. *See also*
learning
"dirty war" 137, 145
discourse dimension 112
divergent learning 2-3, 99-100. *See*
also learning

E

Eastern Revolutionary Movement. *See*
MRO
economic
adjustment 20, 46, 104, 144
model 6-9, 22
modernization 46
reforms 20, 22, 24, 106, 122
elections 15, 18, 23-25, 28-31, 39-40,
45, 47, 50, 56, 59, 73, 77-81, 86,
90-91, 93-94, 100-105, 109-110,
114-120, 123, 132-140, 146
El Gran Viraje. *See Great Turnaround*
elite 17, 25, 65, 76, 108-110, 122
consensus 8, 103, 110, 122
economic 100-101, 106, 139
government 109
group 64
-in-exile, political 101
learning 91
left 51, 56

military 100-101, 139
party 64, 140
traditional 111, 140
Peronist 31
political 4, 9, 51, 63, 99-100, 102-103,
105-106, 109-110, 114, 118-122,
134-135, 141, 143-146
social 4, 106
Emergency Security Measures 75
Encuentro Progresista 89
epistemic communities 3
Espinosa, Malva 7, 37
ETA (Basque Fatherland and Freedom
— Euzkadi Ta Azkatasuna) 84-85
Euzkadi Ta Azkatasuna. *See ETA*
extradition 84, 132

F

FEDECAMARAS (Federation of
Chambers of Commerce) 107
Fermín, Claudio 118, 134
Ferreira, Juan Raúl 79, 84, 90
Fifth Republican Movement. *See*
MVR
fiscal
agreement 19
pact 6, 17
implicit 17
Floreses, Fernando 55
Frei, Eduardo 46, 50-52, 56, 62
Frente Amplio. *See Broad Front*
Frente del País Solidario. *See*
FREPASO
Frente Grande. *See Grand Front*
FREPASO (National Solidarity Front
— Frente del País Solidario) 26, 29
Friederich Ebert Foundation 5

G

Gallegos, Rómulo 100
Gargano, Reinaldo 77, 81, 84, 89
Garretón, Manuel Antonio 7, 37, 133,
141
gender relations 65

generational change 120, 141, 145
Gestido, Oscar 89
Gil Yépez, José Antonio 110, 113-114
globalization 65, 105
governability 4, 7-8, 39, 58, 79, 93,
    95, 99-100, 102, 109, 113, 118-119,
    121-124, 131-135, 142-144
governors 112-114, 122, 134-135, 140
Gran Viraje, el. *See Great Turnaround*
Grand Front (Frente Grande) 29
Great Turnaround (El Gran Viraje)
    104
gremialista 43-44
Grinspun, Bernardo 24
group learning 2. *See also learning*
guerrillas 19, 76, 83, 86
Guzmán, Jaime 48-49, 59

H

Haas, Ernst 3
Halperín Donghi, Tulio 18
Hierro López, Luis 82
Hora del Pueblo. *See Hour of the
    People*
Hospital Filtro 86
Hour of the People (Hora del Pueblo)
    18
human rights 21, 23-24, 32, 39-40,
    42, 46, 55, 65, 131-133, 139
    abuses 132-133, 137-139
    violations 80-81
hybrid
    formula 20, 30
        political 6-7, 15-16, 30, 144
    regimes 136
hyperinflation 19, 22, 24-27, 32, 122,
    132, 137-138, 142-143, 145
hyperinflationary 17, 28

I

ideology, declining 145
Illía, Arturo 24
IMF (International Monetary Fund) 77
implicit fiscal pact 17

Independent Democratic Union. *See
    UDI*
indexation 138
individual learning 2, 38, 93-94. *See
    also learning*
inflation 6, 17, 20, 24, 100, 104-105,
    138, 143
institutional
    framework 1, 6, 20, 39, 43, 46, 57, 64,
        132
    model 56-57, 61
Institutional Pact 103
instrumental learning 61, 119, 138-
    140. *See also learning*
interest-based theory 139
internal
    fights 28
    party democracy 113-114, 117

J

Jácome, Francine 8-9, 99, 133-135
Jarpa, Sergio 48
juntas 24

L

labor unions 16, 18-19, 77, 82-83,
    107, 140
Lagos, Ricardo 40, 133
latent learning 37, 63-64. *See also
    learning*
law
    amnesty 80
        1987 81
    privatization 81, 140
        1991 81
Law of State Reform 83
learning 1-3, 5, 30, 42-44, 73, 81, 89,
    93, 95, 131, 133, 136, 141. *See
    also political*
    attributed 37, 47
    collective 3, 42
    complex 2, 5, 99-100, 103, 120-122,
        131, 139, 141-143, 145
    contemporary 104

learning, continued
defects 62
deficit 140
democratic 3, 6-7, 32, 56, 74, 76, 93, 99,
    112, 120-122, 124, 131, 141, 143, 145
    process 29
    transitions 4
differential 41
divergent 2-3, 99-100
elite 91
from trauma 131-132
group 2-3
historical 100
    experience 55
individual 2, 38, 93-94
instrumental 61, 119, 138-140
latent 37, 63-64
manifest 37, 47, 63-64, 140
mass 146
negative 2, 16-17, 99, 146
    process 17
nondemocratic 4
of the group as a whole 6
over- 9, 37, 62, 99-100, 109, 111, 120-
    123, 132, 134, 141, 143, 146
perceptions of 37
political 3-4, 15, 19, 25, 29-30, 37-38,
    41, 43, 45, 47, 50-53, 55, 65-66, 74,
    76, 99-101, 109, 111, 118, 120, 124,
    135, 145, 146
    elite 93
    process 15, 37-38
positive 17, 49, 64, 74, 142-143
process 1, 3, 6, 21-22, 31-32, 37-38,
    41, 43-44, 46, 112, 120, 122, 137,
    141, 143-146
    individual 38
simple 2, 5, 99, 109, 111, 123, 131, 145
social 84
theories, social 2
theory 2-3, 138-139, 143-144
trauma 5, 49-50, 54, 64, 74, 108, 132,
    136, 138, 141, 143-146,
traumatic 37, 62, 131, 136-137, 143
under military dictatorship 41
valuative 138-139
Left 8, 26, 29, 40-46, 48, 50-58, 60-
    61, 63, 132, 136-137, 139-140, 142,
    145

Left Bloc 40
Leoni, Raúl 103
Levy, Jack S. 3, 5
liberal faction 75
Lusinchi, Jaime 104

M

majoritarian rule 133
manifest learning 37, 47, 63-64,
    140. *See also learning*
market coup 25
marketplace 16, 21
Martínez de Hoz, José M. 20
MAS (Movement to Socialism —
    Movimiento al Socialismo) 103,
    110, 112-117, 122
Masacesi, Horacio 29
Max-Neef, Manfred 38, 52
McCoy, Jennifer L. 1, 120, 131
memory 2, 136
    collective 6, 26, 133
Menem, Carlos Saúl 22, 25-29, 31-
    32, 137-138
Michelini, Rafael 79, 84, 87
military 5, 7-8, 18-20, 23-24, 32, 39,
    42, 44, 46, 54, 58-59, 65-66, 83-84,
    86-87, 90, 100-101, 107, 109, 132-
    133, 136-137, 139, 141-145
    civil- 7, 101, 137, 142, 145
    coup 6-8, 24-25, 41, 55-56, 99-101,
        103, 105, 144
    dictatorship 15, 20-23, 41-42, 74, 76,
        81, 89, 95, 100, 102, 143
    government 20, 23, 25, 39, 48-49, 52,
        54-55, 58, 101, 137
    post- 132, 133
    intervention 15
    regime 7, 16, 20-21, 30-31, 37-38, 40-
        45, 48-50, 57, 59, 61, 64, 66, 80, 101,
        131-132, 138, 140-142
    spending 20
MIR (Revolutionary Left Movement
    — Movimiento de Izquierda
    Revolucionaria) 103

MLN-Tupamaro (Tupamaro National Liberation Movement — Movimiento de Liberación Nacional Tupamaros) 78, 83-86
model economic 49, 64, 106
modernization 46, 65, 112
Moltz, James 3, 139
Montoneros 19
Moreau, Leopoldo 24
Movement of National Liberation See MLN-Tupamaro
Movimiento de Liberación Nacional Tupamaros. See MLN-Tupamaro
Movimiento Participación Popular. See MPP
Movimiento Quinta República. See MVR
Movimiento Revolucionario Oriental. See MRO
MPP (Popular Participation Movement — Movimiento Participación Popular) 78, 86
MRO (Eastern Revolutionary Movement — Movimiento Revolucionario Oriental) 78
multipartyism 79
MVR (Fifth Republican Movement — Movimiento Quinta República) 145

N

National Accord 110
National Accord for Complete Democracy (Acuerdo Nacional para la Democracia Plena) 44
national consensus 107
National Democratic Institute 5
National Labor Confederation. See PIT-CNT
National Party 57, 82, 84, 89-91, 94
National Renovation. See RN
National Solidarity Front. See FREPASO

negative learning 2, 16-17, 99, 146. See also learning
neighborhood associations 16, 140
neoliberal 43, 46, 111-112, 121
policies 20, 26, 138
New Space Party (Nuevo Espacio) 84
Nicolini, Leonardo 88
nondemocratic learning 3. See also learning
Nosiglia, Enrique 24
Novoa, Rodolfo Nin 89
Nuevo Espacio Party. See New Space Party
Nye, Joseph 3, 99

O

oil 104-105, 108, 134, 141
boom 99
exports 101
Olivos Pact (Pacto de Olivos) 29
organizational theory 2, 5
overlearning 9, 37, 62, 99-100, 109, 111, 120-123, 132, 134, 141, 143, 146. See also learning

P

Pacheco Areco, Jorge 75, 84, 89, 93
pact 17-18, 23, 30, 75, 102, 108-111, 113, 119, 134, 136. See also Andean Pact; Institutional Pact; Olivos Pact; Pact for Reform
fiscal 6, 17
implicit 17
-making 9, 134, 141, 143-144
New York 101
party, 1969 19
Pact for Reform 113-114
Pact of Punto Fijo 101, 103-104, 107, 110, 118, 133, 145
Pacto de Olivos. See Olivos Pact
participative political culture 115, 124
participatory/democratic political culture 9

Partido por el Gobierno del
  Pueblo. *See PGP*
Partido por la Democracia. *See PPD*
party
  centralism 102
  system, single-candidate-per- 91
Party for Democracy. *See PPD*
Party for the Government of the
  People. *See PGP*
partyarchy 115
PCV (Venezuelan Communist Party
  — Partido Comunista de Venezu-
  ela) 101
perestroika 44
Pérez, Carlos Andrés 103-106, 110,
  114, 122
Pérez Jiménez, Marcos 101, 109, 133
Perón, Juan 18-19, 27, 30
Peronism 18-19, 25, 30-31, 138
Peronist 18-19, 23, 25-27, 29-32,
  136-138
  politicians 22
  -Radical agreement 29
Peronist Party 19, 22, 24, 30-32
Petkoff, Teodoro 107, 114-116, 119-
  120
petroleum 104
PGP (Party for the Government of the
  People — Partido por el Gobierno
  del Pueblo) 88-89
Pinochet (No-), syndrome 52
Pinochet, Augusto 7, 41-47, 53,
  57-58, 62, 65, 132-133
Pinochetism 43-45, 59
PIT-CNT (National Labor Confedera-
  tion — Plenario Intersindical de
  Trabajadores - Convención
  Nacional de Trabajadores) 85
plebiscite 28, 37-39, 41-45, 56, 76,
  80, 91, 132, 137
Plenario Intersindical de Trabajadores-
  Convención Nacional de
  Trabajadores. *See PIT-CNT*

policy of consensus 40, 62
political
  culture 1, 9, 38-39, 56, 63, 91, 103,
    106-107, 124, 145-146
    delegative 122, 124
    participative 115, 124
  democratization 46
  discourse 5, 62, 76-78, 80, 95, 100
  elite 4, 8-9, 37, 51, 63, 65, 73, 76, 99-
    100, 102-103, 105-106, 109-110,
    114, 118-122, 134-135, 141, 143-146
    -in-exile 101
  fundamentalism 64
  learning 2-4, 15, 19, 21, 25, 29-30, 37-
    38, 41, 43, 45, 47, 50-55, 61, 65-66,
    74, 76, 99-101, 108-109, 111, 118,
    120, 122, 124, 135-136, 145-146. *See
    also political learning*
    process 15, 37-38
  oppositions 131
  participatory/democratic culture 9
  party 3, 5, 7, 15, 17, 28-29, 39, 48, 50,
    52-56, 63, 66, 75-76, 79-80, 88, 91,
    93, 100-101, 103, 105-110, 112-116,
    118-122, 124, 133, 135, 140-141,
    145-146
    system 73, 107
  realignment 134
  realism 64
  -social-economic model 8
  violence 7-8, 19, 23, 30, 73-74, 135-
    136, 144
Popular Participation Movement. *See
  MPP*
Popular Unity. *See UP*
populist 23, 39, 77, 100, 111, 114,
  121, 138
positive learning 17, 49, 64, 74, 142-
  143. *See also learning*
PPD (Party for Democracy — Partido
  por la Democracia) 38, 40, 44, 46,
  51, 53, 58-60, 132
pragmatic 61, 76-77, 95, 109, 112,
  114, 142
pragmatism 47, 62, 74, 94, 112, 142
presidential system 46

privatization 27, 46, 77, 83, 95
  law 81, 140
    1991 81
proportional representation 76, 79,
  113, 116
Proyecto Venezuela. *See Venezuela Project*
psychological theories 2

R

Radical Civic Union. *See UCR*
Radical Party 22-24, 28-30, 136, 138
Radicals 18-19, 23-26, 29-30, 137-138
  Left 8, 77, 84
realignment 8, 73, 110, 134
Red Party (Colorado Party, Colorados)
  75, 82, 84, 86, 88-89, 91, 93
redemocratization 38
  process 37
referendum 80-83, 114, 139-140, 142
Reform of the Social Security System
  83
regionalization 51
Renovación Nacional. *See RN*
Renovación, Peronist Party 31-32, 137
rent-seeking 17
rentier model 108
representidentialization 27
reserved domain 85, 90
Right 7, 26, 38, 40, 42-51, 53-63,
  65, 78-79, 83, 86, 94, 132-133, 140,
  145
RN (National Renovation —
  Renovación Nacional) 37, 44-45,
  47-49, 51, 58-59, 61
Rodríguez, Jesús 30
rules of the game 1, 8, 64, 73-74, 78-
  80, 86-87, 91, 102, 113, 115, 122,
  124, 135
  democratic 4-5, 86, 95, 139, 142

S

Salas Romer, Henrique 134-135
Sanguinetti, Julio María 73, 76, 80,
  83-84, 87-91, 93-94, 135-136
Santoro, Sen. Walter 82
SCM (state-centric matrix) 6-7, 15-16,
  20-23, 30, 32, 100, 102, 104-106,
  108-109, 111, 113, 120, 124, 138
  formula 19
  model 16-17, 20-24
simple learning 2, 99, 109, 111, 123,
  131, 145. *See also learning*
social
  democratization 46
  elites 4
  learning 84. *See also learning*
    theories 2
  market economy 112
  -political-economic models 6
Social Christian Party – Committee of
  Independent Political Electoral
  Organization. *See COPEI*
social security 73, 82, 135, 140
  Reform
    Law, 1995 90
    of the System 83
socialism
  Christian 112
  real 94
socialist 41, 48-49, 60, 77, 84, 112,
  132-133
  bloc 44
  models 77
    political 78
  projects 145
  regimes 78
  sector 44
Socialist Party
  of Chile 37, 46, 51, 55-56, 58, 60, 133
  of Uruguay 75, 77-78
socioeconomic model 43, 47, 65, 141
sociopolitical matrix 39
Sourrouille, Juan 24
state centralism 21
state-centric matrix. *See SCM*

statism 21, 26, 100, 102
Storani, Federico 23, 26, 28
sublemas 79
supra-partisan government 46
symbolic goods 39

T

technical resolution 40
Third Historic Movement 24
transversal party 46
trauma 5, 49-50, 54, 64, 74, 108, 132,
   136, 138, 141, 143-146. *See also*
   learning
   democratic
      breakdown 142
      collapse 134
      failure 131
   dictatorship 135
   economic 32, 138
   high inflation 144
   historical 39, 54, 65, 133
   hyperinflation 137-138, 142
   institutional breakdown 73
   military
      coup 55
      dictatorship 74
   national 122
   of polarization 64
   of repression 5
   overcome 44
   polarization 140
   society 133
traumatic learning 37, 62, 136-137,
   143. *See also learning*
tribes 79
trienio 100-101, 133
tripartism 142
tripartite system 93
Tupamaro. *See MLN-Tupamaro*

U

Ucero, Luis Alfaro 134
UCR (Radical Civic Union — Unión
   Cívica Radical) 25, 29

UDI (Independent Democratic Union
   — Unión Demócrata Independiente)
   37, 43-44, 47-51, 55-57, 59, 62
ungovernability 25, 136
Unión Cívica 88
Unión Cívica Radical. *See UCR*
Unión Demócrata Independiente. *See*
   UDI
Unión Popular. *See UP*
Unión Republicana Democrática. *See*
   URD
UP (Popular Unity — Unión Popular)
   42, 49-50, 55-57, 60, 66
URD (Democratic Republican Union
   — Unión Republicana
   Democrática) 100-101, 134
Uruguay 1, 8, 73-81, 83-84, 87-89,
   91, 95, 131, 135, 137, 142, 144

V

valuative learning 138, 139. *See also*
   learning
Vázquez, Tabaré 78, 85, 88, 95, 139
Velásquez, Ramón J. 105
Venezuela 1, 8-9, 99-100, 102-105,
   107-110, 112-113, 115, 120, 123-
   124, 131, 133-134, 137, 140-141,
   143-145
Venezuela Project (Proyecto Venezu-
   ela) 134
Videla, Jorge Rafael 23
Volonté, Alberto 88, 91

W

White Party (Blancos) 75, 88

Z

Zabalza, Jorge 78, 86
Zamora, Fernando 26